Carnegie Libraries

Carnegie Libraries

Their History and Impact on American Public Library Development

George S. Bobinski

Assistant Dean, School of Library Science
University of Kentucky

American Library Association

Chicago 1969

Z
731
B67

Standard Book Number 8389-0022-4 (1969)
Library of Congress Catalog Card Number 68-54216
Copyright © 1969 by the American Library Association
Manufactured in the United States of America

Dedicated to my wife

Preface

CARNEGIE PUBLIC LIBRARY PHILANTHROPY in the United States began more than eighty years ago in 1886. Many of these library buildings are now being replaced, and the originals either torn down or used for nonlibrary purposes. At times, perhaps, a plaque marks a wall of the new library with a brief statement that this building superseded an earlier one built by Andrew Carnegie, but just as often there is no reminder.

As these landmarks begin to disappear, there still exists no documented history of the Carnegie library philanthropy and no detailed evaluation of its influence upon the history of the United States public libraries. It is to be hoped that this study will, at least in part, help fill this vacuum in library literature.

At the outset it must be said that this book deals only with Carnegie gifts to public libraries in the United States. Andrew Carnegie gave money for public libraries throughout the English-speaking world. He also contributed funds for the erection of some 108 academic library buildings, and made many miscellaneous library gifts to nonpublic libraries. None of these are included in this study, though they are worthy of investigation and their histories and impact should be recorded.

Some explanation is necessary regarding the Carnegie Library Correspondence which was the most important source for this book. In the late 1940's the Carnegie Corporation of New York had all its voluminous correspondence files dealing with Carnegie public library grants microfilmed, and the original files were destroyed. The forty reels of 16mm microfilm contain the correspondence for each of the 1412 communities in the United States which received a grant for one or more public library buildings and for hundreds of other communities which began negotiations for a grant but never received one. There is correspondence here also for more than 50 communities receiving public library building grants in Canada, South Africa, New Zealand, Australia, and the then other English-speaking overseas possessions.

The file on each community ranges from as few as five or six letters and documents to well over a hundred, with the average being about thirty. Found here are letters (many handwritten and often difficult to read), completed applications and questionnaires, newspaper clippings, pictures and drawings of libraries, building dedication programs, copies of annual reports, and so on. In 1961 the microfilm reels began to show signs of some deterioration, and a duplicate set was made by the Carnegie Corporation. The author was fortunate to be able to borrow the original set on an indefinite loan, and he spent many years poring over tens of thousands of pieces of correspondence. Both sets of microfilm reels are now at the Carnegie Corporation offices in New York City.

The citations in the footnotes to the Carnegie Library Correspondence give the name of the town (the file is arranged alphabetically) and the microfilm reel number. This kind of citation means that the information was obtained from many sources in the file on one community. If, on the other hand, the information is from one or more specific letters or documents, then these are cited in detail.

The reader must be cautioned that both Andrew Carnegie and James Bertram, his private secretary, were believers in and practitioners of simplified spelling. Quotations from them, therefore, are not really misspelled or filled with typographical errors, though they may seem to be.

The major portion of this work appeared originally as a doctoral dissertation to meet requirements for a Ph.D. in Library Science at the University of Michigan. Gratitude is expressed posthumously to Professor Rudolph Gjelsness, former Chairman of the Department of Library Science, University of Michigan. His counsel during the earlier years of doctoral work will always be remembered. Appreciation is also extended to the members of my Doctoral Committee: Professors Wallace J. Bonk, Raymond L. Kilgour, William R. Leslie, and particularly Russell E. Bidlack, Chairman, for their interest, critical comments, and helpful suggestions throughout the course of the dissertation.

Grateful acknowledgment is also given to Florence Anderson, secretary of the Carnegie Corporation of New York, for loaning me the original set of the microfilmed Carnegie Library Correspondence and for providing other sources and assistance throughout the years of research and writing.

I should like to thank the following individuals for helpful responses to letters requesting information: Essae M. Culver, Loleta Dawson Fyan, Alvin S. Johnson, Robert M. Lester, Durand Miller, Mary Rothrock, Gretchen Knief Schenk, Carl Vitz, Joseph Wheeler, and Louis R. Wilson. Appreciation is also extended to the hundreds of librarians who responded to many questionnaires.

Finally, my wife's assistance in offering moral support and in typing preliminary drafts is most deeply appreciated. Without her many personal sacrifices it would have been difficult to complete this book.

GEORGE S. BOBINSKI

Lexington, Kentucky
December 28, 1968

Contents

Illustrations

Tables

Carnegie Libraries

Andrew Carnegie (right) and his secretary, James Bertram, at work in the Carnegie home

CHAPTER ONE

Carnegie's Public Library Philanthropy

A<small>NDREW</small> C<small>ARNEGIE</small>, often referred to as the "Patron Saint of Libraries," in his lifetime made new library buildings available to hundreds of communities all over the world. Very few towns which requested such gifts and agreed to his terms were ever refused. He donated $56,162,622 for the construction of 2509 library buildings throughout the English-speaking parts of the world. More than $40,000,000 of this amount was given for the erection of 1679 public library buildings in 1412 communities of the United States.[1] After 1911, library grants were made by the Carnegie Corporation rather than by Andrew Carnegie personally, although he was president of the Corporation until his death in 1919.

Actually this library philanthropy was only a small part of Carnegie benefactions. More than $333,000,000 (90 percent of his fortune) was spent by the Steel King for what he termed "the improvement of mankind." The range of this philanthropy was great and varied, from the Simplified Spelling Board, the more than 7000 church organs, and the Carnegie Hero Fund, to the Carnegie Institute in Pittsburgh, the Carnegie Institution of Washington, the Foundation for the Advancement of Teaching, and the Carnegie Endowment for

4   CARNEGIE LIBRARIES

International Peace.[2] Although the gift of library buildings seems small in comparison, it was perhaps the most dramatic and influential in that it affected millions of people. It also captured the imaginations of Americans everywhere so that even in this day the public is still generally aware of Carnegie's library philanthropy.

Early Public Libraries in the United States

By 1898, when Carnegie began his full-scale program of giving libraries to communities, the public library was already an established, although young and struggling, institution. Earlier proprietary and subscription libraries—all voluntary associations of people of similar background, income, and social level—had given way by this time to stronger institutions supported by taxation and free to all. These early "social libraries," as one authority has termed them, had their beginnings in New England in the fourth decade of the eighteenth century and their golden age of expansion between 1790 and 1850. In a collective sense they had been a public library system based on the ability of the user to pay for the service desired and formed the foundation for the true public libraries that followed them.[3]

The first recognition of the principle that it was the duty of the state to help provide books for the people came in 1835. At that time New York enacted a state law permitting tax-supported, free library service in each school district through a school district library to be used by the general public. Other states followed the example, as shown in Table 1.

But the school district library proved to be ineffective as a true public library. The unit was too small, the amount of tax money raised annually was insufficient, and the number of volumes in these libraries was too meager to attract public interest. However, the libraries did establish certain principles which form the basis of our present public library system: taxation for free library service, state aid to libraries, and recognition of the library as an educational agency.[4]

The town of Peterborough, New Hampshire, is usually

TABLE 1

ENACTMENT OF SCHOOL DISTRICT LIBRARY LAWS*

STATE	YEAR	STATE	YEAR
New York	1835	Missouri	1853
Massachusetts	1837	California	1854
Michigan	1837	Oregon	1854
Connecticut	1839	Illinois	1855
Rhode Island	1840	Kansas	1870
Iowa	1840	Virginia	1870
Indiana	1841	New Jersey	1871
Maine	1844	Kentucky	1873
Ohio	1847	Minnesota	1873
Wisconsin	1848		

*Source: Moses Coit Tyler, "The Historic Evolution of the Free Public Library in America and Its True Function in the Community," in *Contributions to American Library History*, ed. Thelma Eaton (Champaign, Ill.: Illini Bookstore, 1961), p.26–27.

credited with establishing the first municipally supported, free public library in 1833. But it was not until states began passing laws enabling towns to establish and maintain libraries that public libraries can be said to have had their true origins. In 1848 Massachusetts was the first state to pass an act authorizing one of its cities (Boston) to levy a tax for the establishment of a public library. In 1851 this act was extended to apply to all cities and towns in the state. Other states were soon to follow, as Table 2 indicates. By 1896 twenty-nine of the then forty-five states and the District of Columbia had such laws in effect.[5]

Political, economic, social, and intellectual forces in the United States were ripe for the establishment of public libraries and for their further development during the nineteenth century.[6] Foremost was the idea of progress, which was a popular philosophy up to the Civil War period. This was a belief that all men were endowed with unlimited rational capacity and that everyone possessed a natural right to knowledge and the potential to achieve it. The urge for self-improvement had been responsible for the development of social libraries and also helped spur public library growth.

The spread of free public education at all levels was another factor. There was popular enthusiasm for lyceums and other means of adult education and a general popularization

TABLE 2

ENACTMENT OF ENABLING LAWS FOR PUBLIC LIBRARIES*

STATE	YEAR	STATE	YEAR
Massachusetts	1848†	California	1879
	1851‡	Minnesota	1879
New Hampshire	1849	New Jersey	1879
Maine	1854	Montana	1883
Vermont	1865	New Mexico	1884
Ohio	1867	Missouri	1885
Colorado	1872	Kansas	1886
Illinois	1872	Wyoming	1886
New York	1872	North Dakota	1887
Indiana	1873	Pennsylvania	1887
Iowa	1873	South Dakota	1887
Texas	1874	Washington	1890
Connecticut	1875	Mississippi	1892
Rhode Island	1875	Utah	1896
Michigan	1876	District of Columbia	1896
Nebraska	1877		

*Source: U.S. Bureau of Education, *Statistics of Libraries and Library Legislation in the United States, 1895–1896* (Washington, D.C.: Govt. Print. Off., 1897), p.525–26.
† Boston.
‡ All cities and towns.

of knowledge. The forward march of science and technology and increasing specialization in occupations placed further emphasis on reading as a self-improvement. The rise of American literature and the growth in book publishing were still other factors along with the general awakening in the intellectual and cultural life of the nation.

Democracy's growth likewise demanded an enlightened citizenship. Publicly supported libraries were heralded as agencies for the benefit and improvement of all. An informed electorate was a better electorate.

As the nineteenth century progressed, industrialization, urbanization, and rising prosperity were still other developments influencing public library growth. Libraries were an urban phenomenon. Urbanization gave rise to new social and moral problems: crime, alcoholism, gambling, prostitution, and juvenile delinquency. The public library was promoted as a continuing means of moral elevation and as an agency that might prevent, or at least reduce, these problems. The growing prosperity of the nation and the rise of labor unions brought shorter working hours, more leisure, and the financial ability and personal desire to support libraries. Another necessary ingredient was at hand—energetic leaders in each community who recognized the need for a public library and who were able to persuade the majority of their fellow citizens to vote for financial support of the new service.

The importance of philanthropy cannot be overlooked. The period of twenty-five to thirty years after the Civil War was an era of great philanthropy in the United States. The concentration of immense wealth in the hands of a relatively few who had no income or corporate taxes to pay brought about huge surpluses which were expended in large part for charitable, religious, and educational purposes. Libraries benefited greatly. During the twenty-year period from 1880 to 1899, some $36,000,000 were contributed for library purposes. Among these gifts were those of Walter L. Newberry (1887) and John Crerar (1889) in Chicago and of Enoch Pratt (1882) in Baltimore. The Astor, Lenox, and Tilden libraries, each the product of a private gift, united in 1895 to form the New York Public Library.

Numerous small donors gave to libraries as well. Many towns had one or more citizens who donated a building, cash contributions, or collections of books. They gave for many reasons: local pride, gratitude to the community which had helped them to succeed, or the desire to have people as a whole share in the scientific and cultural progress of the time. Sometimes library philanthropy hindered public support, but more often it helped establish and strengthen the local library so that it could prove its importance and eventually receive funds from local taxation.

Thus, in the period between 1848 and 1875, 188 public libraries were established. By 1887 there were 649 public libraries in the twenty states having public library enabling laws.[7] By 1896 there were 971 public libraries with one thousand volumes or more, plus hundreds of others with smaller collections.[8]

The last half of the nineteenth century was also a period of great accomplishment in other library activities. The first national library convention was held in 1853. The U.S. Bureau of Education, beginning with its first annual report in 1870, regularly gathered information and statistics on libraries and gave them a place of prominence in the educational work of the government. Most important was its massive 1187-page report of 1876 entitled *Public Libraries in the United States of America*. This codified existing procedures and sought, in addition, to stimulate interest and emulation by calling attention to library progress all over the world. Then, too, the year 1876 was an important one because the American Library Association was founded, the *Library Journal* was established, the Library Bureau was organized for the manufacture of library supplies, and the first edition of *Dewey's Classification* was published.

In 1884 the first library school in the United States was authorized by Columbia University, and others were soon to follow. The U.S. Bureau of Education gave wide distribution to a *Catalogue of ALA Library: 5,000 Volumes for a Public Library Selected by the American Library Association and Shown at the World's Columbian Exposition*, which it published in two editions in 1893 and 1896. By 1896, also, a new publication, the monthly *Public Libraries*, made its appearance, while the Library of Congress moved into its magnificent new building and began to play an increasingly important role of leadership. Between 1890 and 1897, library associations were organized in sixteen states.[9]

This period was also one of great leadership in the library profession. Much missionary activity for fuller library service was carried on vigorously by leading librarians, such as John Shaw Billings, William Howard Brett, Charles A. Cutter, John Cotton Dana, Melvil Dewey, Charles Coffin Jewett, William F. Poole, and Justin Winsor.

As the nineteenth century drew to a close and before the full-scale Carnegie library philanthropy, a new era began to dawn in public library development. The states became more than just passive agents permitting localities to tax themselves for public libraries. Recognition of the need to provide library services to all the people, including those in the sparsely populated and less prosperous areas, forced the states into the position of playing a more aggressive role. The state governments began to take an active part in the stimulation, guidance, and counseling of local libraries. Between 1890 and 1896, seven states (Massachusetts, New York, New Hampshire, Connecticut, Vermont, Wisconsin, and Ohio) passed new library laws reflecting this change of attitude and established some kind of state agency, often called the State Library Commission, to assume this new role. Just eight years later, in 1904, there were twenty-two states which had moved in this direction.[10]

Carnegie's Motivations toward Library Philanthropy

Andrew Carnegie was born in a weaver's cottage on November 25, 1835, in Dunfermline, Scotland.[11] Because of the rapid industrialization of the textile trade, his father was forced to sell out his business, Carnegie's formal education came to an end, and the family moved to the United States in 1846. They settled in Allegheny, Pennsylvania, a suburb of Pittsburgh. Carnegie's first job (at the age of thirteen) was that of a bobbin boy for $1.20 per week. After one year he became a messenger boy for a local telegraph company. Here he taught himself the art of telegraphy and met important people. Thomas Scott, superintendent of the Pittsburgh division of the Pennsylvania Railroad, hired him as a private secretary and personal telegrapher. Eventually Carnegie took Scott's place when the latter was promoted. In 1861, after Scott became Assistant Secretary of War, Carnegie helped organize the military telegraph department.

Carnegie had wide business interests while associated with the Pennsylvania Railroad from 1853 to 1865. He bought into the Woodruff Sleeping Car Company and introduced the first successful sleeping car on an American railroad. During 1862 he invested in what turned out to be a major oil development in western Pennsylvania. The following year he helped

form the Keystone Bridge Company, which successfully
and profitably began to replace wooden railroad bridges with
structures made of iron.

After he became involved in a small iron-forging company
in Pittsburgh, Carnegie gave up his position with the railroad in 1865 to devote more time to business interests. For
the next thirty-six years he built up the Carnegie Steel Company until it was sold to J. P. Morgan in 1901 for nearly
$500,000,000. Then at the age of sixty-six, healthy, alert,
and keenly interested in politics and literature, Carnegie
retired and devoted the rest of his life to philanthropy and the
securement of international peace. He had married Louise
Whitfield in 1887 and their daughter Margaret was born in
1897. Bronchial pneumonia caused his death on August 11,
1919.

Most biographers attribute Carnegie's success to his genius
for organization, shrewdness of business judgment, ability
to select the proper men for the jobs to be done, faith in the
United States as a land of business opportunity and growth,
and his policy of expanding during the periods of economic
depression. A minority of biographers have characterized
him as greedy, ruthless, and a cruel taskmaster.

A memorandum found among Carnegie's papers after his
death revealed that as early as 1868, at the age of thirty-three,
he made plans to use the surplus of his income for the benefit
of others:

> Thirty-three and an income of $50,000 per annum! By this time
> two years I can so arrange all my business as to secure at least
> $50,000 per annum. Beyond this never earn—make no effort to
> increase fortune but spend the surplus each year for benevolent
> purposes. Cast aside business forever except for others.
>
> .   .   .   .
>
> Man must have an idol—the amassing of wealth is one of the
> worst species of idolatry—no idol more debasing than the worship
> of money.[12]

But it was not until 1889 that he formally declared his philosophy of the trusteeship of wealth or, as it came to be called, the
Gospel of Wealth.

In his first essay written on the subject, "Wealth," Carnegie declared that wealthy men were to live without extravagance, provide moderately for the legitimate needs of their dependents, and then consider all the remainder as surplus funds which they as trustees should distribute in their lifetime for the best promotion of welfare and happiness of the common man. The main consideration was to help those who would help themselves — but only to assist and never or rarely ever to do all, because neither the individual nor the group was improved by almsgiving. Poverty, crime, and ignorance were not to be fought once they had manifested themselves, for this was the function of the government, but rather the trustee was to do his part in uplifting mass intelligence and character. The best and most aspiring poor of the community had to be stimulated to improve themselves. The millionaire should be a trustee for the poor, entrusted with the increased wealth of the community and able to administer it far better than the community could or would.[13]

In his second essay, entitled "The Best Fields for Philanthropy," Carnegie lists seven fields to which the wealthy could devote their surplus in the following order: universities, libraries, medical centers, public parks, meeting and concert halls, public baths, and churches. The best gift which could be given to a community was a free library, "provided the community will accept and maintain it as a public institution, as much a part of the city property as its public schools, and, indeed, an adjunct to these."[14]

Why did Andrew Carnegie select libraries to be among his first and foremost benefactions? One reason was given by a personal friend of the philanthropist, who said that all of Carnegie's gifts were dedicated to causes and movements with which he was especially concerned. Even his most intimate friends could seldom persuade him to give large sums to anything in which he was not personally interested or of which he had not made a personal study. Libraries and books seemed to be of special concern to Carnegie.[15] His father had led his fellow weavers in Dunfermline to pool their contributions for the purchase of books and delegated one of their number to read aloud while the others worked. This collection became the first circulating library in the town. Carnegie frequently spoke with pride of his lineage as the son of a library-founding weaver. It was to the town of Dunfermline that Carnegie gave his first library in 1881.[16]

While Carnegie was still a working boy in Pittsburgh, a Colonel Anderson of Allegheny established in 1850 the J. Anderson Library of Allegheny City to furnish reading for the mechanics and workingmen in the trades. Young Andrew wrote a letter to the newspaper requesting that the library be opened to all working boys, and he was invited to its use. In later years he recalled awaiting Saturday afternoons with intense longing ". . . and it was when reveling in the treasures which he opened to us that I resolved, if ever wealth came to me, that other poor boys might receive opportunities similar to those for which we were indebted to that noble man." [17] Less than ten years after he made this statement Carnegie began his library-giving on a grand scale.

Carnegie's confidence in the value of free libraries as a wise object of philanthropy may also have been stimulated by earlier and contemporary library philanthropists. He praised Ezra Cornell for beginning the distribution of his wealth by establishing a public library in Ithaca, New York, in 1857.[18] He also had high regard for Enoch Pratt's gifts to Baltimore of $1,000,000 with a requirement that the city pay 5 percent of this sum annually to the library trustees for the development of the main library and branches. Carnegie felt that the 37,000 registered borrowers of the Pratt Library were of more value to Baltimore, to the state, and to the nation than all the inert, lazy, and hopelessly poor in all of the United States.[19]

Perhaps Carnegie's library philanthropy was also influenced by his business background. He once told an audience that, far from being a philanthropist, he was making the best bargains of his life. For instance, when he gave a city money for library buildings, he succeeded in obtaining a pledge that the city would furnish sites and maintain the libraries forever. The city's investment was greater than his. "This was not philanthropy but a clever stroke of business." [20]

To all of these motivations must be added one with which Andrew Carnegie was frequently charged. His accusers claimed that he built libraries as monuments of himself for posterity:

> "All th' same, I like Andhrew Carnaygie. Him an' me ar-re agreed on that point. I like him because he ain't shamed to give publicly. Ye don't find him puttin' on false whiskers an' turnin' up his coat-collar whin he goes out to be benivolent. No, sir. Ivry time he dhrops a dollar it makes a noise like a waither fallin' down-stairs with a tray iv dishes. . . . I like Andhrew Carnaygie, an', as he says, he puts his whole soul into th' wurruk."
> "What's he mane be that?" asked Mr. Hennessy.
> "He manes," said Mr. Dooley, "that he's gin'rous. Ivry time he gives a libry he gives himsilf away in a speech." [21]

Extent of the Philanthropy

Andrew Carnegie himself divided his gifts of libraries into two periods, which he called "retail" and "wholesale." The first lasted from 1886 to 1896, and the second covered the years 1898 to 1919.[22] Table 3 gives an analysis of gifts to communities by year.

During the "retail" period, 1886 to 1896, Carnegie gave a total of $1,860,869 for fourteen buildings to six communities in the United States: Allegheny (1886) and Johnstown (1890), Pennsylvania; a main building and eight branches to Pittsburgh, Pennsylvania (1890); and library buildings to Fairfield, Iowa (1892); Braddock, Pennsylvania (1895); and Homestead, Pennsylvania (1896). The Pennsylvania towns were places in which Carnegie industries were located, and each actually received more than a library building. The underlying idea behind these gifts was clearly that of a general community center and library in which art exhibition halls, lecture and recital rooms, organs, and even gymnasiums and swimming pools were available in addition to reading rooms and bookstacks. Furthermore, all these institutions were given endowments which were certainly contrary to library-giving in the "wholesale" period.

The "wholesale" period of library philanthropy lasted from

TABLE 3

COMMUNITIES PROMISED BUILDINGS AND YEAR*

YEAR OF PROMISE	NUMBER OF COMMUNITIES PROMISED BUILDINGS		YEAR OF PROMISE	NUMBER OF COMMUNITIES PROMISED BUILDINGS
1886	1	(Allegheny, Pa.)	1906	62
1890	2	(Johnstown, Pa.)	1907	61
		(Pittsburgh, Pa.)	1908	62
1892	1	(Fairfield, Iowa)	1909	50
1895	1	(Braddock, Pa.)	1910	42
1896	1	(Homestead, Pa.)	1911	89
1898	3		1912	52
1899	26		1913	92
1900	12		1914	78
1901	131		1915	71
1902	129		1916	65
1903	204		1917	42
1904	64		1918	6
1905	64		1919	1

*Compiled from Carnegie Corporation of New York, *Carnegie Grants for Library Buildings, 1890–1917* (New York: Carnegie Corp., 1943), p.21–37.

1898 to 1919. In contrast to the first period, Carnegie gave $39,172,981 to 1406 communities for library buildings during this time. Two quotations show the "wholesale" spirit of the giving. In 1903 Carnegie wrote the following letter to the librarian of the Philadelphia Free Public Library:

DEAR SIR,

After listening to you this morning for a few minutes, I beg to say that it would give me great pleasure to do for the City of Philadelphia what I have done for New York, provided always that Philadelphia will do what New York has done for herself.

I gave to the City of New York funds to build seventy-two branches, the city providing the sites and undertaking to maintain the libraries. You tell me that a complete system of Branch Libraries for Philadelphia would require thirty such Branches and you estimate that Twenty to Thirty Thousand Dollars apiece would be sufficient for these; but I do not think this sum would be enough. You should have lecture rooms in these Branch Libraries and our experience in Pittsburgh is that we have not spent enough upon them.

The last Branches there cost a great deal more than the first.

I think, therefore, it would be well for you to spend Fifty Thousand Dollars apiece for these Branch Library Buildings and it would give me pleasure to provide a Million and a half Dollars, as the same may be needed to erect Thirty Branch Libraries for Philadelphia provided sites be given and the City agree to maintain these Branch Libraries at a cost of not less than One Hundred and Fifty Thousand Dollars a year.

We find in Pittsburgh that the branch libraries are the most popular institution of all, and I think, the most useful. A great Central Library is, of course, needed, but even before it in usefulness, I place the local libraries, which reach the masses of the people.

With best wishes for Philadelphia, which for many years I considered my "second home."

Always very truly yours,[23]

One of Carnegie's biographers records a conversation between Carnegie and James Bertram, his private secretary:

"Here are forty or fifty more libraries, Mr. Carnegie. They need your O.K."
"Have you examined them all, my boy?"
"Yes."
Carnegie would peel a few and ask penetrating questions. Answers showed that Mr. Bertram had done his work well.
"All right, go ahead with them." [24]

A comparison, year by year, of the number of buildings with the amount expended shows that a large number of small libraries were erected during the later years. Actually the small libraries greatly outnumbered the larger ones, but a greater population was served by the larger libraries in the big towns and cities. Thirty-four cities received a main building and one or more branches (34 main buildings and 104 branches) for a total of 138 libraries at a cost of $8,531,870. Twenty-five cities received only branch buildings (191 in number) costing $9,661,621. Thus, 59 cities accounted for

$18,193,491 out of the $41,033,850 spent for all the Carnegie public libraries in the United States.[25]

The vast majority of the 1349 other communities that received only one building were small towns obtaining small structures, as Table 4 clearly shows:

TABLE 4

CARNEGIE LIBRARY COSTS IN COMMUNITIES OBTAINING ONE BUILDING*

COSTS	NUMBER OF COMMUNITIES
$10,000 or less	698
10,001 to 20,000	404
20,001 to 30,000	128
30,001 to 40,000	35
40,001 to 50,000	32
50,000 and up	52

*Source: William S. Learned, *The American Public Library and the Diffusion of Knowledge* (New York: Harcourt, 1924), p.72–73. (Learned calculated a total of 1408 communities receiving grants. Later listings published by the Carnegie Corporation showed this total to be 1412.)

It is interesting to observe that buildings costing less than $20,000 totaled 1102, or two thirds of the 1679 Carnegie library buildings erected and 78 percent of the 1412 communities receiving Carnegie libraries.

Tables 5 to 8 summarize the extent and distribution of Carnegie library benefactions and indicate state and regional rank by the total amount of funds received, by appropriations per 100 population, by the number of communities obtaining grants, and by the number of Carnegie buildings erected.

TABLE 5

CARNEGIE GRANTS FOR PUBLIC LIBRARIES — STATE AND REGIONAL RANK BY TOTAL AMOUNT CONTRIBUTED*

RANK	STATE	AMOUNT	RANK	STATE	AMOUNT
1.	New York	$6,449,200	4.	California	$2,776,987
2.	Pennsylvania	4,621,148	5.	Indiana	2,508,664
3.	Ohio	2,871,483	6.	Illinois	1,661,200

RANK	STATE	AMOUNT	RANK	STATE	AMOUNT
7.	Michigan	$1,655,950	27.	Utah	$255,470
8.	Iowa	1,495,706	28.	South Dakota	254,000
9.	Missouri	1,460,143	29.	Maine	238,950
10.	Massachusetts	1,137,500	30.	Montana	226,700
11.	New Jersey	1,066,935	31.	Florida	198,000
12.	Washington	1,046,000	32.	Alabama	195,800
13.	Wisconsin	1,045,511	33.	Connecticut	191,900
14.	Minnesota	969,375	34.	North Carolina	166,445
15.	Kansas	874,996	35.	Mississippi	145,500
16.	Kentucky	795,300	36.	Arkansas	138,600
17.	Colorado	749,943	37.	Idaho	137,500
18.	Nebraska	706,288	38.	New Hampshire	134,000
19.	Texas	649,500	39.	North Dakota	132,700
20.	Georgia	503,756	40.	South Carolina	124,700
21.	Maryland	500,000	41.	West Virginia	81,500
22.	Oregon	478,000	42.	Vermont	80,000
23.	Oklahoma	464,500	43.	Virginia	78,000
24.	Louisiana	380,000	44.	Arizona	64,000
25.	Tennessee	335,500	45.	New Mexico	32,000
26.	Wyoming	257,500	46.	Nevada	15,000

RANK	REGION†	AMOUNT
1.	Northeast	$14,501,133
2.	Midwest	13,668,032
3.	Far West	4,315,987
4.	Northwest	3,595,097
5.	Southeast	3,061,601
6.	Southwest	1,210,000
	District of Columbia	682,000
	Total	$41,033,850

*Compiled from Carnegie Corporation of New York, *Carnegie Grants for Library Buildings, 1890–1917* (New York: Carnegie Corp., 1943), p.7–18.

†The regions employed in Tables 5–8 and later in Tables 18 and 19 are the same as those used by Louis R. Wilson in *The Geography of Reading: A Study of the Distribution and Status of Libraries in the United States* (Chicago: American Library Assn., 1938), and are as follows:
1. *Northeast:* Connecticut, Delaware, Maine, Maryland, Massachusetts, New Hampshire, New Jersey, New York, Pennsylvania, Rhode Island, Vermont, West Virginia
2. *Midwest:* Illinois, Indiana, Iowa, Michigan, Minnesota, Missouri, Ohio, Wisconsin
3. *Far West:* California, Nevada, Oregon, Washington
4. *Northwest:* Colorado, Idaho, Kansas, Montana, Nebraska, North Dakota, South Dakota, Utah, Wyoming
5. *Southeast:* Alabama, Arkansas, Florida, Georgia, Kentucky, Louisiana, Mississippi, North Carolina, South Carolina, Tennessee, Virginia
6. *Southwest:* Arizona, New Mexico, Oklahoma, Texas

TABLE 6

CARNEGIE GRANTS FOR PUBLIC LIBRARIES — STATE AND REGIONAL RANK BY APPROPRIATIONS PER 100 POPULATION*

RANK	STATE	APPROPRIATION PER 100 POP.	RANK	STATE	APPROPRIATION PER 100 POP.
1.	Wyoming	$114.2	24.	Maine	$30.1
2.	Indiana	77.5	25.	New Hampshire	28.8
3.	Colorado	72.4	26.	Massachusetts	26.8
4.	Washington	66.9	27.	New Jersey	26.4
5.	Iowa	60.3	28.	Vermont	22.2
6.	North Carolina	52.5	29.	Illinois	21.8
7.	Nebraska	51.3	30.	North Dakota	19.5
8.	New York	51.2	31.	Oklahoma	19.4
9.	Utah	50.3	32.	Louisiana	18.0
10.	Oregon	50.1	33.	Georgia	17.3
11.	California	48.9	34.	Nevada	16.5
12.	Pennsylvania	46.7	35.	Arizona	14.7
13.	Kansas	46.5	36.	Florida	13.5
14.	Ohio	43.2	37.	Tennessee	12.8
15.	Montana	42.2	38.	Connecticut	11.9
16.	Missouri	40.2	39.	Texas	11.2
17.	Minnesota	37.8	40.	New Mexico	7.6
18.	South Dakota	36.7	41.	Arkansas	7.5
19.	Wisconsin	35.6	42.	Alabama	7.4
20.	Michigan	34.2	43.	Mississippi	7.2
21.	Idaho	30.9	44.	South Carolina	7.2
22.	Maryland	30.6	45.	West Virginia	4.7
23.	Kentucky	30.4	46.	Virginia	3.2

RANK	REGION	APPROPRIATION PER 100 POP.
1.	Far West	$52.09
2.	Northwest	48.56
3.	Midwest	40.20
4.	Northeast	38.75
5.	Southwest	13.33
6.	Southeast	11.98
	District of Columbia	156.00
	Total for United States	$ 33.60

*Source: Louis R. Wilson, *The Geography of Reading* (Chicago: American Library Assn., 1938), p.172-73.

TABLE 7

CARNEGIE GRANTS FOR PUBLIC LIBRARIES — STATE AND REGIONAL RANK
BY NUMBER OF COMMUNITIES*

RANK	STATE	COMMUNITIES	RANK	STATE	COMMUNITIES
1.	Indiana	155	24.	Maine	17
2.	California	121	25.	Montana	17
3.	Illinois	105	26.	Wyoming	16
4.	Iowa	99	27.	Kentucky	15
5.	Ohio	77	28.	Alabama	14
6.	Nebraska	68	29.	South Carolina	14
7.	Wisconsin	60	30.	Florida	10
8.	Kansas	58	31.	Idaho	10
9.	Minnesota	58	32.	Mississippi	10
10.	Michigan	53	33.	Tennessee	10
11.	New York	41	34.	New Hampshire	9
12.	Massachusetts	35	35.	North Carolina	9
13.	Washington	33	36.	Connecticut	8
14.	Texas	30	37.	North Dakota	8
15.	New Jersey	29	38.	Arizona	4
16.	Colorado	27	39.	Arkansas	4
17.	Missouri	26	40.	Louisiana	4
18.	Pennsylvania	26	41.	Vermont	4
19.	Oregon	25	42.	New Mexico	3
20.	South Dakota	25	43.	West Virginia	3
21.	Oklahoma	24	44.	Virginia	2
22.	Utah	23	45.	Maryland	1
23.	Georgia	20	46.	Nevada	1

RANK	REGION	COMMUNITIES
1.	Midwest	633
2.	Northwest	252
3.	Far West	180
4.	Northeast	173
5.	Southeast	112
6.	Southwest	61
	District of Columbia	1
	Total	1412

*Compiled from Carnegie Corporation of New York, *Carnegie Grants for Library Buildings, 1890-1917* (New York: Carnegie Corp., 1943), p.7-18.

TABLE 8

CARNEGIE GRANTS FOR PUBLIC LIBRARIES—STATE AND REGIONAL RANK
BY NUMBER OF BUILDINGS*

RANK STATE	BUILDINGS	RANK STATE	BUILDINGS
1. Indiana	164	24. Utah	23
2. California	142	25. Maine	17
3. Illinois	106	26. Montana	17
4. New York	106	27. Wyoming	16
5. Ohio	105	28. Alabama	14
6. Iowa	101	29. Maryland	14
7. Nebraska	69	30. South Carolina	14
8. Minnesota	65	31. Tennessee	13
9. Wisconsin	63	32. Connecticut	11
10. Michigan	61	33. Mississippi	11
11. Kansas	59	34. Florida	10
12. Pennsylvania	58	35. Idaho	10
13. Massachusetts	43	36. North Carolina	10
14. Washington	43	37. Louisiana	9
15. Colorado	35	38. New Hampshire	9
16. New Jersey	35	39. North Dakota	8
17. Missouri	33	40. Arizona	4
18. Texas	32	41. Arkansas	4
19. Oregon	31	42. Vermont	4
20. South Dakota	25	43. New Mexico	3
21. Georgia	24	44. Virginia	3
22. Oklahoma	24	45. West Virginia	3
23. Kentucky	23	46. Nevada	1

RANK REGION	BUILDINGS
1. Midwest	698
2. Northeast	300
3. Northwest	262
4. Far West	217
5. Southeast	135
6. Southwest	63
District of Columbia	4
Total	1679

*Compiled from Carnegie Corporation of New York, *Carnegie Grants for Library Buildings, 1890-1917* (New York: Carnegie Corp., 1943), p.7-18.

Some interesting observations may be made from an examination of the tables. Every state was represented except Rhode Island and Delaware. The states which ranked high

TABLE 9

ORGANIZATION OF STATE LIBRARY ASSOCIATIONS AND COMMISSIONS
AMONG THE TOP ELEVEN CARNEGIE LIBRARY STATES COMPARED TO
THE ELEVEN SOUTHEASTERN STATES

STATE	NUMBER OF COMMUNITIES RECEIVING CARNEGIE LIBRARY*	YEAR STATE LIBRARY ASSOCIATION ORGANIZED†	YEAR STATE LIBRARY COMMISSION ORGANIZED‡
	TOP ELEVEN STATES		
Indiana	155	1892	1899
California	121	1893	1903
Illinois	105	1896	1909
Iowa	99	1890	1900
Ohio	77	1895	1896
Nebraska	68	1895	1901
Wisconsin	60	1891	1895
Kansas	58	1901	1899
Minnesota	58	1891	1899
Michigan	53	1890	1899
New York	41	1890	1891
Total	895	Median 1892	Median 1899
	ELEVEN SOUTHEASTERN STATES		
Georgia	20	1897	1897
Kentucky	15	1907	1910
Alabama	14	1904	1907
South Carolina	14	1915	1929
Florida	10	1901	1925
Mississippi	10	1911	1926
Tennessee	10	1902	1909
North Carolina	9	1915	1909
Arkansas	4	1911	1913
Louisiana	4	1910	1920
Virginia	2	1905	1904
Total	112	Median 1905	Median 1910

*Compiled from Carnegie Corporation of New York, *Carnegie Grants for Library Buildings, 1890-1917* (New York: Carnegie Corp., 1943).

†Compiled from Harry G. Cannons, *Bibliography of Library Economy, 1876-1920* (Chicago: American Library Assn., 1927), p.294-304.

‡*Ibid.*, p.358-63, and Fred F. Beach, Ralph M. Dunbar, and Robert F. Will, *The State and Publicly Supported Libraries* (Washington, D.C.: U.S. Office of Education, 1956), p.82-85.

in all tables, particularly in number of communities and buildings, were Indiana, California, Ohio, Illinois, New York, and Iowa. Although the Northeast received the most money, it must be remembered that in this region many large single gifts were made to municipalities (New York City, $5,202,621; Pittsburgh, $1,093,188; Philadelphia, $1,500,000; and so on). Even though the Far West and the Northwest were first and second, respectively, in the amount appropriated per 100 population, the Midwest had the most communities obtaining grants and the largest number of buildings.

New England, the first region to establish a strong and free school system, already had well-established public libraries and received relatively few Carnegie gifts. Of the 971 public libraries of 1000 volumes or more in 1896, 474 were in the five New England states.[26] These same states had only seventy-three communities which received Carnegie buildings. Later it will be seen that very few of these communities established new libraries as a result of the benefactions.

The states that had the smallest number of established libraries also received the smallest number of Carnegie gifts. Note that the Southwest and the Southeast are last in rank on all tables. The eleven Southeast states had just twelve public libraries in 1896, while the four Southwestern states had only two public libraries in the same year. The states in these regions were also among the last to establish free and strong systems of public education.

State library associations and state library commissions were guiding forces helping to build library services. Organizations and agencies such as these spurred library development and applications for Carnegie grants by means of publications, meetings, and constant intercommunication. The year of the organization of such agencies (as shown in Table 9) reflected the relative library sophistication of each state.

Notes

[1] Carnegie Corporation of New York, *Carnegie Grants for Library Buildings, 1890-1917* (New York: Carnegie Corp., 1943), p.8-20.

[2] Robert M. Lester, *Forty Years of Carnegie Giving* (New York: Scribner, 1941), p.6.

[3] Carleton B. Joeckel, *The Government of the American Public Library* (Chicago: Univ. of Chicago Pr., 1935), p.2-8.

[4] *Ibid.*, p.8-14.

[5] U.S. Bureau of Education, *Statistics of Libraries and Library Legislation in the United States, 1895-1896* (Washington, D.C.: Govt. Print. Off., 1897), p.524-25.

[6] Two sources which provide excellent information on the historical background of the public library in the United States are: Jesse H. Shera, *Foundations of the Public Library: The Origins of the Public Library Movement in New England, 1629-1855* (Chicago: Univ. of Chicago Pr., 1949); and Sidney Ditzion, *Arsenals of a Democratic Culture: A Social History of the American Public Library Movement in New England and the Middle States, 1850-1900* (Chicago: American Library Assn., 1947).

[7] Samuel S. Green, *The Public Library Movement in the United States, 1853-1893* (Boston: Boston Book Co., 1913), p.152-53.

[8] U.S. Bureau of Education, *Statistics of Libraries and Library Legislation in the United States, 1895-1896* (Washington, D.C.: Govt. Print. Off., 1897) and William S. Learned, *The American Public Library and the Diffusion of Knowledge* (New York. Harcourt, 1924), p.73.

[9] Martha Conner, *Outline of the History of the Development of the American Public Library* (Chicago: American Library Assn., 1931).

[10] M. G. Toepel, "Legal Responsibility for Public Library Development – United States," *Library Trends*, 9: 11 (July 1960).

[11] Most of the following biographical sketch is based on Burton J. Hendrick, *The Life of Andrew Carnegie* (Garden City, N.Y.: Doubleday, 1932). 2 vols. Cited hereafter as Burton J. Hendrick, *The Life of Andrew Carnegie*.

[12] *Ibid.*, II: 146-47.

[13] Andrew Carnegie, "Wealth," *North American Review*, 148: 653-54 (June 1889).

[14] ———, "The Best Fields for Philanthropy," *North American Review*, 149: 688-89 (Dec. 1889).

[15] Frederick Lynch, *Personal Recollections of Andrew Carnegie* (New York: Revell, 1920), p.135.

[16] Andrew Carnegie, *Autobiography* (Boston: Houghton, 1920), p.48.

[17] ———, "The Best Fields for Philanthropy," *North American Review*, 149: 689 (Dec. 1889).

[18] ———, "Ezra Cornell," in *Miscellaneous Writings of Andrew Carnegie*, ed. Burton J. Hendrick (Garden City, N.Y.: Doubleday, 1933), I: 249.

[19] ———, "The Best Fields for Philanthropy," *North American Review*, 149: 689 (Dec. 1889).

[20] "Mr. Carnegie's Investments," *Library Journal*, 27: 329 (June 1902).

[21] Finley Peter Dunne, "The Carnegie Libraries," in *Mr. Dooley on Ivrything and Ivrybody*, ed. Robert Hutchinson (New York: Dover, 1963), p.228-29.

[22] Burton J. Hendrick, *The Life of Andrew Carnegie*, II: 205.

[23] Andrew Carnegie to James Thomson, Jan. 3, 1903 (Philadelphia, Pa., Carnegie Library Correspondence, Microfilm Reel No.25).

[24] Burton J. Hendrick, *The Life of Andrew Carnegie*, II: 207.

[25] Compiled from Carnegie Corporation of New York, *Carnegie Grants for Library Buildings, 1890-1917* (New York: Carnegie Corp., 1943), p.9-37.

[26] William S. Learned, *op. cit.*, p.84.

CHAPTER TWO

Instruments of the
Carnegie Library Philanthropy

M ANY INDIVIDUALS were involved in the various phases of
Andrew Carnegie's library philanthropy. The most important
of these was James Bertram, Carnegie's private secretary,
who was in charge of the day-to-day operations of the benefactions and in a sense the real power behind them. Carnegie
provided the funds and set up the general guidelines; Bertram
executed them into action. He was the one involved in the
daily contacts and decisions. Andrew Carnegie himself once
wrote that he saw few of the hundreds of daily letters which
Bertram read and answered.[1]

James Bertram

James Bertram was born in Corstorphine, Scotland (now a
part of Edinburgh), on March 17, 1872. He early distinguished himself as a student in the parish school and at
Daniel Stewart's College in Edinburgh, the equivalent to
a current business high school. After graduation, he went to
work in 1888 for the Great Northern and Northeastern Railway Companies at Edinburgh. In 1890, influenced by a family

friend in South Africa, he entered the employ of the Natal Government Railways at Durban as a clerk and later became a stationmaster. After resigning from this post in 1895, he served for sixteen months as secretary to S. Neumann and Company in Johannesburg, where he familiarized himself with assay plans, maps, and mining work in general. He then became mine secretary to the Van Ryn Gold Mines Estate, Limited, also of Johannesburg. Because of a severe attack of enteric fever, he returned to Scotland in 1897 on the advice of his physician.

After he regained his health and strength, Bertram was advised by James Matthew, a former teacher of his, to apply for the position of private secretary to Andrew Carnegie. With a letter of introduction from Matthew, Bertram went to see Dr. Hew Morrison, chief librarian of the Edinburgh Public Library, who had been commissioned by Carnegie to select a secretary for him. Morrison brought Carnegie and Bertram together, and upon his recommendation the latter was engaged for a three-month trial period. Bertram proved satisfactory and was Carnegie's confidential secretary for seventeen years, from 1897 to 1914, and secretary to the Carnegie Corporation of New York from 1911 to 1934.

By 1897 it became generally known that Andrew Carnegie had decided to give away the greater part of his fortune. Applications poured in from all over the world for benefactions, especially for church organs and libraries, as these could be had practically for the asking. To bring order out of the chaos, Bertram organized an office and devised ways and means by which the requests could be handled efficiently. Administrative offices were first installed in Carnegie's home at 5 West 51st Street and later, in 1902, in the new home at 2 East 91st Street. Bertram became an alert, attentive private secretary whose devotion to his chief was evident to all who came in contact with him. He served as a buffer between the hordes of applicants and Carnegie and also as a watchdog on the treasury.

Even after the Carnegie Corporation of New York was organized in 1911 to carry on the Carnegie philanthropy,

Bertram continued in his important role as the appointed secretary of this foundation. Carnegie served as president, and Robert A. Franks, formerly a private financial secretary, became treasurer.[2] Franks took care of the correspondence on library matters in the United States when Bertram was in Scotland with Carnegie during a part of every year. Before the Carnegie Corporation was organized, Franks released funds to individual towns, upon receipt of a communication from Bertram, through the Home Trust Company of Hoboken, New Jersey—a trust company incorporated in 1901 to care for the various financial interests of Carnegie after he retired.[3] These three, Carnegie, Bertram, and Franks, formed the executive committee of the Corporation and met frequently to conduct the business of philanthropy. The annual meeting of the board of trustees merely approved the actions of this group. In 1914 the Carnegie Corporation established its headquarters in offices at 576 Fifth Avenue, and Bertram took over its day-to-day operations.[4]

James Bertram has been well characterized by various contemporaries. Frederick P. Keppell, a former Trustee and President of the Carnegie Corporation, paid tribute to Bertram's integrity, picturesque personality, and dauntless courage in the face of majority opinion.[5] Durand Miller, who worked for Bertram, recalls him as being thrifty, very religious (a staunch Presbyterian), inclined to be irritable, rather brusque in manner, and short and direct in his speech. But he also remembers Bertram mellowing with age and "where he formerly would stand up and fight, in later years he would be content to oppose by having his say and stopping there."[6]

To Robert M. Lester, another contemporary Carnegie Corporation employee, "Bertram was a devoted, meticulous Scot and made a religion out of the Carnegie spirit of giving."[7] Frank P. Hill described him as methodical, systematic, and a stickler for precedent. Bertram believed in going slowly and being sure of his ground. Brevity was his strong trait. He never used a paragraph when a sentence would do, and a word often served to take the place of a sentence.[8]

Bertram's letters were extremely businesslike and at times abrupt and even rude. Certainly, he lacked tact and patience. Upon receiving a letter from a newspaper editor asking for information on how to obtain a library grant for his town, Bertram replied as follows:

> DEAR SIR:
>
> It is an extraordinary fact that after Mr. Carnegie has given some thirty or forty libraries in Indiana, and the detailed applications and also Mr. Carnegie's response have been printed in its daily press, a Newspaper Editor writes and professes ignorance either as to how to proceed or as to what is required.[9]

Whenever a letter he received was not clear to him, Bertram would reply in a style similar to the following answer to a correspondent from Ann Arbor, Michigan:

> DEAR SIR:
>
> There is something missing in your letter of November 22nd/i.e. what it refers to and what is its object.[10]

In response to a request for a copy of an important misplaced letter, he asked, "Do you mean to say that you have lost the letter promising you $10,000? This is extraordinary!"[11]

Bertram assumed that his correspondents should know all there was to know about the procedures of obtaining Carnegie library funds and that his short, terse notes were self-explanatory and clear. But this was not the case as the following letter, an example out of many shows:

> DEAR MR. BERTRAM:
>
> In these letters of yours, I fail to find an instance in which you make a decisive statement. You seem to have the

ability of evading every question put up to you, and it
seems to be your desire that no appropriation be made
for Orland, without coming out and saying it directly in
so many words. Twice the writer has asked you a straight
out and out question, which could and should be answered
by Yes or No, but in both instances you have elected to
evade the questions by referring to some previous letter
which you had written, and by referring to these letters
mentioned, we still fail to find any tangible information,
which will show us just what is expected.[12]

Most applicants accepted Bertram's vagueness and sharp-
ness with tactful grace, by writing polite letters of inquiry
or by quietly acceding to a curt order. But some revolted, and
the letter which follows, an answer to a communication from
Bertram in which he requested a progress report on the
Carnegie grant so that the promise of the gift would not
lapse, shows a most typical reaction:

In answer to your letter of May 14th, I wish to state that
the city of Eaton Rapids has wanted a Carnegie public
library, would like to have one now, and will probably be
wanting one for some time to come.

For the past ten years, the city commission and the library board of Eaton Rapids have been writing you in
regard to this matter. They have endeavored to answer
every question you have asked, furnish you with all necessary and duly signed papers, and have laid awake nights
trying to figure out what would be possible for them to do
that would meet with your approval. This matter has been
given serious consideration about six times, and each time
we have run up against obstacles, and this obstacle or obstacles seems to be James Bertram. We have elected new
mayors, new commissioners and an entire new library
board, figuring that possibly somebody could figure out
just what you want. Now the facts of the case are these:
We want a Carnegie Library; have a site picked out for one
and are willing to do everything within our power, within
reason, to secure this library, but after many efforts, we
have simply given the matter up as an absolute impos-
sibility, as long as you handle these affairs for the Carnegie

Corporation. Every request you have asked has been granted with the exception that [sic] contained in your last letter where you practically ask us to send you a written list with the exact price of every nail, screw, shingle, and grain of sand used in the construction of this building.

Now Mr. Bertram, we desire to be courteous, and would be pleased to have a Carnegie Library building, but have had to throw the whole matter up in absolute disgust on account of your attitude. We are simply unable to get anywhere under your method of handling these matters. If you don't want Eaton Rapids to have this library, very well and good. We will get by and have plenty of first class reading matter from some other source than a Carnegie library.

Suit yourself Mr. Bertram, permit Eaton Rapids to go ahead with this library or not—just as you see fit. Work could be started on this library almost immediately, and it was intended to have it constructed this summer. Suffice to say, however, before we consider this matter entirely closed, we shall get in communication with the chairman of the Board of Directors of the Carnegie Corporation, and endeavor to ascertain just why it is impossible for the city of Eaton Rapids to satisfactorily meet the requirements of the Carnegie Corporation, under the secretaryship of James Bertram.

Trusting you will interpret this letter in the courteous manner in which it is intended, I remain,

Very respectfully[13]

After receiving this caustic missive, Bertram contacted Sarah Bogle, assistant secretary of the American Library Association; gave her all eighty-one pieces of correspondence; and asked her to see what she could do for Eaton Rapids. He indicated that he was not working through the secretary of the Michigan State Library Commission because her advanced age had made her of little influence in Michigan communities.[14] Sarah Bogle, after reading the voluminous correspondence, called the mayor's letter a sample of colossal impertinence and the whole situation a result of small-town ignorance. She traveled to Eaton Rapids to survey the situation. After talking to Mayor Gifford, she blamed it further on the misuse of misinformation and began the resumption of negotiations.[15] Sarah Bogle's activities and those of Adam Strohm, of the Michigan Library Commission (and librarian of the Detroit Public Library), however, came to no avail as negotiations broke down again over costs, and the offer was withdrawn.[16]

Almost all contacts Bertram had with the library world were through correspondence. His aloofness was attributed by one observer to a desire to maintain a strictly impersonal and disinterested attitude toward each and every applicant. He even declined all invitations to attend various library conferences. His view of librarians was that the upper tenth might be, or ought to be, "professional." However, he did not see how the great mass could be so termed or, if they were—in the sense of doctors, lawyers, and engineers—how they could be paid for.[17]

James Bertram's position was difficult. He had to decide on the disposition of a vast sum of money and see that it was properly expended, since every dollar donated had to be well spent. He judged proposals strictly on their merit. Personal relations or considerations never influenced his judgment. No worthy applicant was to be rejected, and, yet, no unworthy one was to be accepted. As a result, some felt that Bertram was inconsiderate, austere, legalistic, and overly critical, but those who knew him well characterized him as sympathetic, sincere, kindly, logical, practical, fair-minded, and socially affable. He was a hard-working secretary who did his job to the best of his ability.[18]

There is no indication that Carnegie ever disapproved of his secretary. On the contrary, he rewarded Bertram with one of two life trusteeships at $5,000 per year in the Carnegie Corporation of New York (Robert A. Franks received the other) and provided him with a $10,000 annuity in his will.[19]

James Bertram died on October 23, 1934, of a blood clot on the brain at the age of sixty-two. Even after death his individuality expressed itself when his will was made public. Upon the death of his wife and in the event of his daughter's death without heirs, the residue of his estate was to go to the

Chancellor of the Exchequer of Great Britain to be applied toward England's debt to the United States. His lawyer stated
that Bertram, who had never become a United States citizen,
wanted to do something for the country of his birth and for
the country of his adoption.[20]

Library Officials

Mention has been made of Bertram's reliance for assistance on certain library officials. These requests for help grew
with each year of Carnegie library philanthropy. Officers
of the American Library Association were consulted, as were
state library commissioners and state librarians—the latter
two groups particularly in Indiana, New Jersey, New York,
Illinois, and Georgia. The League of Library Commissioners
was still another group that Bertram and the Carnegie Corporation relied on, especially when dealing with problem
communities. At times Bertram was impatient with these
officials and felt that they were not powerful enough. He
thought that they should be able to step boldly into local
library problems and resolve them on the spot.

Mrs. Percival Sneed, of the Georgia Library Commission
and head of the Atlanta Carnegie Library, was not only helpful to Bertram in regard to Carnegie library problems in
Georgia, but also served as a consultant on other southern
Carnegie libraries. Henry N. Sanborn, secretary of the Indiana Library Commission, was often called upon to settle
differences and problems in Indiana communities and was
an advisor on out-of-state matters as well.

The most heavily consulted librarian was William Howard
Brett, director of the Cleveland Public Library. Bertram had
implicit confidence in Brett and came to depend upon him
for counsel and criticism. Brett, along with other leading
librarians and architects, aided in the preparation of Bertram's *Notes on Library Bildings,* a guideline of standards on
Carnegie library architecture, written in simplified spelling
and published by the Carnegie Corporation in 1911. Plans
for libraries received from all over the country were fre-

quently referred to Brett by Bertram for review and criticism.[21]

Brett also had an unusual acquaintance with the library laws of all states and was often consulted on them. At the request of the Carnegie Corporation, he collected and abstracted a digest of laws then in operation.[22] They were published in 1916 as an *Abstract of Laws Relating to Libraries in Force in 1915 in the States and Territories of the United States.*[23]

Louise Whitfield Carnegie

Reference should also be made to the role of Carnegie's wife in his public benefactions. Although Carnegie often discussed the philanthropies he had in mind with his wife, she did not seem to play a significant role in his library benefactions except perhaps in the early ones upon which Carnegie acted personally. Here she entered into the library program enthusiastically, even going over the architect's plans for the library buildings with her husband and rejoicing with him in their completion.

The Allegheny Library interested them both, because Carnegie's career began in this town.[24] Carnegie wrote the following to his wife about the project:

> Yesterday I strolled out with Henry Phipps and walked over to see the Library in Allegheny. If ever there was a sight that makes my eyes glisten it was this gem. . . . I saw many people standing gazing and praising and the big words Carnegie Free Library just took me into the sweetest reverie and I found myself wishing you were at my side to reap with me the highest reward we can ever receive on earth, the voice of one's inner self, saying secretly, well done![25]

When the Allegheny Library was opened by the President of the United States in January of 1890, Carnegie wanted his wife by his side, but, unfortunately, she could not be there because of the serious illness of her mother.[26]

Notes

[1] Andrew Carnegie to William A. Courtenay of the Charleston Library Society, March 16, 1905 (Charleston, S.C., Carnegie Library Correspondence, Microfilm Reel No.5).

[2] Frank P. Hill, *James Bertram: An Appreciation* (New York: Carnegie Corp., 1936), p.15–34.

[3] Robert M. Lester, *Forty Years of Carnegie Giving* (New York: Scribner, 1941, p.74–75).

[4] Frank P. Hill, *James Bertram, op. cit.,* p.34–35.

[5] Carnegie Corporation of New York, *Annual Report, 1935* (New York, 1936), p.11.

[6] Durand R. Miller, "My Recollections of J.B." (a typewritten manuscript prepared for Frank Hill on July 31, 1935, when the latter was writing his biography of James Bertram; loaned to the author by Mr. Miller).

[7] Letter from Robert M. Lester to the author, dated Nov. 2, 1965.

[8] Frank P. Hill, *op. cit.,* p.32.

[9] James Bertram to O. H. Downey, editor of *The Herald,* Feb. 15, 1904 (Butler, Ind. Carnegie Library Correspondence, Microfilm Reel No.4).

[10] James Bertram to R. S. Copeland, chairman of the Carnegie Library Committee, Nov. 25, 1904 (Ann Arbor, Mich., Carnegie Library Correspondence, Microfilm Reel No.1).

[11] James Bertram to D. A. Hebel, July 28, 1914 (Aledo [Mercer Township Free Library], Ill., Carnegie Library Correspondence, Microfilm Reel No.1).

[12] Willard Clark, chairman of the Local Library Committee, to James Bertram, March 9, 1918 (Orland, Calif., Carnegie Library Correspondence, Microfilm Reel No.23).

[13] R. D. Gifford, Mayor, to James Bertram, May 24, 1920 (Eaton Rapids, Mich., Carnegie Library Correspondence, Microfilm Reel No.9).

[14] James Bertram to Miss Sarah C. R. Bogle, assistant secretary of the American Library Association, Chicago, Ill., June 2, 1920 *(ibid.).*

[15] Miss Sarah C. R. Bogle to James Bertram, June 17 and Aug. 20, 1920 *(ibid.).*

[16] *Ibid.*

[17] Frank P. Hill, *op. cit.,* p.53.

[18] *Ibid.,* p.66–67.

[19] New York *Times,* Oct. 24, 1934, p.23.

[20] *Ibid.,* Nov. 2, 1934, p.18.

[21] Frank P. Hill, *op. cit.,* p.43.

[22] Linda A. Eastman, *Portrait of a Librarian; William Howard Brett* (Chicago: American Library Assn., 1940), p.67.

[23] Privately printed by the Lezius Printing Co., Cleveland, Ohio.

[24] Burton J. Hendrick and Daniel Henderson, *Louise Whitfield Carnegie: The Life of Mrs. Andrew Carnegie* (New York: Hastings, copr. 1950), p.137–39.

[25] Andrew Carnegie to his wife, Sept. 26, 1889, quoted *ibid.,* p.138.

[26] *Ibid.,* p.139.

CHAPTER THREE

Obtaining a Library Building

THERE IS LITTLE QUESTION of the desperate need for new library buildings in the United States during the late nineteenth and early twentieth centuries. Few public libraries had buildings of their own. Many had undesirable or cramped quarters in the local city hall or in former residences converted for library use. Some contemporary libraries were located in rather unusual places. A millinery shop in Clay Centre, Nebraska; a decrepit wooden shack in Dillon, Montana; the hospital in Dunkirk, New York; a printing shop at Grandview, Indiana; the balcony office of a drugstore in Malta, Montana; a building housing the horses of the fire department at Marysville, Ohio; a physician's reception room in Olathe, Kansas; an old, abandoned church at Onawa, Iowa; a room in the opera house of Sanborn, Iowa; three small rooms over a meat market at Vienna, Illinois — all were typical examples of the ingenuity of townspeople in their efforts to establish local libraries. There was also the case of Chatfield, Minnesota, where the matron of a rest room doubled as librarian. This "library"-rest room was located in a store with the rent, light, and heat paid by the Commercial Club.[1]

Inquiries

A variety of people made inquiries for Carnegie libraries: librarians; library board members; teachers; ministers; and representatives of ladies' library associations, women's club organizations, and commercial clubs. They had heard or read about Andrew Carnegie's library philanthropy, and they, too, wanted to share in this munificence. This was especially true when some nearby town received money for a building, and news of the gift spread in the area.

Carnegie and Bertram both insisted that all business pertaining to the donation of libraries be carried on through the mail. Personal interviews, although requested by many, were granted to few. Now and then there was an exception. Private consultations were occasionally permitted for people of prominence, representatives of communities near Bertram's office in New York City, or in instances where such great complications had developed that a meeting was necessary. When a delegation was sent from Goshen, Indiana, to see Carnegie about a library building, Bertram received them, and they obtained the first Carnegie library in Indiana.[2]

In the original letters of request glowing accounts of the community were usually found, often including descriptions of the cleanliness of the streets and the industrious nature of the inhabitants, along with population figures (sometimes exaggerated) and statistics on the number of churches and schools. The poor financial condition of the city, which made it unable to take on the burden of a library without outside help, was also often mentioned. Supporting letters of request frequently came from congressmen, governors, university presidents, cabinet members, and other officials.

The forty microfilmed reels of Carnegie correspondence are filled with interesting pleas for library buildings. The newspaper editor of Aberdeen, Washington, suggested that Carnegie should give more than the usual amount of money to this community because of the town's Scottish name.[3] The mayor of Berlin, Wisconsin, claimed that a local library could accomplish a great deal of good, because there were at that time more than twenty saloons in the town and not one place where a young man could spend his evenings away from the influence of liquor.[4] Officers of the Commercial Club of Bloomfield, Iowa, on the other hand, boasted that they had had no saloons for thirty years, and this record should certainly qualify their community for a Carnegie gift.[5] The Utopia Club of Columbia, Tennessee, merely asked Carnegie to "drop some bills of some denomination in the addressed envelope" for its library.[6] Corning, New York, wanted a Carnegie library because of the low, moral character of the town and because a rival sister city (Hornell) had obtained one.[7] The Women's Club of Guthrie Center, Iowa, was carrying on a drive to collect one mile of pennies ($844.50) for its library. They requested Andrew Carnegie to put something into an envelope and return it.[8] A citizen of Wiscasset, Maine, appealed to Carnegie's sentiment by asking him to construct and stock a library there because the ship which carried him to America was built in this community.[9]

The appeal from Ponca City, Oklahoma, was typical of the thousands of letters of request on file. Here the ladies of the Twentieth Century Club were " . . . placing a Public Library in our town and knowing of your generosity (which has been felt the world over) and remembering the scriptured injunction 'Ask and ye shall receive' have (in our dire need of funds) over-come our timidity to the extent of asking you for a donation." [10]

Petitioners for libraries often had more in mind than just simple library buildings. Requests for combinations of libraries with city halls or with gymnasiums were very frequent. Banquet rooms, public baths, churches, and YMCA's were still other facilities and agencies which people thought appropriate to share the new Carnegie library structures.

Thus, a committee of businessmen from Lake City, Minnesota, wrote that they were thinking of a library building which would be a good substitute for saloons and might help to counteract their influence. They thought that a restaurant for lunches and soft drinks, a room for games of various kinds, a gymnasium of modern equipment, and a reading and writing room supplied with daily papers and periodicals would be most desirable features.[11]

Officials at Sparta, Michigan, had a similar notion. They wanted a building with two floors and a basement. The basement was to be equipped with a bowling alley and lunch counter where men and boys could purchase coffee and sandwiches in place of beer and pretzels. The first floor was to contain a library and reading rooms, and on the second floor, lecture and entertainment rooms were to be located.[12]

None of these requests was granted. Libraries only were provided. James Bertram refused the appeal for the inclusion of a gymnasium in the library from Fort Benton, Montana. If libraries were provided with gymnasiums, he replied, it would open the door to requests for art galleries, museums, and similar appendages. People interested in these added facilities would ask for library buildings as a means of obtaining them. They would then try to make these features paramount or, at least, competitive. He felt this would result in continual conflict between those individuals interested in the library and those concerned with the auxiliary functions added to the building.[13]

The procedures of applying for and obtaining library buildings became more formalized as time went on. During the early period of library philanthropy, Carnegie acted upon requests personally. Then, as letters of application began to pour in, James Bertram handled all the details. From 1911 on, the Carnegie Corporation managed the distribution of the benefactions.

Very often the responses to the letters of inquiry were not immediate, particularly in the early years of giving. At times it was because Carnegie and Bertram were both abroad. Rev. A. L. Weaver from Syracuse, Indiana, began his second letter with an apt quotation, "If at first you don't succeed, try, try again."[14] The Carnegie library correspondence is filled with repeated and persistent letters requesting information and funds.

Usually the original request came from a person other than

the mayor or the municipal council, and the standard reply
in James Bertram's simplified spelling (see Appendix A-1)
stated that the mayor or council should write an official letter
of application declaring what the community would be willing to do in providing a site and in levying a tax for the support of the library. Carnegie found it desirable at all times to
deal directly with the city rather than with a library board.
When a pledge of revenue was received from a library board
(even if the board were legally entitled to give it), Carnegie
authorities insisted on the endorsement of the city so that
there would be no doubt that everyone supported the library. If the board of education happened to be the legal
authority for managing the library and levying the tax, a
pledge from them was required plus a resolution of endorsement from the city council.

Requirements

Library grants were limited to English-speaking countries.
Carnegie believed that Great Britain and America were great
sister republics struggling with the same problems of capital
and labor, laws regulating commerce and manufacture,
taxation, improved housing for the poor, and education of
the people. Also, the voice of the people counted in these
countries. He apparently felt that these two nations had already developed a general public library system and were,
thus, the most promising fields for library philanthropy.[15]

Each community requesting a library received a Schedule
of Questions to complete. The three versions of this questionnaire, as noted in the Carnegie library microfilmed correspondence, are presented in Appendix A-2. The key questions were those requesting the town's population and asking
whether or not it already had a library. If a library was in
operation, there were inquiries on its size in volumes and
floor space, the annual book circulation, and its receipts and
expenditures for the most recent year. Carnegie officials also

wished to know if a site was available for the requested build-ing and how much the community was willing and legally able to tax itself for the annual support of the library. James Bertram frequently stated that Carnegie made no offers of libraries. The benefactor merely considered the offers which communities made, and he responded to what a town was willing to do if funds for a library building were received. Bertram was insistent that the Schedule of Questions was not an application form and that it not be so called. He was quite determined, also, that the questionnaire be filled out completely and accurately.

After the completed forms were examined, some towns were refused donations of buildings for various reasons. Carnegie did not wish to contribute to state libraries or state historical society libraries, nor did he generally favor build-ings for proprietary or subscription libraries. For example, he was reluctant to give funds to the endowed subscription library of Charleston, South Carolina. Carnegie declared that it should be made a public library and that its books should not be reserved for persons already enlightened. Nevertheless, he did contribute a token $5000 toward a $75,000 library building in spite of his objections.[16]

Still other questions or comments were made by Bertram based on the Schedule of Questions. If it seemed evident that the current library accommodations were adequate, Bertram would ask for pictures and a full description of the existing library. Bay City, Michigan, was at first refused money for a building in 1906, because library quarters were considered ample.[17] Initial appeals from St. Paul, Minnesota, were also rejected, for Carnegie felt that there were local philanthropists who should give first. However, ten years later, in 1914, he did donate funds for branch libraries to this city.[18] Independence, Kansas, was answered with the fol-lowing:

> Your statement of the extraordinary development of Independence is not borne out by the fact that only one thousand dollars a year can be guaranteed to support the library.[19]

Still another sharp reply went to Greenfield, Indiana, officials:

> A request for $30,000 to erect a library building for 5000 people is so preposterous that Mr. Carnegie cannot give it any consideration.[20]

And Madison, Nebraska, was asked to give particulars of $939 listed as "miscellaneous receipts." Its accounting was probably typical of the financing of contemporary subscription libraries:[21]

Membership fees of 139 members brought	$136.00
Cash donations netted	559.12
Proceeds from the Library Hog	86.05
(The weight of a gift hog was guessed for 25¢ a try at the County Fair with the hog going to the winner.)	
From the sale of Library Maid	17.60
(A gift Jersey heifer sold at auction.)	
Proceeds from entertainment by a local Company provided	52.00
The Fourth of July Tag Sale by the ladies	77.77
Library fines produced	11.25

Regardless of persistent interrogation by Carnegie's secretary, most communities did receive funds for a building. The welcome news was conveyed in form letters (see Appendix A-3) which stated that Carnegie would be glad to give a stipulated amount if the city provided a suitable site for the building and agreed by a resolution of its council to support a public library annually at a cost of no less than 10 percent of the total sum contributed.

Location

Locating and acquiring a site and gaining approval of the building plans were the most frequent stumbling blocks in obtaining a Carnegie library. Bertram and the Carnegie Corporation offered little interference in site selection except to suggest that it should be satisfactory to the community, owned by it, and large enough to allow for expansion of the building if necessary. Carnegie officials did request a letter

**SPEAKING OF LIBRARIES, HOW WOULD YOU LIKE TO BE
THE MAIL MAN?**

Pioneer Press, St. Paul, Minnesota

Requests pour in for Carnegie libraries

describing the site and its area and stating that it was purchased and paid for so that title was vested in the community.
Many localities misunderstood this request and sent deeds,
title abstracts, and other documents to show proof of owner-
ship.

Simple as these stipulations may seem, a controversy over
the location of the library occurred in about one out of every
three requests for a building. Frequently it was a question
of local politics. Hundreds and even thousands of names on
petitions as well as many individual letters were sent to Carnegie praising one site over another or bitterly opposing
a certain library location. Usually, however, neither Carnegie nor Bertram questioned the site decision of local
officials. They claimed that if citizens were unhappy with the

choice, they could turn these officials out of office. The citizens did just this in Goodland, Kansas, where the local administration was defeated in the regular election as a result of its previous stand on the library location.[22]

Other factors often created dissension. Occasionally a realtor or one of the members of the library board wanted to dispose of a piece of land for the library site. Sometimes there was a desire on the part of each neighborhood to have the library building in its own area. Towns with rivers bisecting them seemed to be particularly prone to disputes about the library location. Such bitter controversies occurred in Rockford and Aurora, Illinois, as well as in Waterloo, Iowa. In the latter case the new library was to be located on an island in the river dividing the town into two factions. But, then, Carnegie raised his gift from $30,000, to $40,000, and finally up to $45,000 so that two libraries could be built, one on each side of the river.[23]

Library sites were frequently donated, or money was given to purchase the land. But just as often sites were bought by the municipality from public funds. Quite often these sites were put up to a vote. At Allegan, Michigan, four locations were listed on the ballot.[24] And, at Needham, Massachusetts, even the sick and the maimed turned out to attend a stormy town meeting on the proposed library site.[25]

Carnegie officials were anxious that site disputes be settled always in a manner acceptable to the majority. In Excelsior Springs, Missouri, the dispute over the site became a row between "wet" and "dry" elements. Bertram wrote that the officials should choose a site upon which the whole community could agree, and that they should delay a decision rather than take any action which might allow ill feeling to continue and thus interfere with the success of the library.[26] Such controversies sometimes lasted a long time. In other instances (as will appear later) they were never settled, and as a result the money was not obtained.

Kendallville (Indiana) *Daily,* March 23, 1908

Carnegie stands ready with library offers

Annual Maintenance Pledge

The annual maintenance agreement of 10 percent of the total amount contributed by Carnegie was another stumbling block. Andrew Carnegie was unyielding in this requirement.

> I do not think that the community which is not willing to maintain a Library had better possess it. It is only the feeling that the Library belongs to every citizen richest and poorest alike, that gives it a soul, as it were. The Library Buildings which I am giving are the property of all the members of the community which maintain them.[27]

The pledge had to be for 10 percent of the gift amount. Statements as to mills or other wording were not accepted. This pledge, which was required in writing, was often sent back because it was not properly worded. Eventually a form pledge was drawn up and sent to each community for its use (see Appendix A-4).

A minimum of $1000 annual maintenance was usually required, though there were exceptions to this rule. But even though Carnegie made it a condition that 10 percent of the sum he provided for a building had to be spent annually by the community for maintenance, he was not prepared to give ten times any sum the community chose to provide for this purpose.

Carnegie frowned on endowment income or gifts paying for any or all of the annual support clause. Whenever such a procedure was suggested, he would recommend that the town or city build the library without his financial aid, as it would not otherwise contribute any tax money for the library's support. In the case of Eatonton, Georgia, for example, Carnegie withdrew his $6000 benefaction because the community was planning to use a prospective $5000 endowment fund for the annual support of the library. When the endowment gift was retracted, he renewed his original library building grant.[28]

At times legal difficulties stood in the way of communities acceding to the 10 percent clause. There were still states (especially in the very early days of Carnegie philanthropy) that had no enabling laws authorizing communities to levy taxes for library support. In Kentucky an enabling act had to be passed before Louisville could tax itself for the Carnegie library. This delayed the acceptance of the gift for about two years.[29] The Carnegie donation to Union, South Carolina, necessitated the enactment of a state law which required that taxpayers in each community vote on the acceptance of the gift and the guarantee of the income to the library in perpetuity.[30] In Utah the law was changed to give power to cities to levy a higher tax for libraries when Provo City, Utah, was refused a Carnegie gift because of low maintenance potentiality.[31] The Pennsylvania state legislature had to approve an act authorizing the Philadelphia city council to enter into contracts with the trustees of the public library so that the arrangements necessary for receiving the Carnegie gift could be carried into effect.[32]

Ohio presented even more difficulty. When Lebanon, Ohio, was in the process of obtaining a gift, local objectors raised the whole question of whether a village could lawfully accept a gift of money for a library building and agree to maintain it at not less than a specified sum per year (especially since a statute in Ohio provided that a council could not enter into any obligation involving the payment of money without the necessary funds in the treasury). The Court of Common Pleas declared that this statute was not applicable, but the Circuit Court reversed the judgment. The State Supreme Court, however, decided in favor of Carnegie libraries, and they were legalized in Ohio.[33]

As in the case of the site, and probably even more often, the annual maintenance frequently came up to a vote, since it usually meant an increase in taxes or a new tax to be imposed on the populace.

Amount of Money Donated

Small towns, particularly those under 1000 population, were not eligible for Carnegie library grants, since separate library buildings were not considered a necessity for such localities. However, it was possible, and, indeed, urged by Carnegie officials that such small communities join together with townships so that their officials could request funds for a joint or a county library. As an example, Cresco, Iowa, joined with Albion, Freemont, Howard Center, Orleans, and Vernon Springs townships for a Carnegie library grant.[34] Indiana was a state where this kind of cooperation was prevalent. Difficulties frequently arose, however. Often certain towns in a county would not want to support a county library, or adjoining townships would not cooperate with the desire of townspeople to enlarge their population in order to qualify for a Carnegie library.

The amount of money donated was dependent on the population of the town according to the last official United States census, the standard being about $2 per capita. An allowance was made for a possible population increase based on the annual average increase of the country. Bertram used only the United States census figures. In 1903 he declared that the local population statements, if believed, would give the United States a population of 150,000,000 (instead of 75,994,575).[35]

Some officials felt their towns unfairly reported by the census and fought back with letters of appeal and statistics of their own. They would cite what other towns of similar size had received from Carnegie and complain about how much less they, in turn, were obtaining. Post-office receipts, school-attendance figures, and population estimates of the city directory or chamber of commerce were sent as further evidence of the inaccuracies of census figures. Some communities were not even listed on a previous census, because they had been established only recently. If it was necessary, Bertram employed one other measure to supplement census information. He would request the assessed valuation of a town for each year since the last census and the percentage of the true valuation upon which the assessment was based. Action was delayed on some applications until results of the 1910 census became available. Elmira, New York, waited for the 1920 census and received a $40,000 increase over the original $70,000 Carnegie allocation in 1916 but, even so, had to add $40,000 of its own funds to complete the library building.[36]

Dissatisfaction with the amount of money received brought requests not only for increases in the original amount but also for additional funds after the building had been begun in order to finish it. However, there were a few towns which did not spend all the funds allotted. Pawnee City, Nebraska, accepted and used only $5800 out of its $7000 donation.[37] Lyons, Kansas, was offered $10,000 but took only $6000, since the legal tax levy authorized just $600 per year for maintenance.[38]

Increase of Controls

After the site was provided and the pledge of annual support was made, the townspeople who obtained gift funds before 1908 had little else to concern themselves with except to build the library anyway they wished. But as the donations of Carnegie buildings continued, there were more and more stipulations, regulations, and procedures as well as greater scrutiny by James Bertram.

By about 1908 he began requiring that building plans be submitted for approval before construction began. Still another requirement, beginning about 1914, was a pledge signed by the mayor that the projected building would not exceed a specified cost. Construction expenses often exceeded the gift amount, and every imaginable excuse was used to ask for further donations to finish the building. Frequent pleas were also made that the money was used on the building proper and none was left for the furnishings, since these had never been considered as part of the building cost. The resulting deficit had to be met by Carnegie so that the library would not open incompletely furnished or with a debt to be paid for out of current income. This situation was avoided by requiring the approval of plans accompanied by a pledge specifying the exact cost of the building, complete and ready to occupy. After this regulation was put into effect, Carnegie was rarely asked to pay deficits and, in fact, never did pay them.[39]

In the case of Mitchell, Indiana, the mayor for personal reasons refused to sign a statement that the library building would not exceed a certain cost. The Carnegie library correspondence indicated that the vast majority of the residents wanted the library. The Indiana library commissioner, after being asked by Bertram to investigate the situation, requested that an exception be made here, since in Indiana the power to levy taxes for library purposes rested entirely in the hands of the library board. In a rare instance of breaking a rule, Bertram accepted a pledge signed by the chairman and the secretary of the library board.[40]

Delays and Confusion

Seattle, Washington, received a promise of funds in 1901 for a main library building less than a week after its old main building had been destroyed by fire.[41] South Norwalk, Connecticut, prematurely began construction of its library in 1908 before resolutions and building plans had been approved. Bertram was horrified, but after some officials made a special trip to his office, everything was worked out satisfactorily.[42]

Normally, however, events did not move so quickly. On the contrary, procedures for Carnegie library philanthropy moved rather slowly. At times it took a lengthy period from the original offer to the actual completion of the building. For example, in Columbus, Wisconsin, seven years went by after the first promise before the matter was taken up a second time. Then, eight more years elapsed before the library building was finally completed.[43] Grand Haven, Michigan, also had a long history of offers, rejections, and neglect from 1903 to 1913.[44] In later years a four-year time limit was set up by the Carnegie Corporation from the time of promise to the completion of the building.

Numerous letters scattered over a long period of time are common in the Carnegie library correspondence. The Cuthbert, Georgia, file, for example, has ninety-three letters and documents in it, and this is by no means an extreme case.[45] Bertram often complained about all this excessive correspondence. He lost his temper with officials at Kendallville, Indiana, and told them that they had been wasting his time for nine years with lengthy, frequent communications and had paid no attention to directions.[46]

Often the delay was caused by confusion on the part of local officials as to what to do next. What was meant by the maintenance resolution and in what form was it to be? To whom should they turn for help on library building planning? Or, even more important, just how should they proceed in the details of obtaining a grant? The letter that follows is typical:

> Some few months ago the Woman's Reading Club of this place wrote you concerning a Carnegie Library. When the long looked for letter arrived we were not to say a little disappointed for we had asked in as simple and con-

cise a manner as possible, just *how* to go about the work. We were and still are, looking for information.

The reply sent, saying we should have our town council make application stating what the community is willing to do for its part, does not help much, for they do not know what is expected or required of them. If they do not know, and we can not inform them we are still in the dark.

I think you will find this place is worthy of your support. The community have manifested their willingness to help. Some hundred have even told what they will give towards it.

The town Council have given us to understand (verbally) that they will do their part, and now if you will be so kind as to tell us just what to do *Firstly, Secondly,* etc. we will work like trojans.

Hoping this letter will not seem out of place, and begging for an *early* reply.[47]

In exasperation Bertram referred the clubwomen of Hobart, Indiana, to their state library commission for help.

James Bertram did not simplify or expedite matters with the impatience and lack of tact which many of his letters display. Whenever anyone appealed for further information or assistance, he would refer them to the original letter of promise. This, presumably, afforded the answers to all questions regarding procedure in connection with Carnegie library gifts. In reply to a query from Enterprise, Oregon, Bertram wrote that the letter of promise was "so clear that it should not need elucidation." [48] When the president of the library board of Whiting, Indiana, wrote saying that the letter of promise did not state just who would erect the library building, Bertram replied:

There is no reason why you should not understand the letter sent, as it is very plain. Mr. Carnegie said he would give the money for the building. If he had intended you to understand he would erect the building himself, he would have said so.[49]

Frequently not just one but a combination of many different problems arose during Carnegie library negotiations causing long delays. For instance, the Sidney, Nebraska, village governing board requested and received a grant of $6500 for a building in 1913. It proceeded to pass a library ordinance and tax levy and to appoint a library board. Being ignorant of state law in this regard, the officials were not aware that their procedures in these actions were illegal. Then, one of their number took the whole matter in hand personally by engaging an architect and contractor to begin construction. As the work progressed, the official made modifications on the approved plans and raised building costs. The library board protested to the Carnegie Corporation and declared that under Nebraska law it was the only body empowered to disburse the library funds which, in any case, had been illegally taxed. The village board was then voted out of office, and the building stood abandoned and incomplete. It took action by the state library commission to settle local differences amicably and complete the Carnegie library building.[50]

At Athol, Massachusetts, the original request in 1902 resulted in an offer of $15,000. But the Carnegie library was voted down because of differences of opinion on the location, a feeling that the annual pledge was too high, and labor opposition. The question was taken up again in 1916 resulting in a willingness on the part of the Carnegie Corporation to make $22,000 available. Athol requested an additional $3500 but did not receive it. When the library building was finally completed in 1918, the community had to add its own funds to cover rising costs.[51]

Grants Pass, Oregon, voted against a tax levy for a $12,500 building in 1903. The matter was taken up again in 1910 and 1913 without further action. In 1917 an attempt was made to form a county library, but everything was delayed until 1921 because of World War I and building-plan problems.[52]

The task of managing the mechanics of Carnegie donations was a great one. The Carnegie library correspondence gives a good picture of all the problems, confusion, and delay. In addition to official letters, the file contains both signed and anonymous letters to Carnegie from people in a community considering a library building. An attorney from Goodland, Kansas, wrote to Andrew Carnegie saying that "the set that is after you now are a set of grafters, and it is not for the good that the city can get out of it but for what benefit they can get out of it. In the next place the city cannot levy tax enough to maintain the library." [53] And an anonymous letter mailed from Albion, Indiana, declared:[54]

> I beg to write you as one having great interest in the Library question at Albion, Ind. the people are greatly incensed at some of the methods followed by the Board, and there is a very dissatisfied feeling prevailing, if I might suggest, the Corporation go slow in giving their bequest, or retrait [sic] all together as there is going to be some underhand work done about the building. While I know anonymous letters do not sound good you will find this to be an exception to the rule in as much as it is truthful and from
>
> An interested party

Telegrams also abound in the correspondence. Townspeople sent telegrams entreating additional sums because the bids exceeded the gift amount, asking why there had been no reply to a letter of application, or just notifying Carnegie that a special election had approved a tax levy for the library. Bertram did not like the use of these dispatches and declared that this was no way to do business. Handwritten letters, likewise, annoyed him. He wrote the following postscript on a letter to one woman correspondent, "Please use the typewriter and business note paper. Your letter of Jan. 31st is nine pages which is too much for busy people to turn over to get at the facts of the case." [55]

To add to the confusion, letters, plans, photographs, and drawings often seemed to go astray in the mail. Sometimes a change in the administration of a local mayor or library board brought about a complete loss of correspondence, and Bertram was called upon to provide copies of previous letters.

Bertram tried to keep track of progress on community activities in regard to obtaining a library. He apparently scanned professional library magazines, particularly the *Library Journal's* monthly section dealing with news of new buildings. He frequently wrote to the editor of *Library Journal* asking him for the source of false or questionable information pertaining to Carnegie library grants. Various news-clipping services covering Carnegie libraries were also subscribed to. He also would write follow-up letters to communities which he had not heard from in some time to inquire about the progress on their library buildings.

Consummation

The gift money was never sent in advance nor in one large sum but rather in smaller amounts as work on the building progressed. Bertram would send a letter to Robert F. Franks, Carnegie's cashier and later treasurer of the Carnegie Corporation, authorizing payment and, at the same time, would instruct the community to call for payments from Franks. A request was also made at this point that once the building was erected, an unmounted photograph should be sent to Bertram, showing the front and side elevations, with a complete set of plans on a reduced scale, preferably on a sheet not more than twelve by sixteen inches.

Even the laying of the cornerstone was not without problems. Officials of Eatonton, Georgia, sent for a cornerstone from Dunfermline, Carnegie's place of birth, but unfortunately it arrived in many broken pieces.[56] Some communities asked for permission to have Masons lay the cornerstone. In such cases Bertram declared that this was a local decision and that Andrew Carnegie had no objections.

Very often library officials would request a picture or a bust of Carnegie to display in their new building. These were not given freely but had to be purchased from commercial outlets, of which Bertram would supply the names and addresses. Frederick, Oklahoma, was not satisfied with a portrait of

Andrew Carnegie; it wanted a life-size photograph of him for the library wall.[57] Ponca City, Oklahoma, went further and requested a photograph of Carnegie in a Highland costume.[58]

Building dedications were usually large, imposing affairs with many distinguished guests and speakers. Andrew Carnegie was frequently invited but rarely attended. Occasionally he was asked to send a message to be read. As in the case of Warren, Ohio, he would usually reply by requesting the main speaker "to assure the good people of Warren that although absent in body I am with them in spirit" [59] and to express his best wishes for the success of the library and the prosperity of the people. Sometimes he would depart from this standard greeting and mail one in the style sent to the president of the Public Library Board of Brookings, South Dakota, to whom he wrote:

> . . . Brookings is to enter into enjoyment of its new library building. What a blessing came to man when the improvement in printing enabled our forefathers to realize that the best of man's work was hereafter to be preserved in books, and further, that in civilized nations like ours the general mass of the people are able to read such books and enjoy the treasures of literature.
>
> Shakespeare puts it thus, "my library, dukedom large enuf." [60]

Communities would often send Carnegie mementos of building openings. Officials at Muncie, Indiana, sent a souvenir silver spoon with a picture of the Carnegie library in the bowl to Carnegie's little daughter along with a plea for an additional $5000 to finish paying for a $50,000 building. Their request was granted.[61] Announcements, programs, and newspaper clippings of library dedications sent to the Corporation give a graphic picture of the festive occasions which closed periods of negotiations, arrangements, and construction for each community as the Carnegie libraries were opened to the public.

54   CARNEGIE LIBRARIES

Notes

[1] Dr. W. A. Moore, secretary of the Library Association, to the Carnegie Corporation of New York, May 27, 1913 (Chatfield, Minn., Carnegie Library Correspondence, Microfilm Reel No.5).

[2] E. E. Mummert and I. O. Wood to Andrew Carnegie, Dec. 20, 1900 (Goshen, Ind., Carnegie Library Correspondence, Microfilm Reel No.12).

[3] Undated editorial clipping from the *Aberdeen Sun* (Aberdeen, Wash., Carnegie Library Correspondence, Microfilm Reel No.1).

[4] Mayor H. G. Truesdale to Andrew Carnegie, April 28, 1902 (Berlin, Wis., Carnegie Library Correspondence, Microfilm Reel No.3).

[5] Commercial Club (signed by S. A. Lorenz, president; K. F. Baldridge, secretary; and S. F. McLeuwell, treasurer) to Andrew Carnegie, May 17, 1911 (Bloomfield, Iowa, Carnegie Library Correspondence, Microfilm Reel No.3).

[6] Wilkes Holcomb to Andrew Carnegie, Jan. 10, 1911 (Columbia, Tenn., Carnegie Library Correspondence, Microfilm Reel No.66E).

[7] Fay H. White to Andrew Carnegie, April 6, 1911, and April 17, 1914 (Corning, N.Y., Carnegie Library Correspondence, Microfilm Reel No.67).

[8] Effa Crawford of the Women's Club to Andrew Carnegie, June 23, 1915 (Guthrie Center, Iowa, Carnegie Library Correspondence, Microfilm Reel No.68).

[9] Marion Howard Prentiss to Andrew Carnegie, April 15, 1903 (Wiscasset, Maine, Carnegie Library Correspondence, Microfilm Reel No.68).

[10] Mrs. W. F. Oates to Andrew Carnegie, March 27, 1908 (Ponca City, Okla., Carnegie Library Correspondence, Microfilm Reel No.25).

[11] J. M. Underwood, E. H. Smith, and third illegible name to James Bertram, Feb. 25, 1909 (Lake City, Minn., Carnegie Library Correspondence, Microfilm Reel No.16).

[12] W. C. Whitney to James Bertram, April 7, 1915 (Sparta, Mich., Carnegie Library Correspondence, Microfilm Reel No.29).

[13] James Bertram to Miss Gertrude Buckhaus of the Montana Library Commission, also librarian of the University of Montana, Feb. 15, 1916 (Fort Benton, Mont., Carnegie Library Correspondence, Microfilm Reel No.10).

[14] Rev. A. L. Weaver to Andrew Carnegie, Feb. 2, 1911 (Syracuse, Ind. Carnegie Library Correspondence, Microfilm Reel No.31).

[15] Burton J. Hendrick, *The Life of Andrew Carnegie*, p.199–200.

[16] James Bertram (for Andrew Carnegie) to Rev. Robert Wilson, president of the Library Society, April 18, 1911 (Charleston, S.C., Carnegie Library Correspondence, Microfilm Reel No.5).

[17] James Bertram to William L. Clements, Dec. 11, 1905 (Bay City, Mich., Carnegie Library Correspondence, Microfilm Reel No.2).

[18] St. Paul, Minn., Carnegie Library Correspondence, Microfilm Reel No.27.

[19] James Bertram to A. C. Steck, Dec. 28, 1904 (Independence, Kans.,
Carnegie Library Correspondence, Microfilm Reel No.15).
[20] James Bertram to George H. Cooper, Feb. 19, 1904 (Greenfield, Ind.,
Carnegie Library Correspondence, Microfilm Reel No.12).
[21] A. E. Ward, secretary of Library Association, to Andrew Carnegie,
Jan. 28, 1911 (Madison, Nebr., Carnegie Library Correspondence, Microfilm Reel No.18).
[22] Goodland, Kans., Carnegie Library Correspondence, Microfilm Reel
No.12.
[23] Waterloo, Iowa, Carnegie Library Correspondence, Microfilm Reel
No.37.
[24] Allegan, Mich., Carnegie Library Correspondence, Microfilm Reel No.1.
[25] Needham, Mass., Carnegie Library Correspondence, Microfilm Reel
No.21.
[26] James Bertram to Purd B. Wright, librarian, Aug. 11, 1915 (Excelsior
Springs, Mo., Carnegie Library Correspondence, Microfilm No.10).
[27] Andrew Carnegie to the Gentlemen of the Committee (Trustees) of the
Free Public Library, March 18, 1904 (Connelsville, Pa., Carnegie Library
Correspondence, Microfilm Reel No.7).
[28] Eatonton, Ga., Carnegie Library Correspondence, Microfilm Reel No.9.
[29] Louisville, Ky., Carnegie Library Correspondence, Microfilm Reel
No.18.
[30] Union, S. C., Carnegie Library Correspondence, Microfilm Reel No.30.
[31] Provo City, Utah, Carnegie Library Correspondence, Microfilm Reel
No.26.
[32] I. G. Rosengarten, president of the Board of Trustees, to James Bertram,
April 18, 1903 (Philadelphia, Pa., Carnegie Library Correspondence, Microfilm Reel No.25).
[33] W. Chester Maple, secretary of the Library Trustees, to James Bertram,
March 16, 1906 (Lebanon, Ohio, Carnegie Library Correspondence, Microfilm Reel No.16).
[34] Cresco, Iowa, Carnegie Library Correspondence, Microfilm Reel No.7.
[35] James Bertram to Melvil Dewey, State Librarian, Albany, N.Y., Feb. 20,
1903 (Oneida, N.Y., Carnegie Library Correspondence, Microfilm Reel
No.23).
[36] Elmira, N.Y., Carnegie Library Correspondence, Microfilm Reel No.9.
[37] Pawnee City, Nebr., Carnegie Library Correspondence, Microfilm Reel
No.24.
[38] Lyons, Kans., Carnegie Library Correspondence, Microfilm Reel No.18.
[39] James Bertram to Les K. Johnson, chairman of the Library Board, Feb.
8, 1916 (Vernon, Texas, Carnegie Library Correspondence, Microfilm Reel
No.32).
[40] Mitchell, Ind., Carnegie Library Correspondence, Microfilm Reel
No.20.
[41] Seattle, Wash., Carnegie Library Correspondence, Microfilm Reel
No.29.

⁴²South Norwalk, Conn., Carnegie Library Correspondence, Microfilm Reel No.29.

⁴³Columbus, Wis., Carnegie Library Correspondence, Microfilm Reel No.7.

⁴⁴Grand Haven, Mich., Carnegie Library Correspondence, Microfilm Reel No.12.

⁴⁵Cuthbert, Ga., Carnegie Library Correspondence, Microfilm Reel No.7.

⁴⁶Kendallville, Ind., Carnegie Library Correspondence, Microfilm Reel No.15.

⁴⁷Mrs. Fannie Werner to James Bertram, Jan. 27, 1913 (Hobart, Ind., Carnegie Library Correspondence, Microfilm Reel No.14).

⁴⁸James Bertram to Dr. Clyde T. Hockett, May 14, 1913 (Enterprise, Ore., Carnegie Library Correspondence, Microfilm Reel No.10).

⁴⁹James Bertram to F. N. Gavit, president of the Public Library Board, Jan. 25, 1905 (Whiting, Ind., Carnegie Library Correspondence, Microfilm Reel No.34).

⁵⁰Sidney, Nebr., Carnegie Library Correspondence, Microfilm Reel No.29.

⁵¹Athol, Mass., Carnegie Library Correspondence, Microfilm Reel No.2.

⁵²Grants Pass, Ore., Carnegie Library Correspondence, Microfilm Reel No.12.

⁵³C. C. Perdieu to Andrew Carnegie, July 4, 1911 (Goodland, Kans., Carnegie Library Correspondence, Microfilm Reel No.12).

⁵⁴Anonymous writer to James Bertram, Sept. 9, 1916 (Albion, Ind., Carnegie Library Correspondence, Microfilm Reel No.1).

⁵⁵James Bertram to Mrs. Sabelle W. Gyde, Feb. 19, 1908 (Wallace, Idaho, Carnegie Library Correspondence, Microfilm Reel No.33).

⁵⁶Eatonton, Ga., Carnegie Library Correspondence, Microfilm Reel No.9.

⁵⁷S. J. Mathies, secretary of the Library Board, March 6, 1916 (Frederick, Okla., Carnegie Library Correspondence, Microfilm Reel No.11).

⁵⁸Mrs. W. G. Walls to Andrew Carnegie, undated (Ponca City, Okla., Carnegie Library Correspondence, Microfilm Reel No.25).

⁵⁹Andrew Carnegie to John Sullivan, U.S. Attorney, Cleveland, Ohio, Dec. 16, 1905 (Warren, Ohio, Carnegie Library Correspondence, Microfilm Reel No.33).

⁶⁰Andrew Carnegie to William H. Powers, president of the Public Library Board, Jan. 18, 1915 (Brookings, S.Dak., Carnegie Library Correspondence, Microfilm Reel No.4).

⁶¹Clipping entitled "Souvenir Silver Spoon Brought Good Return" from the Muncie, Ind., *Star*, Feb. 28, 1904 (Muncie, Ind., Carnegie Library Correspondence, Microfilm Reel No.21).

CHAPTER FOUR

Carnegie Library Architecture

Until 1908, once the site was provided and the annual maintenance pledge was signed, the community built its library as it saw fit. Further requests for funds, particularly those in the early years or those for small amounts, were usually granted with little question. Then, as James Bertram began to examine building plans, especially those of towns desiring great increases of money, he noted signs of poor library planning. From 1908 on he requested plans be submitted for approval in order to correct these abuses.

Carnegie himself was aware of some of the architectural monstrosities going up as libraries. On a clipping from a Denver newspaper showing a drawing of the projected main library promised in 1902, he wrote, "I am sorry to have my money wasted in this way — This is no practical library plan. Too many pillars." [1]

Specifications

In later years Bertram wrote Carnegie a memorandum reporting the policy involving close supervision of library plans. In his note he indicated that relatively few libraries had been constructed before 1898. As a result there were no architects experienced in building libraries, particularly those for small or medium-sized towns. All too many buildings were planned with expensive exteriors and inefficient, uneconomical interiors. When well-known librarians began to urge architectural supervision, Bertram decided to prevent building blunders instead of attempting to correct them.

Conferences with leading authorities from the library and architectural professions brought about agreement on certain standards in library architecture. The result was a leaflet entitled "Notes on Library Bildings" which was sent from 1911 on as a guide to each community along with the promise of funds. These "Notes" and "judicious pressure on architects and communities" usually resulted in a desirable building.[2]

Many communities themselves had constantly requested assistance in their architectural planning from the earliest days of Carnegie library gifts. Unfortunately, library architectural control began rather late. By the end of 1907, 762 out of 1412 communities had already been promised Carnegie library buildings. When the "Notes" came out in 1911, 916 communities had been promised funds for libraries.

The six editions of the "Notes on Library Bildings" varied only slightly in presentation and information. They provided certain minimum standards for the main requirements of accommodations in the libraries built with Carnegie funds. Each community was to obtain the greatest amount of usable space consistent with good taste in building. The best results for a small library could be obtained in a rectangular-shaped building with a basement and one floor (other-shaped buildings would require extra attention and planning to avoid waste of space). The main floor, 12 to 15 feet high, would accommodate the bookstacks, the circulation desk area, and suitable space for reading by adults and children. Rear and side windows were to be about 6 to 7 feet from the floor, thus permitting shelving all around. The floor could be subdivided as desired by means of bookstacks. Glass partitions built in above these stacks would provide quiet if, for instance, a

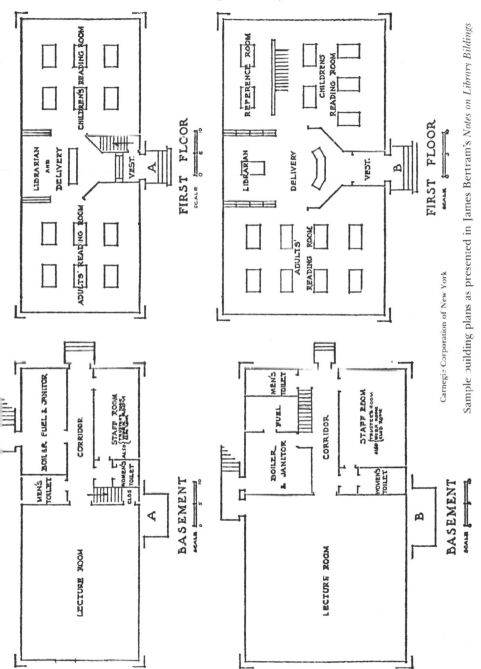

Carnegie Corporation of New York

Sample building plans as presented in James Bertram's *Notes on Library Bildings*

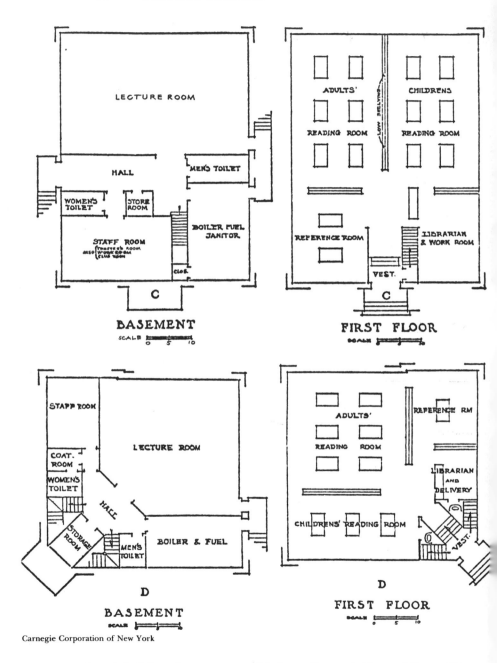

BASEMENT

SCALE 0 5 10

FIRST FLOOR

SCALE

BASEMENT

SCALE

FIRST FLOOR

SCALE 0 5 10

Carnegie Corporation of New York

Sample building plans as presented in James Bertram's *Notes on Library Bildings*

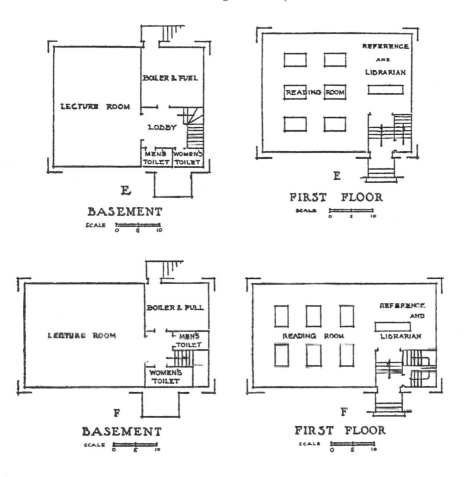

NOTE

Elevations of plans submitted for approval should clearly sho the floor and ceiling lines of basement and main floor, and the natural and artificial grade lines.   Floor plans should sho, clearly designated, all roof supports and similar obstructions of the accommodation.

Carnegie Corporation of New York

Sample building plans as presented in James Bertram's *Notes on Library Bildings*

separate children's department was to be established on the main floor.

Library planners were admonished to guard against the waste of space at the building entrance. The earlier Carnegie libraries frequently provided for large, elaborate entrance-ways that were costly and space-consuming. What often resulted was a corridor 12 to 18 feet wide running from the entrance to a circulation desk 20 feet inside the building. In a small library with little heavy traffic, an entry half this size was ample. The circulation desk was to be located close to the entrance and placed so that the librarian could supervise as much of the library as possible. A small vestibule entering into one large room allowed two large, well-lighted areas or spaces on either side of the passageway in which readers were undisturbed by library traffic and circulation-desk conversation.

The basement was to be about 9 to 10 feet high and about 4 feet below the natural grade level. Storage, work, and lecture rooms as well as the heating plant and rest rooms would be located here. Care was to be taken so as not to allot too much valuable space to cloakrooms, toilets, and stairs.

The "Notes" were written with smaller buildings in mind. A more spacious building required larger and more varied treatment but no modification of primary purposes. For such a library a small stackroom, about one third of the width of the main portion, could be placed at the rear, giving an inverted T-plan. Or such a rear wing could be added for a stackroom at minimum expense and without seriously interfering with library services in a building which had to be expanded. The librarian's office logically belonged between this stackroom and the delivery desk.

No suggestions were made about the exterior, but the implication was for the architect to keep to a plain, dignified structure and not aim at exterior effects that might make a practical and economic layout of the interior impossible. Bertram warned against building "Greek temples" instead of libraries.[3]

Some additional rules not specifically covered by the "Notes" are found throughout the microfilmed correspondence.

Andrew Carnegie had no interest in buying residences or other existing buildings for conversion into libraries. Except for a few small communities or some very small branches, no frame buildings were built as libraries. Building costs were not to include shrubs, walks, or other ground improvements. The installation of fireplaces was discouraged in the Carnegie libraries. Bertram felt that a fireplace installed for appearance only took up important wall space which would be adequate to shelve 500 to 600 books. If the fireplace were for actual use, it would be chiefly for the comfort of two or three people in its vicinity to the exclusion of others. It would be better to have an adequate heating plant in the basement.[4] Smoking rooms also were not approved by Bertram as being appropriate or necessary in library buildings. Finally, the building was to be exclusively for library purposes and not for any other, not even for related municipal or educational offices.

Problems

James Bertram became deeply involved in architectural control. The Carnegie library correspondence is filled with lengthy letters from him offering suggestions or requesting changes in building plans. A typical and frequent phrase of his after receiving some proposed plans was, "but these will not do." Another representative Bertram response went to Anthony, Kansas:

> It is all very well for you to plan your building as a dance hall, club, YMCA, dining room, kitchen, etc., but remember Mr. Carnegie is paying for a Library Building and not for this kind of miscellaneous general convenience.[5]

Bertram told Derby Neck, Connecticut, officials that a small town like theirs should have and needed only a small cottage as a library building. He cited the many, tiny communities in New England, with only a few hundred dollars annually to spend on the library, that had been given expensive structures by benevolent persons who had spent their boyhoods there. He called these libraries "white elephants" on the hands of the people and stated that small cottage-type libraries, costing $2000 or $3000, could more easily have been maintained for practical use to the community.[6]

Rockford, Ohio, library officials were asked, "With regard to the plans you sent, will you kindly tell me the reason for enclosing the Librarian in a small room with walls a foot thick surrounding him?"[7] And Bertram criticized the Franklin, Texas, library building plan for being merely an auditorium with two small library rooms attached to it.[8]

Some communities did not pay attention to Bertram's building suggestions or to the "Notes on Library Bildings." He chided Geneva, Nebraska, for examining nearby library buildings instead of being guided by the "Notes" that had been sent to them. He admitted that many of the library buildings previously built were done so without critical review of the plans, and that they currently would probably not be approved.[9] Bertram expressed discouragement with Dixon, California, when he received a night letter asking what particular parts of their last revision of plans were contradictory to his ideas, after they had just had the matter explained in detail and after having "Notes" in their hands.[10] Not only did many communities tend to ignore the "Notes," but a few, like Broken Bow, Nebraska, apparently even built libraries which were different from those approved by the Carnegie Corporation.[11]

Generally Carnegie officials never interfered in the choice of an architect. Bertram had close contact with two New York City architects, Edward Tilton and Henry Whitefield, and often called upon them for advice and consultation. He would also on occasion suggest their names, as well as others who had successful library planning experience, to communities requesting such information, though he never formally recommended an architect. Bertram did not want to communicate or correspond with architects in regard to building plans and would deal only with the civic or library authorities who were their employers.

But Bertram was not averse to criticizing architects. Such criticism and his own personal involvement in library architectural control can be seen in a letter to the mayor of West Tampa, Florida, in which he wrote:

> I have looked at probably two thousand library plans and I have never had so much trouble with any set of plans as with yours. This arose from the fact that you employed a gentleman who had never drawn library plans before, and that I practically had to have them drawn by correspondence, and of course take no responsibility whatever for the result, either architecturally or financially. What has been secured is as economical and satisfactory a layout of accommodation as could be secured under the circumstances.[12]

Bertram praised the Newman, California, architect on his talent for expressing beauty and dignity, but with only an $8000 appropriation for a building he suggested that the more important features were utility and economy of space.[13] He was a bit more caustic in regard to the Centralia, Washington, architect:

> Yours of June 12th received, with plans. No wonder the people do not like the plans, which in no way interpret the ideas exprest in Notes on Library Bilding. A school-boy could do that better than the plans show. If the architect's object had been how to waste space instead of how to economize it, he could not have succeeded better.

After some specific examples of what was wrong, Bertram continued:

> If the Architect cannot make a better attempt at interpreting the notes on Library Bilding, I shall be pleased to put you in communication with architects who have shown their ability to do so.[14]

Lusk, Wyoming, began to put up a Carnegie Library without an architect, much to the discomfort of Bertram. He so informed the president of the Wyoming Library Association with the hope that she would use her influence to dissuade such action.[15]

In addition to problems with architects, there were difficulties with contractors and builders. At times contracts and lengthy specifications were sent to Bertram unnecessarily. Sometimes contractors would abandon or be dismissed from a new library project with the building not only incomplete but also with the original allocation overspent. The Syracuse, New York, correspondence contains numerous newspaper clippings and letters criticizing exhorbitant legal, architect's, and inspectors' fees pertaining to the Carnegie library. It seems that there were inspectors for everything, and it was suggested that these were merely political appointees.[16] The librarian of Wichita, Kansas, resigned in protest over the furniture selection, the interior decoration, and what to her were faults in the library building construction.[17]

One of the most frequent architectural problems, prior to the requirement of a cost resolution pledge, was that funds were exhausted before the completion of the building or the acquisition of furnishings and equipment. That this happened often is dramatized by a letter from Andrew Carnegie to the chairman of the Mount Vernon, New York, Carnegie Library Building Committee:

> Yours of January 11th received. You have broken the record this morning by your note. In all my experience, having provided funds for about thirteen hundred and fifty libraries, I have never had a Chairman of a Building Committee report a surplus, and I have very often had to meet a deficit.[18]

He went on to say that the $75 surplus could be spent for useful books.

Bertram's most common response to petitions for additional funds was to request the community to see what could be done with the available funds before Mr. Carnegie was called upon to add to his donation. If the demand for an increase persisted, a list of expenditures encumbered and

Houston Public Library

An early Carnegie library building at Houston, Texas

another list of requirements were requested from the community. Such lists were scrutinized very carefully by Bertram, and he did not hesitate to slash those items which in his opinion were unnecessary. Thus, to the Lima, Ohio, list of $5000 worth of items to complete their building, he replied in part, "I think it is somewhat impertinent to enter in list of cost of a library the cost of a piano."[19] If an increase were granted to a community, it first had to raise the annual maintenance proportionately to the new total amount.

Often a community would wish to add its own funds to those of Carnegie. This was permissible, but its own contribution had to be spent before any part of the Carnegie donation was touched, and the pledge for annual support still had to be based on the total spent for the building. For example, when Eveleth, Minnesota, added $15,000 to the

$15,000 Carnegie gift, it not only had to expend its contri-
bution first but also had to pledge an annual support of
$3000.[20] Many towns, however, did not request permission to
add their own funds to those of Carnegie, and in such cases
there was usually no maintenance pledge increase.

If a town purposely overbuilt or added nonlibrary features,
there would be no help from Carnegie. The request for an
additional $15,000 to $17,000 from Spartanburg, South
Carolina, was answered with the following:

> Yours of the 5th received. This seems to be one of the
> worst cases of projecting a fine building irrespective of what
> it is to cost and where the money is to come from. Mr.
> Carnegie sometimes gives a thousand or two more than he
> has promised where the town is able and willing to give a
> correspondingly increased maintenance fund but to make
> up the amount you wish is out of the question.[21]

When Greenfield, Indiana, spent all its $7500 gift on the
building shell and asked for an additional $2000 for neces-
sary heating, wiring, plumbing, and furniture, the money
was refused.[22] Further funds were also refused Eufaula,
Alabama, which added another floor to its library building as
an unauthorized auditorium and then asked Carnegie for this
extra $3000 expense.[23] After Bertram reviewed the justi-
fication of Parkersburg, West Virginia, for an additional
$2000 (it had already been granted one increase from $25,000
to $34,000), he replied:

> Yours of December 1st received. Glancing over the
> photographs you have sent, the carpets, easy chairs, re-
> ception room, etc. give one more the idea of a private
> house than a Free Public Library. In a busy city library one
> would expect more benches and tables and fewer carpets
> and arm chairs. In the newspaper room there only appears
> to be half a dozen newspapers. Why is a "reception room"
> needed? Why should there be a "board room?" Cannot the
> committee meet in the librarian's office? Altogether, we are
> perfectly sure that a Library Building to give all the public

service needed by Parkersburg could have been erected for $25,000, certainly within $30,000.[24]

When the additional funds necessary to complete or to furnish the library did not come from Carnegie, public-spirited local citizens would usually contribute whatever was necessary, or, if it were a small amount, perhaps the general fund of the municipal treasury would suffice. In the case of Freeport, Illinois, the extra money was received from the board of education in exchange for permanent, free office space on the second floor of the library.[25] But after Carnegie's refusal to provide an additional $3000 to Casper, Wyoming, the building stood empty for a number of years. Following appeals of the governor of Wyoming on behalf of his home town, Carnegie relented and provided the extra $3000 for an additional $300 per year pledge.[26]

It is paradoxical that in the last years of Carnegie donations, from about 1915 to 1920, a period during which building prices were rapidly rising, there should be such severe strictures on keeping within building costs through the mayor's pledge. Conversely, during the early years of Carnegie's gifts of library buildings, up to about 1904, it was relatively easy to obtain an increase.

Building Additions

By about 1908 some of the communities with early Carnegie libraries began to make requests for the expansion of their buildings. Before Bertram would consider such an application, he would ascertain whether the original donation had been used to provide the maximum accommodation possible for the money (consistent with good architectural taste) and whether the space within the existing walls was laid out with maximum efficiency and economy for library purposes. Then, of course, there had to be a sizable population increase as well as evidence that the library was being used heavily and that not enough space was available for books and readers. The Carnegie Corporation would cooperate with a town in the joint operation of correcting faults in and adding to an existing library building with the community paying for the correction and the Corporation doing so for the addition.

In reality, then, the earlier Carnegie library towns were penalized for not planning their buildings correctly. Yet, the reason they did not build their libraries well was because they had no one to help them. Now they were forced to re-model at their own expense.

As an example, White Plains, New York, had to spend $4000 of its own funds for alterations of its building in 1916 before the Carnegie Corporation donated $18,000 for an addition to the library that originally cost $18,000 in 1904. Since the total cost of the building now totaled $40,000, the annual maintenance pledge had to be raised to $4000.[27] On the other hand, the 1917 request of Fort Collins, Colorado, for money to expand its library was refused, because the community would not rearrange and redo the old library interior which had been very poorly planned.[28]

Some of the poor architectural features of these early libraries were criticized in Bertram's letters. In answer to a request for expansion from Eureka, California, he replied that the library had a great deal of wasted space, including a dome and a large lobby which was a lobby to nothing at all. Also, two double stairways to the basement led to nothing of importance, because an 8-foot clearance made this place an impracticable cellar rather than a useful basement.[29] The 1899 Carnegie Library in Fort Worth, Texas, was censured for an art gallery which took up one sixth of the total library area, a large lobby and wide vestibule across the building, and a second floor which was not entirely devoted to library purposes.[30]

Branch Libraries

After Carnegie had been giving libraries on a wholesale scale for a few years, he changed his views on donating funds for large main libraries in big cities in favor of providing funds for branch libraries. He felt there was a tendency for

TABLE 10

CITIES RECEIVING CARNEGIE LIBRARY MAIN
BUILDINGS AND/OR BRANCHES*

STATE AND MUNICIPALITY	BUILDINGS	AMOUNT
CALIFORNIA		
Los Angeles	6	$210,000
Oakland	M + 4	190,000
San Francisco	M + 7	750,000
San Jose	2	57,000
Santa Cruz	M + 3	29,000
Santa Monica	M + 1	25,000
COLORADO		
Colorado Springs	M + 1	60,000
Denver	M + 8	360,000
CONNECTICUT		
Bridgeport	2	50,000
New Haven	3	60,000
DISTRICT OF COLUMBIA		
Washington	M + 3	682,000
GEORGIA		
Atlanta	M + 3	202,000
Savannah	M + 1	87,000
ILLINOIS		
Danville	2	65,000
INDIANA		
East Chicago	2	40,000
Evansville	3	60,000
Gary	M + 2	90,000
Indianapolis	5	100,000
IOWA		
Sioux City	M + 1	85,000
Waterloo	2	45,000
KANSAS		
Kansas City	M + 1	100,000
KENTUCKY		
Louisville	M + 8	450,000
LOUISIANA		
New Orleans	M + 5	350,000
MARYLAND		
Baltimore	14	500,000
MASSACHUSETTS		
Lynn	2	50,000
Somerville	M + 2	123,000
Springfield	M + 3	260,000
Worcester	3	75,000

TABLE 10—*continued*

STATE AND MUNICIPALITY	BUILDINGS	AMOUNT
MICHIGAN		
Detroit	M + 8	$ 750,000
MINNESOTA		
Duluth	M + 2	125,000
Minneapolis	4	125,000
St. Paul	3	75,000
MISSISSIPPI		
Meridian	M + 1	38,000
MISSOURI		
St. Joseph	2	50,000
St. Louis	M + 6	1,000,000
NEBRASKA		
Lincoln	M + 1	87,000
NEW JERSEY		
Camden	M + 2	120,000
East Orange	M + 2	116,000
Elizabeth	M + 1	130,810
Montclair	2	60,000
NEW YORK		
New York	66	5,202,621
NORTH CAROLINA		
Greensboro	M + 1	40,446
OHIO		
Cincinnati	10	286,000
Cleveland	15	590,000
Dayton	2	65,000
Toledo	5	125,000
OREGON		
Portland	7	165,000
PENNSYLVANIA		
Philadelphia	25	1,500,000
Pittsburgh	M + 8	1,160,614
TENNESSEE		
Nashville	M + 3	175,000
TEXAS		
Dallas	M + 1	76,000
Houston	M + 1	65,000
VIRGINIA		
Norfolk	M + 1	70,000
WASHINGTON		
Bellingham	2	36,000
Seattle	M + 7	430,000
Spokane	M + 3	155,000

TABLE 10—*continued*

STATE AND MUNICIPALITY	BUILDINGS	AMOUNT
WISCONSIN		
Madison	M + 1	$90,000
Racine	M + 1	60,000
Superior	2	70,000

*Compiled from Carnegie Corporation of New York, *Carnegie Grants for Library Buildings, 1890–1917* (New York: Carnegie Corp., 1943), p.9–37, and Carnegie Corporation of New York, *Carnegie Corporation Library Program, 1911–1961* (New York: Carnegie Corp., 1963), p.25–64.

such central buildings to be too lavishly designed and monumental.

The Carnegie gift of $500,000 to St. Louis for a main building had been supplemented by $1,000,000 in city funds.[31] Yet it contained only about as much effective space as the Springfield, Massachusetts, main library which was built for $350,000.[32] San Francisco's main library cost $1,153,000, with only $375,000 contributed by Carnegie.[33] Denver overspent by $50,000 on its central library and took $30,000 from its book fund to help make up the deficit. By 1913 Denver reported that the main library was unsafe and needed repairs. Carnegie did not give further help in these instances, but he did give funds for branch libraries.[34]

When requests came in for building additions, branches were sometimes suggested as a better means of expanding library service. Such was the case when Bertram made the reply to Easton, Pennsylvania: "You say that everybody can get to the Easton Library for a five cents fare. No doubt, but there is no reason why there should be a five cent tax on every book taken out by a great many people." [35] The total distribution of branch libraries built with Carnegie funds during these years is shown in Table 10.

Notes

[1] Undated clipping (from unidentified newspaper) entitled "Work Soon To Begin on Carnegie Library" (Denver, Colo., Carnegie Library Correspondence, Microfilm Reel No.8).

[2] A corrected first draft of a letter from James Bertram to Andrew Carnegie, undated, in Carnegie Corporation of New York files.

[3] Taken from the various editions of the "Notes on Library Bildings" as found in the microfilmed Carnegie Library Correspondence.

[4] James Bertram to Mrs. Eliza A. Tinkle, secretary of the Library Board, July 16, 1917 (Flora, Ind., Carnegie Library Correspondence, Microfilm Reel No.10).

[5] James Bertram to W. E. Blackburn, April 11, 1912 (Anthony, Kans., Carnegie Library Correspondence, Microfilm Reel No.1).

[6] James Bertram to W. F. Osborne, March 15, 1906 (Derby Neck, Conn., Carnegie Library Correspondence, Microfilm Reel No.8).

[7] James Bertram to W. F. Pixler, chairman of the Board of Trustees, Feb. 21, 1912 (Rockford, Ohio, Carnegie Library Correspondence, Microfilm Reel No.27).

[8] James Bertram to Mayor R. M. Cole, May 17, 1913 (Franklin, Texas, Carnegie Library Correspondence, Microfilm Reel No.11).

[9] James Bertram to Sara E. Wilson, secretary of the Library Board, Nov. 13, 1911 (Geneva, Nebr., Carnegie Library Correspondence, Microfilm Reel No.11).

[10] James Bertram to Walter H. Parker, April 19, 1912 (Dixon, Calif., Carnegie Library Correspondence, Microfilm Reel No.8).

[11] Broken Bow, Nebr., Carnegie Library Correspondence, Microfilm Reel No.4.

[12] James Bertram to Mayor James D. McFarlane, July 15, 1913 (West Tampa, Fla., Carnegie Library Correspondence, Microfilm Reel No.34).

[13] James Bertram to Mrs. Helen Price Gregory, town clerk, Oct. 25, 1915 (Newman, Calif., Carnegie Library Correspondence, Microfilm Reel No.21).

[14] James Bertram to Mayor J. P. Guerrier, July 4, 1911 (Centralia, Wash., Carnegie Library Correspondence, Microfilm Reel No.5).

[15] James Bertram to Grace R. Hobard, president of the Wyoming Library Association, Laramie, Wyo., May 28, 1912 (Lusk, Wyo., Carnegie Library Correspondence, Microfilm Reel No.18).

[16] Syracuse, N.Y., Carnegie Library Correspondence, Microfilm Reel No.31.

[17] Wichita, Kans., Carnegie Library Correspondence, Microfilm Reel No.34.

[18] Andrew Carnegie to W. F. Gay, Jan. 16, 1905 (Mount Vernon, N.Y., Carnegie Library Correspondence, Microfilm Reel No.20).

[19] James Bertram to G. M. Sprague, secretary of the Library Association, Dec. 26, 1908 (Lima, Ohio, Carnegie Library Correspondence, Microfilm Reel No.17).

[20] Eveleth, Minn., Carnegie Library Correspondence, Microfilm Reel No.10.

[21] James Bertram to John B. Cleveland, Library Committee, Sept. 21, 1904 (Spartanburg, S.C., Carnegie Library Correspondence, Microfilm Reel No.30).

[22] Greenfield, Ind., Carnegie Library Correspondence, Microfilm Reel No.12.

[23] Eufaula, Ala., Carnegie Library Correspondence, Microfilm Reel No.10.

[24] James Bertram to George D. Heaton, secretary of the Board of Education, Dec. 6, 1905 (Parkersburg, W.Va., Carnegie Library Correspondence, Microfilm Reel No.24).

[25] Freeport, Ill., Carnegie Library Correspondence, Microfilm Reel No.11.

[26] Casper, Wyo., Carnegie Library Correspondence, Microfilm Reel No.5.

[27] White Plains, N.Y., Carnegie Library Correspondence, Microfilm Reel No.34.

[28] Fort Collins, Colo., Carnegie Library Correspondence, Microfilm Reel No.10.

[29] James Bertram to Mrs. Lillian E. Irons, president of the Library Board, Dec. 27, 1915 (Eureka, Calif., Carnegie Library Correspondence, Microfilm Reel No.10).

[30] James Bertram to W. B. Paddock, president of the Library Board of Trustees, Nov. 23, 1910 (Fort Worth, Texas, Carnegie Library Correspondence, Microfilm Reel No.11).

[31] St. Louis, Mo., Carnegie Library Correspondence, Microfilm Reel No.27.

[32] "Table of Available Square Feet of Floor Space for Library Purposes: New York, Boston, St. Louis, Springfield," worked out by William Howard Brett, librarian of the Cleveland Public Library, and enclosed with letter from James Bertram to H. M. Utley, librarian of the Detroit Public Library, Nov. 15, 1912 (Detroit, Mich., Carnegie Library Correspondence, Microfilm Reel No.8).

[33] San Francisco, Calif., Carnegie Library Correspondence, Microfilm Reel No.28.

[34] Denver, Colo., Carnegie Library Correspondence, Microfilm Reel No.8.

[35] James Bertram to Fred R. Drake, vice-president, Public Library Board, July 11, 1906 (Easton, Pa., Carnegie Library Correspondence, Microfilm Reel No.9).

CHAPTER FIVE

Unusual Public
Library Philanthropy

ANDREW CARNEGIE once wrote that an endowed institution was liable to become the prey of a clique, and the public might never acquire a sincere interest in it. He compared an endowed library to an endowed church, at best half and generally wholly asleep. People would never appreciate what was wholly given to them as much as that to which they themselves contributed.[1] Yet Carnegie broke this rule, and another against building libraries in combination with community centers, when he gave library funds to special Pennsylvania towns which were of a personal or business interest to him and his iron industry. He lived to see both these broken rules create the very situations he predicted.

Special Carnegie Library Buildings

When Carnegie returned from a visit to Scotland in the autumn of 1881, he was still excited about the wide acclamation his gift of a public library to the town of Dunfermline had received. Almost immediately he offered Pittsburgh funds for a library building, but, as described in the next chapter, the

offer was at first declined. Then, in 1886, Allegheny, where
the Carnegie family had spent its early years of struggle, requested and received $331,012 for an endowed library-and-
community-center building to serve a population of 78,682.
The dedication in 1890 became a national event, with President Benjamin Harrison making the main address. In 1913
Carnegie donated an additional $150,000 for a building ex-
pansion.[2]

When Allegheny became a part of Pittsburgh in 1909, all
governmental units merged except the library. Local politicians successfully prevented the Allegheny library from being
merged with the Pittsburgh Public Library until 1956. Many
of the staff appointments, including that of the head librarian,
were used as political rewards in the wards comprising the
former Allegheny area. A great deal of opposition to the mer-
ger came also from older residents, who argued that Carnegie
donated the library to Allegheny and not to Pittsburgh.[3]

Other Pennsylvania towns were also recipients of money
from Carnegie for combination library-and-community-cen-
ter buildings. In 1895, $357,782 was donated to Braddock
(population, 1890, 8561) for such a building, which included
a swimming pool, gymnasium, bathing rooms, billiard rooms,
a music hall with organs, and reading rooms.[4] The one at
Homestead (population, 1890, 7911) was built and endowed
by a contribution of $322,067 in 1896.[5] The town of Carnegie
received $30,000 for a site, $118,000 for the building,
$13,000 for books, and an endowment of $93,000 for a total
of $254,000 in 1898. By 1912 there was still no local tax sup-
port for the library, and Carnegie contributed an additional
$100,000 for the endowment fund. Thus, a total contribution
of $354,000 had been made to a community with a population
of 10,000 in 1910.[6] The building in Duquesne (population,
1900, 9036) cost $310,000 in 1901.[7] Lavish giving declined a
little by 1914 when Edgewood (population, 1910, 2596) was
provided $90,500 ($12,500 of which went for the library
proper) for an unendowed community center and library.[8]

Although a number of other towns received special consideration in Carnegie public library philanthropy, their

buildings were neither endowed nor included community centers. Carnegie's library for Johnstown, Pennsylvania (population, 1890, 21,805), cost $55,332 in 1890, with no maintenance pledge required for its support but with a small charge for books checked out for home use.[9] A personal appeal from Senator Joseph F. Wilson, who was also president of the Jefferson County Library Association, induced Carnegie in 1892 to contribute $30,000 for a library building in Fairfield, Iowa (population, 1890, 3391).[10]

Five towns received special funds from Carnegie in 1899. Beaver Falls, Pennsylvania (population, 1890, 9735), obtained $50,000 for a building and was required to pledge only $3000 annual support. A normal grant for a town of 10,000 people would have been $20,000–$25,000.[11] Connellsville, Pennsylvania (population, 1890, 5629), received a $50,000 grant, but the city officials refused to levy a tax for the library. Even after the townspeople voted financial aid to the library, the officials refused to support it until the building was completely finished. Funds had run out, and they did not want to incur any additional expense. Carnegie in a personal letter then added $25,000 more for the completion of the library structure.[12]

Carnegie implied that since he had spent two-week vacations in East Liverpool, Ohio (population, 1890, 10,956), for many years in his youth, he contributed more than the usual amount ($50,000) for a library building located there.[13] McKeesport, Pennsylvania (population, 1890, 20,741), was another town where Carnegie industry was located. Carnegie's gift of $50,000 in 1899 was more than usual for a town of this size, and he required only a $3000 annual support pledge. Charles Schwab, Carnegie's close business associate, donated $2500 for books. Just a few years later the city asked Carnegie for a music-hall addition, hoping that this might stimulate interest in the library among the populace, but the request was not granted.[14]

Steubenville, Ohio (population, 1890, 13,394), received a $50,000 library gift in 1899, later raised to $62,000, for which only a $4000 annual pledge was requested. There are indications in the Steubenville correspondence that Carnegie's generous gift resulted from his early days as a telegraph operator in that town.[15]

On the other hand, some communities received contributions for only part of the cost of the library buildings. In most instances this occurred when pleas were made to Carnegie for funds to add to those which already were available but which were not sufficient to complete the library. A list of such towns is found in Table 11.

TABLE 11
CARNEGIE GIFTS TOWARD PARTIAL COST OF PUBLIC
LIBRARY BUILDINGS*

TOWN	YEAR	AMOUNT
Augusta, Maine	1895	unrecorded
Charleston, S.C.	1914	$ 5,000
Eveleth, Minn.	1911	15,000
Franklinville, N.Y.	1914	2,200
Gardiner, Maine	1897	2,500
Mountain Iron, Minn.	1914	8,000
Orange, N.J.	1915	1,500
Oyster Bay, N.Y.	1901	1,000
Pittsburgh, Texas	1898	5,000
Raymond, N.H.	1906	2,000
Wauwatosa, Wis.	1905	6,000
West Goldsboro, Maine	1908	500

*Compiled from Carnegie Library Correspondence and from Carnegie Corporation of New York, *Carnegie Grants for Library Buildings, 1890–1917*, (New York: Carnegie Corp., 1943), p 25–37.

A number of libraries which had been destroyed by fire were quickly replaced by Carnegie philanthropy. Among these benefactions were a $30,000 gift to Marlborough, Massachusetts, in 1902; $50,000 (later raised to $220,000) to Seattle, Washington, in 1901; and $25,000 to St. Cloud, Minnesota, in 1901.[16] Chelsea, Massachusetts, was provided with $60,000 for a new building, and the $20,000 insurance money on the burned-out library was used for new books to stock the Carnegie building.[17]

In a few cases a library building was provided for both a town and a college located in it. Thus, at Athens, Ohio, $30,000 was given to Ohio University in 1903 for a library to be used by local residents as well as by university personnel and students. Ohio University, the village, and the local board of education pledged $1000 each in annual support.[18] And in 1903, $50,000 was given to Cornell College and Mount Vernon, Iowa, for a library to be used by college and community.[19]

Carnegie Libraries for Negroes

Andrew Carnegie and James Bertram were acquainted with the mores of the South and its local segregation laws. Generally libraries there were for the white population only, and this (not the total population) was the basis for Carnegie library gifts. Although Carnegie was pleased when provisions were made for Negroes, he never attempted to foster integration with his donations.

Only a small percentage of the 132 southern communities which received Carnegie libraries provided library service to Negroes. Louisville, Kentucky, was the first community to have a separate Negro branch library in 1908. It was followed by branches for Negroes in Atlanta, Georgia; Houston, Texas; Knoxville, Tennessee; Meridian, Mississippi; Nashville, Tennessee; New Orleans, Louisiana; and Savannah, Georgia. There was, also, such a branch at Evansville, Indiana.[20]

Other communities made different arrangements for Negroes. In Jackson, Tennessee, they were permitted to borrow books but not to use them in the library.[21] In Jacksonville, Florida, a separate Negro department was located in the basement of the library.[22]

The attitudes of the southern whites are exemplified in four different situations. Charleston, South Carolina, was reluctant to establish a free public library (replacing an endowed subscription library) because officials feared Negroes

would want to use it.[23] Union Springs, Alabama, declared
that the colored people would not be allowed to use the library building, but if they expressed a desire for a library of
their own, no doubt provision would be made for them.[24]
In preliminary correspondence, officials from Rome, Georgia,
indicated that Negroes would have access to the library, since
it would be illegal to collect public funds and not have facilities available for both races. But after the library was built,
they put in an application for a Negro branch. The request
was not granted, because the city wanted to buy an existing
building for use as a library.[25] Jackson, Mississippi, representatives were more blunt. They said Negroes were too illiterate
for library facilities; the educational level of the colored
people had to be raised first.[26]

Negroes often protested about their lack of facilities in
most Carnegie libraries of the South. Mrs. S. S. H. Washington wrote to Carnegie for financial support of a private Negro
library set up by her club, because Negroes in Montgomery,
Alabama, were not allowed in the Carnegie library.[27] James
Bertram answered that he was sorry, but support could be
given only to libraries maintained by cities and towns.[28] When
Tampa, Florida, did not provide separate library service to
Negroes, as it had implied it would, the NAACP wrote a letter
of protest to Andrew Carnegie.[29] In reply, the Carnegie
Corporation of New York stated that it did not interfere in
such local matters; it was always willing, however, to consider
applications from communities for Negro branches.[30]

Many of these libraries for Negroes took years of negotia-
tion. Negroes in Atlanta, Georgia, began asking for permission to use the main building soon after it was completed
in 1902. The city wanted its colored residents to provide the
site for their own branch. But Negro leaders refused because
they felt this responsibility belonged to the municipality.
Finally, after a long lapse of time, a Negro branch was built
in 1921 with city, county, and private subscription adding
$25,000 to Carnegie's original offer of $25,000.[31] A request
for a Negro branch at Greensboro, North Carolina, was
accepted by Carnegie in 1905 and again in 1915. After the

latter date, there was a controversy over the site, and the Carnegie Corporation canceled the offer in 1921. It was, however, renewed (the only renewal on record) in 1922 after many entreaties. When the Negro branch was built, the $10,000 Carnegie gift had to be supplemented by $4575 from the Negro board of education, $250 from the city, and $250 from private sources.[32]

Special Carnegie Gifts to Public Libraries

Andrew Carnegie, although well known for his gifts for library buildings, was nevertheless severely criticized for not providing the books to go with them. Yet, particularly in the earlier years, he did occasionally give money for library books, endowments, and operations. A tabulation of these special gifts is shown in Table 12.

TABLE 12
SPECIAL CARNEGIE GIFTS*

TOWN	YEAR	AMOUNT	PURPOSE
Athens, Pa.	1899	$ 250.00	Books
Avalon, Pa.	1899	117.40	Library fund
Belmont, N.Y.	1895	1,000.00	Library fund
Blue Rapids, Kans.	1899	500.00	Books
Boston, Mass.	1900	Unknown	Books (Purchase of the Galatia Coll. of books related to the history of women with subsequent gifts for maintenance)
Bridgeville, Pa.	1899	50.00	Books
Bucyrus, Ohio	1899	500.00	Books
Butler, Pa.	1899	100.00	Books
Cartersville, Pa.	1899	50.00	Books
Charleroi, Pa.	1900	1,500.00	Books
Chartiers Township, Pa.	1900	1,500.00	Books
Cocoanut Grove, Fla.	1904	Unknown	35 vols. of the Encyclopaedia Britannica

TABLE 12—*continued*

TOWN	YEAR	AMOUNT	PURPOSE
Conneautville, Pa.	1899	$ 100.00	Books
	1902	100.00	Books
Deersville, Ohio	1899	200.00	Books
Denison, Texas	Unknown	Unknown	Pay off debt on library
Eastport, Maine	1899	600.00	Books
Erie, Pa.	1899	6,000.00	Books
Fernandina, Fla.	1899	20.00	Books
Hagerstown, Md.	1903	25,000.00	Endowment for the development of the already est. extension work of the Wash. Ct. Lib.
High Bridge, N.Y.	1904	100.00	Books
Kennett Square, Pa.	1902	2,000.00	To clear mortgage
Manassas, Va.	1899	1,000.00	Books
Milton on Hudson, N.Y.	1903–8	1,000.00	Books
New York, N.Y.	1900	1,000.00	Books
Peterborough, N.H.	1902	5,000.00	Books (to honor first U.S. public library)
Piqua, Ohio	1913	10,000.00	To replace books lost in flood
Redlands, Calif.	Unknown	500.00	Books (Indian Coll.)
Royersford, Pa.	1899	200.00	Books
Seaboard Air Line R.R., Ga.	1899–1909	4,000.00	Books for Andrew Carnegie libraries at schools and stations along Seaboard Air Line R.R. lines
Sheridanville, Pa.	1900	1,000.00	Books
Thomaston, Conn.	1905	1,700.00	Clear off indebtedness
Waco, Texas	1899	1,000.00	Library fund

*Source: Carnegie Library Correspondence, Microfilm Reels 1-35, 66E, 67-68, 86-87.

84   CARNEGIE LIBRARIES

Library Grants in U.S. Possessions

Carnegie funds were provided for two public library buildings in two outlying possessions of the United States. San Juan, Puerto Rico, received a $100,000 grant on October 4, 1901. Honolulu, Hawaii, was the recipient of a $100,000 offer on November 29, 1909.

Notes

[1] Andrew Carnegie, *North American Review*, 149: 689 (Dec. 1889).

[2] Burton J. Hendrick, *The Life of Andrew Carnegie*, II: 253.

[3] Ralph Munn, Pittsburgh head librarian, to F. Keppell, Carnegie Corporation president, May 3, 1938 (Allegheny, Pa., Carnegie Library Correspondence, included in Pittsburgh, Pa., Carnegie Library Correspondence, Microfilm Reel No.25).

[4] William M. Stevenson, *Carnegie and His Libraries* (Pittsburgh, 1899). Privately printed.

[5] Carnegie Corporation of New York, *Carnegie Grants for Library Buildings, 1890–1917* (New York: Carnegie Corp., 1943), p.27.

[6] Carnegie, Pa., Carnegie Library Correspondence, Microfilm Reel No.5.

[7] Carnegie Corporation of New York, *Carnegie Grants for Library Buildings, 1890–1917* (New York: Carnegie Corp., 1943), p.25.

[8] Edgewood, Pa., Carnegie Library Correspondence, Microfilm Reel No.9.

[9] Johnstown, Pa., Carnegie Library Correspondence, Microfilm Reel No.15.

[10] Fairfield, Iowa, Carnegie Library Correspondence, Microfilm Reel No.10.

[11] Beaver Falls, Pa., Carnegie Library Correspondence, Microfilm Reel No.3.

[12] Connellsville, Pa., Carnegie Library Correspondence, Microfilm Reel No.7.

[13] Andrew Carnegie to George E. Sunnis, Dec. 11, 1905 (East Liverpool, Ohio, Carnegie Library Correspondence, Microfilm Reel No.9).

[14] McKeesport, Pa., Carnegie Library Correspondence, Microfilm Reel No.18.

[15] Steubenville, Ohio, Carnegie Library Correspondence, Microfilm Reel No.30.

[16] Marlborough, Mass.; Seattle, Wash.; and St. Cloud, Minn., Carnegie Library Correspondence, Microfilm Reels No.19, 29, and 27.

[17] Chelsea, Mass., Carnegie Library Correspondence, Microfilm Reel No.5.

[18] Athens, Ohio, Carnegie Library Correspondence, Microfilm Reel No.2.

[19] Letter from B. E. Richardson, librarian of Cornell College, to the author, n.d.

[20] James Bertram to Mr. F. L. Adams, secretary of the Board of Trustees,

March 14, 1915 (West Tampa, Fla., Carnegie Library Correspondence, Microfilm Reel No.34).

[21] Booker T. Washington, Tuskegee Institute, to James Bertram, Dec. 8, 1909 (Jackson, Tenn., Carnegie Library Correspondence, Microfilm Reel No.15).

[22] Booker T. Washington, Tuskegee Institute, to James Bertram, Dec. 30, 1909 (Jacksonville, Fla., Carnegie Library Correspondence, Microfilm Reel No.15).

[23] Robert Nelson, president of the Charleston Library Society, to Andrew Carnegie, May 5, 1911 (Charleston, S.C., Carnegie Library Correspondence, Microfilm Reel No.5).

[24] Mayor J. D. Norman to James Bertram, Dec. 23, 1910 (Union Springs, Ala., Carnegie Library Correspondence, Microfilm Reel No.32).

[25] Rome, Ga., Carnegie Library Correspondence, Microfilm Reel No.27.

[26] Edward L. Bailey, superintendent of schools, to James Bertram, Jan. 24, 1911 (Jackson, Miss., Carnegie Library Correspondence, Microfilm Reel No.15).

[27] Mrs. S. S. H. Washington, of the Sojourner Truth Club, to Andrew Carnegie, Nov. 16, 1908 (Montgomery, Ala., Carnegie Library Correspondence, Microfilm Reel No.20).

[28] James Bertram to Mrs. S. S. H. Washington, Nov. ?, 1908 (Montgomery, Ala., Carnegie Library Correspondence, Microfilm Reel No.20).

[29] Mr. Oswald Garrison Villard, treasurer, NAACP, New York, to Andrew Carnegie, Nov. 16, 1914 (Tampa, Fla., Carnegie Library Correspondence, Microfilm Reel No.31).

[30] James Bertram to O. G. Villard, Nov. 25, 1914 (Tampa, Fla., Carnegie Library Correspondence, Microfilm Reel No.31).

[31] Atlanta, Ga., Carnegie Library Correspondence, Microfilm Reel No.2.

[32] Greensboro, N.C., Carnegie Library Correspondence, Microfilm Reel No.12.

CHAPTER SIX

Reaction to Carnegie Library Donations

FORMAL EXPRESSIONS OF GRATITUDE for Carnegie gifts, stiffly starched resolutions, testimonials of esteem in the form of honorary degrees from colleges, and laudatory speeches on public occasions and library dedications became commonplace occurrences in the life of Andrew Carnegie. Statues of him adorned many libraries, and the one in Atlanta was even purchased with the penny contributions of children. Tokens of appreciation were sent to him by people in all walks of life. President Theodore Roosevelt declared, at the dedication of the District of Columbia main public library building, that Carnegie could consider himself "thrice blessed" for using his wealth to benefit all the people, and that in no way could more benefit be done than through gifts of libraries.[1]

Expressions of Gratitude

Library circles, in general, praised all aspects of Andrew Carnegie's gifts of libraries and did not seem to question his money-making methods. Their attitude was that it was not for them to say whether the money given in this way could have been more wisely expended, but, rather, whether they as trustees made the best possible use of it. Librarians and library journals emphasized the awakening effect these gifts had on dormant minds. People began thinking about libraries and their importance and services.[2] Melvil Dewey stated that Carnegie had been investing in libraries "with the same ideas that made him in an age of steel invest in steel and make the best steel in the world and then command the markets of the world for it. His wisdom has done five times as much as his wealth in the conditions he has put with his gifts."[3] In recognition of Carnegie's contribution to the library field, he was made an honorary member of the American Library Association and of many state library associations.

There is no question that Carnegie appreciated these expressions of gratitude. The walls of his study were covered with mementos and resolutions of thanks. Indeed, James Bertram made a point of requesting the larger cities to produce these documents in fancy form. He indicated to John Thomson, librarian of the Philadelphia Free Library, that Carnegie was always pleased to receive resolutions in such a way that they could be framed and hung in his study.[4] Bertram even returned the resolution of thanks sent by St. Louis and asked for a more appropriate one which could be framed. He suggested that William H. Brett of the Cleveland Public Library be contacted on how to prepare one that would please Carnegie.[5]

Opposition

In Towns Receiving Carnegie Grants

Notwithstanding these expressions of gratitude, opposition to Carnegie gifts of libraries began early. As soon as Andrew Carnegie returned from his trip to Scotland in the autumn of 1881 (after his gift of a library to Dunfermline), he wrote a letter to the mayor of Pittsburgh offering $250,000 for a library building, providing the city furnished a site and

88	CARNEGIE LIBRARIES

appropriated $15,000 annually for the library's support. Pittsburgh balked because it had no power to raise taxation money for maintaining such an institution. Still another reason for the delay was a feeling by some that Carnegie was merely glorifying himself and building a great monument to his own fame.[6]

The Pittsburgh *Dispatch* declared itself against the need for a library. Although the newspaper soon reversed its opinion on this point, it still fought against a "Carnegie" library. It claimed that Pittsburgh would not be able to get more money from a John Smith or a William Brown for the library in the future. Besides, the *Dispatch* continued, in sixteen years the $15,000 a year levy would equal the $250,000 that Carnegie was offering.[7]

In 1887, when representatives of the Pittsburgh city council sought an interview with Carnegie to inform him that an enabling act had been passed by the state legislature and his terms could now be met, he replied, "No, I do not think that $250,000 is enough for Pittsburgh. I'll quadruple the amount and make it an even million."[8] Opposition continued with controversy over the appointment of the members of the library commission. Carnegie wanted a commission composed of twelve residents of the city chosen by himself plus nine Pittsburgh officials. The compromise effected enabled each side to have an equal number on the commission.[9] In September of 1892 the labor organizations of Pittsburgh circulated petitions asking the city council to return the money.[10] Although Carnegie added further funds for branch libraries and lavished millions for accompanying museums, institutes, and schools for Pittsburgh, criticism of his benefactions did not cease.

In 1906, City Controller John B. Larken strongly objected to an increase in the library appropriation from $98,000 to $250,000. He even recommended that the annual appropriation be withdrawn altogether and the library be reorganized to form an annex to the technical school. Larken declared, "The library has, after ten years of open house on appropriation from the city of more than $1,100,000, 194,000

MISS DETROIT:—"DON'T ANDY; IT'S TOO HOT. GIVE ME AN ICE CREAM SODA."
Detroit Journal, July 2, 1901

Bountiful grants for those interested

volumes on its shelves and a pay roll as long as the moral law." The city controller felt that Pittsburgh could not afford the sixty-three cents it was costing to circulate each volume and that private support was the only alternative. Eventually, Larken was willing to allow $125,000 for the operation of the library, but he was outvoted for a final appropriation of $200,000.[11]

The controversy over the Detroit Carnegie grant was even more severe and much more prolonged. Early in 1901 informal discussions between Detroit library commissioners and city officials led to unanimous feeling that the city ought to raise at least $1,000,000 by the issue of bonds for a modern main library building on a new site to take the place of its 1877 crowded structure. Since legislative authority to carry out this project was necessary, a bill was drawn up and presented to the state legislature providing for the incorporation of the library board, authorizing it to take and hold property by gift or otherwise, and also authorizing the issue of bonds not exceeding $1,000,000 for library purposes. The legislature, being in session, passed the bill immediately.[12]

The first mention of Carnegie appeared in the February 8 issue of the *Detroit Journal* in an article headlined "Carnegie Might Give Detroit a Library." It stated that an unidentified Washington man approached Carnegie about the matter and felt certain that the latter would be glad to give a library building if the city assumed the necessary obligations. The library board began correspondence with Carnegie and then sent one of their number to New York to see him. An offer of $750,000 was made, and the board accepted it.[13]

There was immediate reaction in the newspapers on the following day. The *Detroit Journal* headlined its first page "Shall Detroit Take Mr. Carnegie's Gift?" and then followed with an attack on Carnegie and the board, assuming that the library would have to be named after Carnegie. It questioned the authority of a "Little Coterie of Citizens" to send a man to Carnegie with credentials setting forth that he represented the citizens of Detroit and asking the city to become a recipient of the plutocrat's largess. The paper quoted city treasurer Thompson as saying:

> We ought to be able to take care of ourselves, I should think. Who told Mr. Carnegie that we were worthy objects of charity, I wonder? It doesn't seem to me that anybody was ever given authority to go begging for a city as big and prosperous as this one is. . . .
> It doesn't seem to me as though it would be a proper thing for this town to accept a big chunk of money as a gift from a man who has made his money the way Carnegie did.[14]

The next day, on its editorial page, the *Journal* continued the attack by asserting that the chief asset of a library was its books. They were what made it an educational institution.

Mr. Carnegie gave money only for buildings, and the question to consider was whether he was helping education or multiplying proud mausoleums to himself.[15]

The *Detroit Free Press* came out in favor of the offer,[16] as did the newspaper, *Today*. In an editorial, the latter stated that no beggary was implied. Detroit would have to wait a long time before any of her own rich citizens would match such a gift. Mr. Carnegie's citizenship was too wide to consider him an outsider to Michigan. After all, anyone who paid railroad fare or bought anything on which freight was paid had helped to contribute to Andrew Carnegie's wealth. Carnegie had also drawn much from the great ore deposits of the state. Now he was redistributing some of his wealth, and Detroit should get her share.[17]

Labor opposition was also immediate. C. H. Johnson, secretary of the Street Railway Employees, stated that, "Carnegie ought to have distributed his money among his employees while he was making it. No man can accumulate such wealth honorably. It may be legally honest, but it's not morally honest."[18] Not only did the Detroit Trades Council vote against acceptance of the Carnegie library gift by the city, but they also reviled the donor. Even the two delegates who favored the gift explained that it was because they feared the money would melt if Carnegie took it with him to the hereafter. The following resolution was adopted with little dissent:

> Whereas, It has come to our notice that several of our city officials have solicited Andrew Carnegie for a donation to erect a public library, and,
> Whereas, the shooting of innocent men and making of widows and orphans at Homestead is still fresh in our memories, therefore be it
> Resolved, That we request the mayor and other officials interested to assert their manhood and independence by refusing to accept of Andrew Carnegie his offer of unjust gains.[19]

Meanwhile the library board wrote to Carnegie asking if he would be willing to furnish money to build one branch building immediately. Everyone was awaiting the submission of a bond issue to the electorate in the November, 1902, election for $500,000 to buy sites for a new main library building and eight branches. The money for the purchase of one of these sites was now available from city funds. Carnegie answered that he would give money now if the common council would adopt a resolution formally accepting his offer and making an annual maintenance pledge. But the failure of the City Savings Bank, which held all the city library funds, put an end to any further consideration of buying a branch site. The matter had to await the formal vote.[20]

Opposition to the Carnegie offer was not limited to labor or one newspaper. One of Detroit's most prominent businessmen decried the necessity of spending $500,000 for libraries:

> Men who have no money of their own, who do not expect to have any of their own, and who, if they had it, would not know how to take care of it are delirious with desire to spend the people's money.
>
> An influenza of extravagance has attacked the officialdom of the city.[21]

The bond issue was passed in November, 1902, by a 7574 to 4730 majority. But the board of estimates approved the bond issue only by the close vote of 18 to 17, and 20 votes were needed for passage. Efforts were then made to have the common council submit the question to the new board of estimates, which assumed office in January, 1903. But, instead, it again submitted the bonding proposal to the electors at the April, 1903, vote, and it was defeated 8338 to 6900.[22]

By 1905 the main building of the Detroit Public Library system was extremely inadequate. When it was built in 1877, it was planned for a collection of 25,000 books and a population of 100,000. These figures had now grown by 800 percent and 400 percent, respectively.[23]

It was not until April, 1907, that the library board submitted two propositions to the voters. They turned down the acceptance of the Carnegie offer, 7860 to 7783, but passed the issuance of $750,000 in bonds for a library building, 7408 to 6323.[24] But no bonds were issued, because such an

THE LIBRARY COM'S.—"SURELY YOU OUGHT TO BE WILLING TO ADD THESE TO YOUR BURDEN, TO HELP ANDY BUILD ONE OF HIS MONUMENTS."

Detroit Journal, Dec. 10, 1902

Those obligatory community maintenance pledges

act would then have carried the bonded debt beyond the charter limits.[25]

Finally, in March, 1910, the common council adopted a resolution by a vote of 31 to 3 to accept the Carnegie offer and agreed to comply with his requests. The board of estimates approved $240,000 to be raised by bonds: $25,000 immediately and $215,000 after a vote to increase the bond limit. This vote failed to carry.[26] In 1911 the Michigan State Supreme Court ruled that the city could issue bonds for library purposes to an amount over and above the limit applying to bond issues for general municipal purposes. Library bond issues fell into the same class as school bonds, and the library commission was a corporation separate from the city proper.[27]

Carnegie had stipulated that his $750,000 had to be used in two parts, not more than half toward a main building and the rest for branches. Eight branches were built between 1911 and 1917, each costing $40,000, except the one honoring the former librarian, Henry M. Utley, which cost $58,659.[28]

The controversy over the location of the main building was renewed. Some wanted it to be moved north along Woodward Avenue, and others wanted it to remain downtown. When the Art Museum site was chosen on Woodward Avenue, the main building of the library was planned opposite it. The site cost $414,000. A million-dollar building was planned, but it had to be enlarged to include the Clarence Burton Historical Collection.[29]

The foundation of the new building was completed by 1915 and the structural steel put up, but then work ceased for lack of funds. The Carnegie gift and the $750,000 bond issue, approved after the Supreme Court decision of 1911, were not enough. It took three additional bond approvals—$750,000 in 1916, $250,000 in 1917, and $750,000 in 1919—to complete the building as costs rose from year to year.[30] By 1921 Detroit had a main library building that cost $2,775,000 exclusive of site. Carnegie contributed one eighth of the amount. The library had sixteen branches, half of which had been built with Carnegie funds.

From Indianapolis, Indiana, a lifelong resident wrote that

in his opinion there existed neither a popular desire for a free gift nor a lack of means to provide for branch libraries. He felt that efforts for a Carnegie gift sprang from a misguided appetite for notoriety on the part of a few public officials.

> If you will investigate, I think you will find that the better thought of this community does not endorse the move to secure this gift but rather looks upon it as being in bad taste. Personally I deplore the effort and feel that the gift, if made, would stunt the growth of civic pride and the higher ideals of good citizenship.[31]

The Central Labor Union of Indianapolis also opposed the Carnegie gift, because they felt that the philanthropist's dollars had an objectionable taint.[32]

In many instances opposition was bitter and prolonged, not so much against a Carnegie library as against the whole question of an additional tax burden. The Taxpayers Association of New Rochelle, New York, protested the Carnegie gift not only on the basis of its proposed poor location, but more strongly because of their claim that the second floor of the present building in operation as a library was unused and provided adequate space for expansion. The Association also questioned the legality of the bonds issued for purchasing the site. The group failed to obtain an injunction and later was defeated when the State Supreme Court sustained the building contract.[33]

The opposition to Carnegie library grants was varied. In some cases there was still doubt over the need for a public library. More often the opposition was to a "Carnegie" library, either because the donor was a "foreign" philanthropist building memorials to himself or because of a suspicion (especially held by Labor) that his money was tainted. Some communities were under financial or legal limitations preventing them from taxing themselves to support the library. In others there was opposition to the annual 10 percent support because of the added tax burden. Delay was common. It was not unusual for more than one of the above factors, together with those previously discussed in earlier chapters concerning site and building problems, to prolong the time it took to obtain libraries up to three, six, and even nine years. A detailed examination of the correspondence of the 1412 United States towns which received Carnegie public libraries indicates that in about half of these some kind of difficulty was experienced, with a consequent lapse of much time before a building was accepted and constructed.

Complaints of Poor Financial Support and Misuses

Soon after a Carnegie library was built, it was not uncommon for Carnegie and Bertram to receive letters expressing concern about poor financial support or indicating that the 10 percent annual support pledge was not being met. One newspaper account described the library at Americus, Georgia, as a showy building bearing Carnegie's name and declared that it was certainly not a public library. Americus had not fulfilled its maintenance pledge, and even if it had, the amount pledged would not have been enough. Ten percent of the original cost of $20,000 was no more than enough to provide for the upkeep of the building, to say nothing of the purchase of books and other library materials.[34] The librarian from Ardmore, Oklahoma, nine years after the Carnegie gift of 1903, wrote about the poor condition of the library, its inadequate financial support, and its use by the high school for classes. She reported that debts had accumulated for the repair of the building (for conversion to classroom use) and for books purchased three years before.[35]

A frequent drain on the annual maintenance pledge was the need to use these funds for the completion of the library building. The community would use up all the Carnegie funds on the building, which would still be standing either unfinished or unfurnished. Frequently, the annual support pledge was then used for these purposes rather than for books and salaries. In Ashtabula, Ohio, for example, the first two years of the city appropriation was spent for furnishing the library.[36]

In some cases the annual support pledge was not kept because of local politics or changes in administration. At Eureka Springs, Arkansas, the Carnegie library first stood unfinished for a very long time after funds had been overspent and then was not properly supported. All this resulted from a controversy over the legal technicalities of a previous administration's having or not having the right to make certain library appropriations.[37] At Gloversville, New York, the city council refused to make an annual appropriation in 1911 unless the library board turned the library over to the direct control of the city. A reporter from the Gloversville newspaper tried to interview Carnegie in New York City but could not get past Bertram, who declared that Carnegie was incensed and felt that this wrong would be righted through the shame and the indignation of the people in Gloversville.[38] In 1915, the common council at Amsterdam, New York, was unhappy about making the annual $2500 library appropriation and seriously considered using the money for rebuilding a jail condemned by state authorities or turning the library into a new jail. However, the matter was reconsidered and eventually the usual appropriation was made to the library.[39]

Librarians were not without ingenuity in supplementing the annual maintenance pledge. The library in Fort Worth, Texas, sold advertising space on the backs of its fiction books to local businessmen and rented out one library room as an art gallery at $300 per year. The proceeds from both these enterprises went for additional library books.[40]

Although the 10 percent support was usually not enough, there was a tendency for communities to assume that it was. The League of Library Commissioners corresponded with James Bertram in 1915 requesting the Carnegie Corporation to state that the stipulated 10 percent was only a minimum, and that the amount needed to run a library varied not only with the section of the country but also with the cost of the building. For instance, it cost more than half as much to maintain a library in a $10,000 building as it did to support one in a $20,000 building. The Corporation reprinted per-

98   CARNEGIE LIBRARIES

tinent parts of this correspondence and distributed them
with each promise of funds.[41]

Actually, by this time, Carnegie Corporation officials and
trustees became so disturbed over the whole question of
the annual maintenance pledge that they began to send
questionnaires to the Carnegie library towns. The first one,
which was mailed in 1915, served as the pattern for those
sent in 1917 and 1920. All of these requested information
for each year since 1907 on the following:

Income
   Taxes
   Fines
   Other sources   _____
                          Total

   Rate of levy (in mills)

Expenditures
   Books and binding
   Newspapers and periodicals
   Salaries and wages
   Other   _____
                          Total

Number of persons on staff
Number of card holders
Number of volumes
Date of completion of building
   Amount donated by Andrew Carnegie or the
      Carnegie Corporation of New York
   Amount spent from other sources to complete
      building

Many communities failed to return the questionnaires,
but indications were that some 10 percent of the Carnegie
library communities were currently failing to live up to their
annual support obligations.[42] Others had defaulted upon
occasion in the past but were currently supporting their
libraries according to the agreement. There were, however,
certain states (Alabama, Illinois, Kansas, Kentucky, Ohio,
Oklahoma, Texas, Virginia, and West Virginia) where the

derelictions had become so serious that the Carnegie Corporation of New York felt justified in declining further grants until public opinion in favor of honoring commitments was brought to bear upon the delinquent communities.[43]

The state of Ohio was refused further grants because there were twenty-three communities (out of seventy-seven) that were not living up to their maintenance obligations by 1917. Here the state library had fallen under political control and offered no leadership or guidance.[44] The story was much the same in Texas. The larger towns, such as Dallas, Fort Worth, Houston, and San Antonio, supported their Carnegie libraries well, but the small, struggling pioneer towns did not. There was no central state authority to act upon the recalcitrants.[45] Indeed, one observer came across the prosperous town of Benton, Texas, with a population of 6000, that had a $10,000 Carnegie library toward which the community was contributing $15 a month. Many of Benton's citizens manifested pride in their good library; and the librarian displayed with satisfaction her tattered array of all but worthless books and praised the generosity of the town in its support of the library.[46]

In contrast, Indiana, which stood first in the number of grants received, also placed first in the results of the questionnaire. Not one of its 155 Carnegie communities had defaulted on a pledge. California, which had second place in the number of grants received, was a close second on the questionnaire results.[47] Both of these were states with effective state library commissions.

In other cases there was not only the problem of poor financial support of the Carnegie library, but, more drastic, the nonuse of the building for its intended function. An unidentified Texas town serves as an extreme example. Funds for a library building were granted, but when the structure was being brought to completion a new town council was elected. It promptly repudiated the maintenance pledge, contending that no previous council could bind its successors. The new library received some gift books, and the aged daughter of a Confederate general volunteered to serve two hours a week as librarian. After two weeks people stopped coming, and the so-called librarian closed the building.

Soon the town became afflicted by an epidemic of depredations by tramps. The sheriff found that they had burrowed into the basement of the library and were warming themselves over a fire which was started with books and maintained with bookshelves. After the tramps had been chased out of town, the council decided to put the building up for sale at an auction. The only bidder was a barber who felt that the basement would be fine for barber chairs and a hair-dressing shop, and the main floor, with the bookstacks removed, would be perfect as a meeting hall for organizations like the Odd Fellows. The barber was about to receive the building for $1000 when someone in the audience declared that the money would have to be returned to Andrew Carnegie. The auction was closed, and the building boarded up by a twelve-foot-high fence with no entrance.[48]

Clarksville, Texas, defaulted on its pledge completely, and the building was shut down after the first year for lack of funds. It stood abandoned with its windows broken. A local newspaper editor wrote to Andrew Carnegie asking to buy it in order to put it to other use. Carnegie answered him with a request not to give up the fight for reestablishing the library, but the city did eventually sell the building.[49]

In Grove City, Pennsylvania, the Carnegie library was taken over by Grove City College. The building was completed by the school at a cost of $2000 added to the $30,000 originally given to the community.[50]

Middlesboro, Kentucky, did not open its library building because of the heavy financial burden on the city. The Women's Club wrote to James Bertram stating that the club would like to open the library building and sponsor it. Then, the Christian Scientists wanted to use the building for their religious services. Bertram found all this unbelievable and wrote to the president of the Kentucky Library Association for clarification. In the meantime the request of the First Baptist Church of Middlesboro for an organ was denied by Carnegie because of the town's library situation. It was not until three and one half years later that the library building was completed and opened for use, but financial problems continued to plague it for many years.[51]

At Mound Bayou, Mississippi (almost entirely a Negro community), the $4000 Carnegie building was erected in 1910 but was never used as a library, presumably because of lack of financial support. Instead, it was rented out for meetings and also used by a Masonic group.[52] In Union City, Tennessee, the city council and the school board both claimed jurisdiction over the Carnegie library. The school board won and used the building as a schoolhouse.[53]

In 1920 certain city officials of Perry, Oklahoma, wanted to return to the Carnegie Corporation the original $10,000 grant made in 1909 and be released from their contract. They called the library a "white elephant" as it could not be used for anything else, the State Supreme Court having decided that the building must be used for library purposes only. Bertram immediately contacted the American Library Association, the Oklahoma Library Commission, and the Oklahoma Library Association for assistance. Carl Milam, executive secretary of the American Library Association, investigated the town, which was very close to his place of birth. He reported that the trouble was all part of a plot on the part of some members of the city commission who wanted to usurp the power of the library board.[54]

No doubt, some towns received buildings before library interest was sufficiently developed. Many communities were totally ignorant about the techniques and problems of running and supporting a public library. Falling under the spell of Carnegie philanthropy, they applied for a building. Here was something for nothing, or, at least, so it seemed. Pride, too, impelled communities to apply for buildings so that they would not be outdone by neighboring cities which had received gifts.

Other factors which caused particular states to rank low because they did not keep their pledges or support their Carnegie libraries well, were political conditions and inadequate state laws enabling the establishment of public-supported local libraries. In some states library commissioners were political appointees, usually without any knowledge of library affairs and, thus, unmindful of their obligations or the need for action in such matters.

The Carnegie Corporation did have a compendium of the laws relating to libraries of all states as of 1915, prepared by W. H. Brett. They published it with the hope that those interested in bettering unsatisfactory conditions in their states could—by consulting this volume and securing the cooperation of such organizations as the American Library Association—have laws drafted modeled on those of the progressive states.[55]

In applying for a Carnegie library, it was extremely difficult, if not impossible, for a group to draw up an agreement which could bind any particular municipal body for longer than the life of that council or board. Carnegie probably considered it to be a gentleman's agreement. But attempts were made to bring the communities into line. Offending municipalities became the subject of correspondence from state library associations and commissions. Bertram once stressed the importance of such bodies when he wrote that "the success of these library buildings provided by Mr. Carnegie or the Corporation in a great measure depends upon advice, encouragement, propaganda and supervision by the state authorities and state library commissions."[56]

The suspension of library donations in certain states had an immediate reaction. Many towns had applications in progress which were suddenly stopped. For example, negotiations on five additional branches for Cincinnati were terminated, as were those for Youngstown, Fort Worth, and Houston. Often officials from such penalized communities would turn against the offenders in their states and bombard them with letters and verbal pleas to resume their Carnegie obligations.

Organized Labor and the Left

Organized labor and the political Left were in open and frequently outspoken opposition to Carnegie and Carnegie

libraries. A vocal segment of organized labor accused him of
building libraries and then reducing wages to pay for them.
At a Pittsburgh rally against the acceptance of the Carnegie
library, a union leader cried out that he " . . . would sooner
enter a building built with the dirty silver Judas received for
betraying Christ than enter the Carnegie Library." [57]

The Homestead, Pennsylvania, steel strike of 1892 prompt-
ed Eugene V. Debs to cry "shame" upon the workers who had
uncritically accepted gifts " . . . from the hands of their slain
comrades. We want libraries, and we will have them in
glorious abundance when capitalism is abolished and workingmen are no longer robbed by the philanthropic pirates of
the Carnegie class. Then the library will be as it should be,
a noble temple dedicated to culture and symbolizing the
virtues of the people." [58]

District Attorney Jerome of New York supported the
viewpoint of labor when he declared that it was unwise to
take millions from the pockets of the toilers down in Homestead and build useless libraries. It would be better to forget
the name of Carnegie and leave the money with the men who
earned it. They lived in miserable hovels and needed money
for their loved ones. [59]

Upton Sinclair was moved to contribute the following
poem to a Socialist organ when Carnegie made New York
his library offer:

> 'Twas on a lofty throne of jewels piled,
> She sat, the mistress of Manhattan Isle,
> And Andrew Armky, the champion slight,
> A modest, mild, unwarlike hero he,
> Poured words of tender pleading in her ear: —
> Oh, come with me, fair lady, sovereign bride,
> And we will wisdom's lofty pleasures taste;
> A thousand libraries thine shall be,
> A thousand books thy bridal bed shall form,
> And thou shalt dine three times a day on Lamb,
> With Bacon garnished, and shalt know the joys
> Of pure beneficent philanthropy,
> And daily in the papers thou shalt read
> Of the new libraries, in cities vast,

In villages, and Indian wigwams too,
In Texas ranches and Esquimaux huts,
In Heaven, Hell, and stations in between.[60]

However, Samuel Gompers, president of the American Federation of Labor, probably reflected the typical attitude of labor in his remarks on the subject. When Toronto was considering the acceptance of a public library from Carnegie, a local labor leader wrote to Gompers for his opinion on the matter. He replied that the matter was one of entire indifference to him and the AFL. Carnegie had made his money at the expense of labor. It was probably useless to persuade him to devote his wealth to more useful and important purposes. It was best not to interfere with his plans for, "After all is said and done, he might put his money to a much worse act. Yes, accept his library, organize the workers, secure better conditions and particularly, reduction in hours of labor and then workers will have some chance and leisure in which to read books." [61]

The negative reception to his gifts from the laboring class was a blow to Carnegie's hopes and expectations. In speaking of the great library philanthropist Enoch Pratt, Carnegie said that the mass of toilers would be sure to see in such men as Pratt their best leaders and most invaluable allies.[62] Carnegie believed that the distribution of wealth through the establishment of cultural agencies like libraries rendered gains of a higher spiritual type and, therefore, were better than wage increases. Men did not live by bread alone, and five or ten cents a day more income scattered over many thousands would produce little good.[63] Far better for the workers to receive their share of the profits in the form of a public library which was built for their benefit, supported by their taxes, and subject to their control as citizens. It was at the opening of the Allegheny Free Library on February 13, 1890, that Carnegie declared:

> I wish that the masses of working men and women, the wage-earners of all Allegheny, will remember and act upon the fact that this is their library, their gallery, and their hall. The poorest man, the poorest woman, that toils from morn till night for a livelihood,

as thank Heaven, I had that toil to do in my early days, as he walks this hall, as he reads the books from those alcoves, as he listens to the organ, and admires the works of art in this gallery, equally with the millionnaire and the foremost citizen, I want him to exclaim in his heart, "Behold, all this is mine. I support it, and I am proud to support it. I am joint proprietor here." [64]

Other Criticisms

Criticism was not limited to organized labor or the Left but was widespread in all levels of public opinion. It was not confined to the question of the morality of Carnegie's methods for making money and his subsequent purchase of fame with his library monuments. Some of his critics also protested that he was donating the money for buildings but was not providing the books and brains to go with them.

Mark Twain records a visit to Carnegie during which "Father Andy" talked himself almost to death about attentions which he received because of his philanthropy. It was not possible to divert him from his subject as he flew from one memento to another, buzzing over each like a "happy hummingbird." Some of these, Twain thought, were merely sorrowful, transparent tokens of reverence for his money-bags. "He has bought fame and paid cash for it, he has deliberately projected and planned out this fame for himself; he has arranged that his name shall be famous in the mouths of men for centuries to come. He has planned shrewdly, safely, securely, and will have his desire. . . ." [65]

The accusation was frequently made that Carnegie required his name to be used for every building he donated. This was not the case, and apparently he preferred that the name of the city followed by "Free Public Library" be used. Only 27 percent of the Carnegie-built libraries used his name. Twelve states with 265 libraries donated by Carnegie did not use his name at all. Indiana, with 155 libraries, was among these. Four other states, with 129 libraries, used it almost always, with Iowa doing so in all its 99 libraries.[66] But whether the library was named after Carnegie or not, it was known as the Carnegie Library to many local residents.

Actually, not only was it unnecessary for a library built

with Carnegie funds to be named after him, but, sometimes, it was named for someone else. In the case of Aberdeen, South Dakota, Carnegie wrote, "Hope library will be called after my friend Alexander Mitchell who was very kind to me in my youth." [67] Mitchell was born in Aberdeen, Scotland; migrated to Milwaukee; and then founded Aberdeen, South Dakota.[68] At Bellevue, Ohio, H. C. Stahl offered $5000 to pay for the site and equip the library on condition that the building be called the Carnegie-Stahl library.[69] There was never any objection on the part of Carnegie to this or other similar arrangements.

Suggestions for Improvement of Carnegie Gifts

Some critics claimed that Carnegie thought more of the bronze medallion of himself which frequently adorned the libraries he built than of the books and librarians that were their breath of life. They said that the good of his gifts was almost entirely outbalanced by evil effects. He was establishing libraries that were going to ruin, because library buildings without books were mockeries. The finest library building when administered by a broken-down clerk, retired policeman, or minister at a salary equal to that of a bricklayer's assistant could not produce the best results.[70]

The Philadelphia *Times* declared that Carnegie had the unusual facility of putting the cart before the horse. His offer of a library was compared to an offer of a handsome carriage on condition that the receiver would provide a pair of horses and maintain them with a coachman, footman, and all else needed in perpetuity. The newspaper went on to say that a building is the last necessity for a library. First, must come books and, second, an endowment or income for further purchase of books and operation of the library. In the early stages of library organization, any building would do. Only after the library was well established and supported was a new building to be considered. "A building alone, entailing a large expenditure without anything to put in it, would be a questionable gain." [71]

JOY ON THE GOLF LINKS.

"HURRAH! WHAT'S MORE APPROPRIATE FOR A BICENTENARY MEMORIAL THAN A NEW PUBLIC LIBRARY?"

Detroit News, July 2, 1901

Library buildings or Carnegie memorials?

Suggestions were made that a Carnegie Committee select the best books being published yearly, purchase them, and send them to all the Carnegie libraries. The purchase of 1000 copies each of such books and the distribution of them to the 1000 Carnegie libraries would encourage the publication of fine books and ensure wide reading of them. It was estimated that an expenditure of $50,000 a year would place fifty good books on the shelves of each library.[72]

Ezra Pound accused the local Carnegie library boards of having the wrong attitude on book selection. They judged consumption only by quantity, by the number of times a book circulated, and not by the amount of change it caused in the mind of the reader. He, too, called for a central selecting committee, which could possibly have books printed at a lower price and sold in great quantity to Carnegie libraries. He claimed that these libraries made no provisions for the serious student and ". . . at twenty-two, stranded in Devil's Island, Indiana, I could make some use of the local Carnegie Library, but at forty it would probably be utterly useless to me."[73]

Mencken summed the matter up aptly when he wrote:

Go to the nearest Carnegie Library and examine its catalog of books. The chances are five to one that you will find the place full of literary bilge and as bare of good books as a Boston bookshop. Almost everywhere these Carnegie libraries are in charge of local notables and among these notables there are always plenty of wowsers. Andy, himself, was a skeptic and hoped to spread the enlightenment by giving the populace access to sound literature but today his money is being used to keep sound literature out of its reach. . . . There are, of course, Carnegie libraries that are intelligently run, but certainly there can't be many. When the rest are heard of at all it is in dispatches to the effect that the numbskulls who operate them have just burned the works of Jane Addams because she has doubts about the Mellon idealism, or sued someone for spreading the report that they have bought the collected works of James Branch Cabell.[74]

The Carnegie Library Correspondence is filled with appeals to Andrew Carnegie, written after the completion of the building, for more gift money to buy books. There are dozens of such appeals for help from "bookless" libraries. The Tampa, Florida, library opening was delayed for lack of furnishings and books.[75] Brush, Colorado, appealed for more funds for their completed building by writing that "the number of empty shelves in our reading rooms would plead eloquently to him [Andrew Carnegie] could he see them."[76]

Bertram's answer to such appeals was always the same. If the annual maintenance appropriation was not enough to provide for all the necessary books, it should be raised, or there should be a drive for voluntary contributions in the community. He further said that after Andrew Carnegie gave the money for the library building, he thought the citizens should do the rest and that no institution was a success unless a few individuals worked heart and soul for it. Subscription lists, entertainments, lectures, and many other ways could be found to augment the tax funds.[77]

Alvin Johnson, a close observer of the Carnegie libraries (see Chapter VIII), felt that Carnegie could not give funds for books because the book was perishable. No fortune, however great, could arrange for a steady flow and permanent supply of books. Johnson believed that it was Carnegie's aim to make library buildings freely accessible to all, with the hope that the forces of public opinion would compel the local governments to supply books.

Johnson also believed that Carnegie did not care about the kind of books which were stocked in his libraries. Those in demand and those selected by librarians would do. An eager and persistent youth could find enough to suit his needs in any collection of thousands of titles. The philanthropist seemed unconcerned about the existence of multitudes of mediocre books on the shelves of the gift buildings. He was content to leave the fate of bad books to the law of natural selection.[78] Carnegie once declared that "every free library in these days should contain upon its shelves all contributions bearing upon the relations of labor and capital from every point of view—socialistic, communistic, co-operative and individualistic: and librarians should encourage visitors to read them all."[79]

Criticism extended not only to the lack of books in Carnegie libraries but also to the lack of professionally trained librarians. As early as 1890, Melvil Dewey asked Andrew Carnegie for funds to help the New York State Library School. But Carnegie declined, declaring that no difficulty was being experienced in finding persons naturally adapted for this kind of work in the Pennsylvania libraries receiving new building grants. Dewey wrote back predicting that Carnegie would some day become a friend and supporter of educational programs for librarians.

By 1900 there were almost 5400 public, school, academic, and special libraries in the United States, but only some 377 graduates of all the library training schools were employed in them. As the need for more and better-trained librarians became evident, Carnegie changed his attitude and did provide some assistance. In 1903 he gave endowment funds for the establishment of a library school at Western Reserve University and also gave financial assistance to the Training School of the Carnegie Library of Pittsburgh. The Atlanta, Georgia, Carnegie Library School and the New York Public Library Training School also received some funds in 1905 and 1911 respectively.[80] But not until after the close of Carnegie library-building philanthropy in 1917 was any concentrated effort made by the Corporation to improve training for librarianship.

Apparently, Carnegie never regretted his gifts of libraries. When asked by a magazine reporter if he were satisfied with the results of his philanthropy, he gave a loud and affirmative, "Yes." Proudly he cited the many letters received from parents thanking him for the libraries and describing the change these had made upon their children.[81] In 1914, speaking at the twenty-fifth anniversary of the Braddock Library, he said:

> I don't know how every one thinks about the way I spend money but I'm willing to put this library and institution against any other form of benevolence. It's the best kind of philanthropy I can think of and I'm willing to stand on that record. This is a grand old world and its always growing better. And all's well since it is growing better and when I go for a trial for the things

done on earth, I think I'll get a verdict of "Not Guilty" through my efforts to make the earth a little better than I found it.[82]

Notes

[1]"Dedication of the Washington (D.C.) Carnegie Library Building," *Library Journal*, 28: 18 (Jan. 1903).

[2]For two examples of contemporary library opinion, see: Melvil Dewey, "The Future of the Library Movement in the United States in the Light of Andrew Carnegie's Recent Gift," *Journal of Social Science*, 39: 139 (Nov. 1901); J. P. Dunn, "Tainted Money," *Public Libraries*, 18: 186–87 (May, 1913).

[3]Melvil Dewey, "Purpose of Carnegie Gifts," *Library Journal*, 30: 80 (Sept. 1905).

[4]James Bertram to John Thomson, librarian of the Philadelphia Free Library, Feb. 9, 1903 (Philadelphia, Pa., Carnegie Library Correspondence, Microfilm Reel No.25).

[5]James Bertram to Frederick Crunden, St. Louis Public Library, Nov. 14 and Nov. 18, 1903 (St. Louis, Mo., Carnegie Library Correspondence, Microfilm Reel No.27).

[6]Burton J. Hendrick, *The Life of Andrew Carnegie*, II: 253–54.

[7]"Pittsburg (Pa.), The Carnegie Library," *Library Journal*, 12: 300 (Aug. 1887).

[8]*Ibid.*

[9]Pittsburgh, Pa., Carnegie Library Correspondence, Microfilm Reel No.25.

[10]Sidney Ditzion, *Arsenals of a Democratic Culture*, (Chicago: American Library Assn., 1947), p 161

[11]"Pittsburg (Pa.) Carnegie Library," *Library Journal*, 31: 144 (March 1906).

[12]Henry Munson Utley, *The Public Library: Mr. Carnegie's Offer To Provide the Means for Erecting a New Building* (Detroit: Detroit Public Library, 1903), p.1.

[13]*Ibid.*

[14]*Detroit Journal*, July 1, 1901.

[15]*Ibid.*, July 2, 1901.

[16]Editorial in the *Detroit Free Press*, July 2, 1901.

[17]*Today* (Detroit), July 2, 1901.

[18]*Detroit Journal*, July 3, 1901.

[19]*Ibid.*, Aug. 15, 1901.

[20]Detroit, Mich., Carnegie Library Correspondence, Microfilm Reel No.8.

[21]*Detroit Journal*, Dec. 10, 1902.

[22]Henry Munson Utley, *op. cit.*, p.6.

[23]Detroit Public Library, *Annual Report, 1905*, p.10.

[24]*Detroit News*, April 2, 1907.

[25]Detroit Public Library, *Annual Report, 1909*, p.5.

[26]———, *Annual Report, 1910*, p.8.

[27]———, *Annual Report, 1911*, p.6.

112   CARNEGIE LIBRARIES

28———, *Annual Report, 1918–1919*, p.13.

29———, *Annual Report, 1913–1914*, p.5–6.

30———, *Annual Report, 1916–1917*, p.9; *Annual Report, 1918–1919;* p.3.

31 J. P. Fringel, president of the Indiana Trust Co., to Andrew Carnegie, Jan. 28, 1908 (Indianapolis, Ind., Carnegie Library Correspondence, Microfilm Reel No.15).

32 Clipping entitled "Opposed to Carnegie Money for a Library" from the *Indianapolis News*, Feb. 11, 1903 (Indianapolis, Ind., Carnegie Library Correspondence, Microfilm Reel No.15).

33 New Rochelle, N.Y., Carnegie Library Correspondence, Microfilm Reel No.22.

34 Clipping entitled "One of Carnegie's Libraries" from the Augusta, Ga., *Herald*, ?, 1909 (Americus, Ga., Carnegie Library Correspondence, Microfilm Reel No.1).

35 Myrtle Jones, librarian, to Andrew Carnegie, Feb. 12, 1912 (Ardmore, Okla., Carnegie Library Correspondence, Microfilm Reel No.1).

36 Ashtabula, Ohio, Carnegie Library Correspondence, Microfilm Reel No.2.

37 Eureka Springs, Ark., Carnegie Library Correspondence, Microfilm Reel No.10.

38 Gloversville, N.Y., Carnegie Library Correspondence, Microfilm Reel No.12.

39 "Editorial," *Library Journal*, 40: 226 (April 1915).

40 Mrs. Charles Scheuber, librarian, to Andrew Carnegie, undated letter (probably March 1905) and another on Sept. 28, 1907 (Fort Worth, Texas, Carnegie Library Correspondence, Microfilm Reel No.11).

41 Correspondence between League of Library Commissioners and James Bertram on file at the Carnegie Corporation of New York: J. I. Wyer to James Bertram, Oct. 28, 1915; James Bertram to J. I. Wyer, Nov. 1, 1915; J. I. Wyer to Carnegie Corporation, Nov. 15, 1915; James Bertram to J. I. Wyer, Nov. 24, 1915. See also Theodore W. Koch, *A Book of Carnegie Libraries* (New York: Wilson, 1917), p.17–18.

42 Carnegie Endowment for International Peace, *A Manual of the Public Benefactions of Andrew Carnegie* (Washington, D.C.: Carnegie Endowment, 1919), p.300.

43 Obtained from an examination of the Carnegie Library Correspondence, Microfilm Reels No.1–35, 66E, 67, and 68.

44 Joseph L. Wheeler, "The Library Situation in Ohio," *Library Journal*, 45: 877 (Nov. 1, 1920).

45 Elizabeth Howard West, "Texas Libraries," *Library Journal*, 48: 269 (Jan. 15, 1923).

46 Alvin S. Johnson, *A Report to Carnegie Corporation of New York on the Policy of Donations to Free Public Libraries* (New York: Carnegie Corp., 1919), p.53–54, 56.

47 "Carnegie Local Derelictions re Contracts," *Library Journal*, 42: 585 (Aug. 1917).

[48] Alvin S. Johnson, *Pioneer's Progress: An Autobiography* (New York: Viking, 1952), p.235-36.

[49] Clarksville, Texas, Carnegie Library Correspondence, Microfilm Reel No.6.

[50] Grove City, Pa., Carnegie Library Correspondence, Microfilm Reel No.86.

[51] Middlesboro, Ky., Carnegie Library Correspondence, Microfilm Reel No.19.

[52] Mound Bayou, Miss., Carnegie Library Correspondence, Microfilm Reel No.20.

[53] Union City, Tenn., Carnegie Library Correspondence, Microfilm Reel No.32.

[54] Perry, Okla., Carnegie Library Correspondence, Microfilm Reel No.24.

[55] Carnegie Endowment for International Peace, *loc. cit.*

[56] James Bertram to Mary C. Spencer, Michigan state librarian, June 13, 1917 (Albion, Mich., Carnegie Library Correspondence, Microfilm Reel No.1).

[57] Sidney Ditzion, *loc. cit.*, citing the Sept. 10 and 17, 1892, issues of the *Commoner and Glassworker* (Pittsburgh).

[58] *Ibid.*, p.163, quoting from letter by Eugene V. Debs, entitled "Crimes of Carnegie," in *The People*, April 7, 1901.

[59] Frank Pierce Hill, "One Phase of Library Development," *Library Journal*, 21: 8 (Aug. 1906).

[60] Sidney Ditzion, *op. cit.*, p.163, quoting from *The Comrade* (n.d.).

[61] "Public Libraries and Labor Unions," *Iowa Library Commission Quarterly*, 3: 32 (April 1903).

[62] Andrew Carnegie, *North American Review*, 149: 690 (Dec. 1889).

[63] ———, *The Empire of Business* (New York: Doubleday, 1902), p.143.

[64] Sarah K. Bolton, *Famous Givers and Their Gifts* (New York: Crowell, 1896), p.82.

[65] Samuel L. Clemens, *Mark Twain in Eruption: Hitherto Unpublished Pages about Men and Events*, ed. Bernard De Voto (New York: Harper, 1940), p.309.

[66] William S. Learned, *The American Public Library and the Diffusion of Knowledge* (New York: Harcourt, 1924), p.74.

[67] Quoted in letter from James Bertram to Miss M. L. Crouch, University of Illinois Library School student at Urbana, Dec. 12, 1929 (Aberdeen, S.Dak., Carnegie Library Correspondence, Microfilm Reel No.1).

[68] U.S. Senator James H. Kyle to Andrew Carnegie, Feb. 13, 1901 (Aberdeen, S.Dak., Carnegie Library Correspondence, Microfilm Reel No.1).

[69] Bellevue, Ohio, Carnegie Library Correspondence, Microfilm Reel No.3.

[70] Robert Johnson, "Public Libraries and Mr. Carnegie," *Library Journal*, 32: 440-41 (Oct. 1907).

[71] An editorial from the *Times* (Philadelphia) of June 4, 1901, quoted in the *Norristown Daily Times* of June 5, 1901, and found in the Norristown, Pa., Carnegie Library Correspondence, Microfilm Reel No.67.

[72] "Library Suggestion," *Dial*, 46: 69-71 (Feb. 1, 1909).

[73] Ezra Pound, "Where Is American Culture?" *Nation*, 126: 443 (April 18, 1928).

[74] "Carnegie Libraries Go under Fire," *Wilson Library Bulletin*, 3: 261 (May 1928). Reprinted by permission. Copyright © 1928 by The H. W. Wilson Company.

[75] Tampa, Fla., Carnegie Library Correspondence, Microfilm Reel No.31.

[76] Brush, Colo., Carnegie Library Correspondence, Microfilm Reel No.4.

[77] James Bertram to Dr. C. E. Boynton, Jan. 25, 1906 (Reading, Pa., Carnegie Library Correspondence, Microfilm Reel No.26).

[78] Alvin Johnson, "Andrew Carnegie, Educator," *Journal of Adult Education*, 8: 7–8 (Jan. 1936).

[79] Sarah K. Bolton, *op. cit*, p.86–87. No citation given.

[80] Sarah K. Vann, *Training for Librarianship before 1923* (Chicago: American Library Assn., 1961), p.58–59, 63, 118–20.

[81] Andrew Carnegie, "Library Gift Business," *Collier's*, 43: 14 (June 5, 1909.

[82] G. H. Lamb, "Mr. Carnegie and the Free Library Movement," *Pennsylvania Library Notes*, 10: 3 (Jan. 1920).

CHAPTER SEVEN

Libraries Which Never Materialized

Communities which did not obtain a Carnegie public library building after having requested and received a tentative offer of one by Carnegie or his officials are rarely mentioned and have never been considered in any detail. Which were these municipalities, and where were they located? What were their populations? When and what was the original offer? Did the locality already have an established public library? And, of most significance, why was the offer rejected or allowed to lapse? These are the questions this chapter will attempt to answer.

Table 13 gives a tabulation of the 225 communities which did not follow through on available Carnegie grants. Some municipalities had received Carnegie public library buildings but had allowed other offers of Carnegie funds for expansion or additional buildings to lapse. These towns are not listed in the table, although a number of them are mentioned throughout this book. No doubt many other communities probably discussed the possibility of applying formally for a Carnegie library grant but never progressed further than this. Table 13 comprises solely the localities which formally contacted Carnegie or the Carnegie Corporation and ex-

TABLE 13

Unaccepted Carnegie Library Offers

COMMUNITY	STATE	POPULATION	AMOUNT
1. Ada	Oklahoma	4,349 (1910)	$ 12,500
2. Albany	New York	94,151 (1900)	150,000
3. Almont	Michigan	675 (1910)	8,000
4. Alpena	Michigan	12,706 (1910)	25,000
5. Alva	Oklahoma	3,688 (1910)	10,000
6. Amory	Mississippi	2,122 (1910)	10,000
7. Andrews	Indiana	746 (1900)	5,000
8. Appleton	Minnesota	1,221 (1910)	7,000
9. Ashfield	Massachusetts	985 (1900)	3,000
10. Auburn	Indiana	3,396 (1900)	12,500
11. Auburn	Nebraska	2,664 (1900)	10,000
12. Augusta	Georgia	20,913w(1900)*	50,000
13. Bainbridge	Georgia	1,903w(1910)	10,000
14. Batesville	Indiana	1,384 (1900)	8,500
15. Beaumont	Texas	6,474w(1900)	25,000
16. Beaver	Pennsylvania	1,552 (1890)	50,000
17. Belding	Michigan	3,282 (1900)	10,000
18. Belmond	Iowa	1,224 (1910)	7,500
19. Bement	Illinois	1,530 (1910)	10,000
20. Benicia	California	2,751 (1900)	10,000
21. Bethany	Missouri	2,093 (1900)	10,000
22. Bicknell	Indiana	(520)†	6,500
23. Big Stone Gap	Virginia	2,194w(1910)	10,000
24. Birmingham	Alabama	21,832w(1900)	100,000
25. Birmingham	Michigan	1,170 (1900)	8,000
26. Blairsville	Pennsylvania	3,126 (1890)	15,000
27. Bluefield	West Virginia	8,950w(1910)	22,000
28. Bottineau	North Dakota	888 (1900)	7,500

TABLE 13—*continued*

DATE OF PROMISE		PREV. PUBLIC LIB.	PUBLIC LIB. EST. BY 1923?	REASON	SOURCE
Sept.	29, 1911	Yes		Wanted more funds	M.R. No.1
April	3, 1902	Yes		Voted down twice by electorate	M.R. No.66E
Nov.	9, 1916	Yes		Local philanthropist	M.R. No.1
April	30, 1912	Yes		Council against 10% support	Questionnaire
May	15, 1916	Yes		World War I and rising building costs	M.R. No.1
Jan.	6, 1911	No	No	Unknown	
April	8, 1907	Yes		Unknown	
Feb.	6, 1915	Yes		Unknown	
Jan.	18, 1910	Yes		Local philanthropist	M.R. No.66E
Jan.	14, 1909	Yes		Local philanthropist	M.R. No.66E
Jan.	29, 1906	No	Yes	Council against 10% support	M.R. No.66E
Jan.	22, 1903	No	No	Local philanthropist	M.R. No.66E
Jan.	31, 1913	No	No	Council against 10% support	M.R. No.2
July	19, 1905	No	No	Voted down by electorate	Questionnaire
June	1, 1903	No	No	Council against 10% support	M.R. No.66E
Sept.	17, 1897	No	Yes	Financially unable to support at 10%	M.R. No.66E
March	20, 1903	No	Yes	Local philanthropist	Questionnaire
Jan.	28, 1916	No	Yes	Local philanthropist	M.R. No.3
March	14, 1913	Yes		Legally unable to give 10% support	M.R. No.3
March	20, 1903	No	Yes	Unknown	
July	20, 1903	No	No	Unknown	
Feb.	25, 1908	No	No	Council against 10% support	M.R. No.66E
March	29, 1911	Yes		Unknown	
April	21, 1909	Yes		Unknown	
March	14, 1903	Yes		Unknown	
June	20, 1899	Yes		Council against 10% support	M.R. No.66E
April	8, 1911	No	Yes	Unknown	
Nov.	20, 1908	No	Yes	Unknown	

TABLE 13 — *continued*

COMMUNITY	STATE	POPULATION	AMOUNT
29. Bountiful	Utah	1,442 (1900)	$ 5,000
30. Brookport	Illinois	1,443 (1910)	5,000
31. Brunswick	Maine	5,210 (1900)	12,000
32. Bunker Hill	Illinois	1,279 (1900)	7,500
33. Burley	Idaho	(1,410)	10,000
34. Burr Oak	Michiga ᵢ	744 (1900)	5,000
		752 (1910)	8,000
35. Burton	Ohio	727 (1910)	7,500
36. Camden	Maine	2,825 (1900)	6,000
37. Camilla	Georgia	1,827 (1910)	7,500
38. Canandaigua	New York	6,151 (1900)	10,000
39. Canton	North Carolina	1,393 (1910)	5,000
40. Cape May	New Jersey	2,257 (1900)	10,000
41. Carbon County	Wyoming	9,589 (1900)	10,000
(Rawlins)		2,317 (1900)	
42. Carbondale	Pennsylvania	13,536 (1900)	25,000
43. Caruthersville	Missouri	2,315 (1900)	10,000
44. Chardon	Ohio	1,542 (1910)	8,000
45. Charleston	West Virginia	19,910w(1910)	45,000
46. Charlottesville	Virginia	3,836w(1900)	20,000
47. Chase City	Virginia	1,662 (1910)	6,500
48. Chicopee	Massachusetts	19,167 (1900)	15,000
49. Chillicothe	Missouri	6,905 (1900)	20,000
50. Chisholm	Minnesota	7,684 (1910)	15,000
51. Claremore	Oklahoma	2,866 (1910)	10,000
52. Clarion	Pennsylvania	2,164 (1890)	16,660
53. Clearfield	Pennsylvania	5,081 (1900)	10,000
54. Cleveland	Tennessee	3,041w(1900)	10,000

TABLE 13 — *continued*

DATE OF PROMISE	PREV. PUBLIC LIB.	PUBLIC LIB. EST. BY 1923?	REASON	SOURCE
Jan. 18, 1910	No	No	Unknown	
Jan. 27, 1914	No	No	World War I and rising building costs	M.R. No.4
July 13, 1903	Yes		Local philanthropist	M.R. No.66E
Jan. 19, 1905	Yes		Site problems or controversy	M.R. No.66E
Nov. 9, 1916	No	Yes	World War I and rising building costs	M.R. No.4
April 19, 1909	Yes		Voted down by electorate	Questionnaire
June 24, 1911	Yes		electorate	
April 2, 1913	Yes		Unknown	
Jan. 31, 1910	Yes		Local philanthropist	Questionnaire
Nov. 3, 1913	No	No	Unknown	
Aug. 16, 1901	Yes		Voted down by electorate	M.R. No.66E
Dec. 7, 1911	No	Yes	Unknown	
July 30, 1903	No	Yes	Unknown	
Feb. 1, 1909	No	No	Financially unable to support at 10%	Questionnaire
March 8, 1901	Yes		Council against 10% support	M.R. No.66E
Feb. 2, 1903	No	No	Voted down by electorate	M.R. No.66E
Dec. 3, 1912	Yes		Council against 10% support	M.R. No.5
March 14, 1913	Yes		Wanted more funds	M.R. No.3
July 3, 1901	No	Yes	Unknown	
Nov. 9, 1916	No	No	Financially unable to support at 10%	M.R. No.5
Jan. 23, 1907	Yes		Architectural problems	M.R. No.66E
May 9, 1908	No	No	Local philanthropist	M.R. No.66E
May 6, 1911	No	Yes	Architectural problems	M.R. No.67
Feb. 3, 1917	Yes		Architectural problems	M.R. No.6
July 25, 1900	No	Yes	Council against 10% support	M.R. No.67
July 14, 1901	No	No	Unknown	
Feb. 2, 1903	No	No	Unknown	

TABLE 13 — *continued*

COMMUNITY	STATE	POPULATION	AMOUNT
55. Cleveland Heights	Ohio	(2,100)	$ 10,000
56. Coeur d'Alene	Idaho	508 (1900)	
		7,291 (1910)	13,000
57. Cohoes	New York	23,910 (1900)	25,000
58. Collinwood	Ohio	(3,629)	17,500
59. Columbia	Tennessee	3,336w(1900)	10,000
60. Commerce	Texas	2,664w(1910)	10,000
61. Corning	New York	13,730 (1910)	25,000
62. Crockett	Texas	1,693 (1910)	9,000
63. Cumberland	Maryland	16,128w(1900)	25,000
64. Darien	Connecticut	3,116 (1900)	5,000
65. Deep River	Connecticut	1,634 (1900)	5,000
66. De Funiak Springs	Florida	(1,300)	10,000
		2,017 (1910)	10,000
67. De Kalb	Illinois	5,904 (1900)	15,000
68. Denton	Texas	3,673w(1900)	10,000
69. Dover	New Jersey	5,938 (1900)	20,000
70. Dunmore	Pennsylvania	12,583 (1900)	15,000
71. Du Quoin	Illinois	4,353 (1900)	10,000
72. Eaton	Ohio	3,155 (1900)	10,000
73. Eaton Rapids	Michigan	2,103 (1900)	10,000
		2,094 (1910)	10,000
74. Edgar	Nebraska	1,080 (1910)	8,000
75. El Dorado Springs	Missouri	2,137 (1900)	10,000

TABLE 13—*continued*

DATE OF PROMISE	PREV. PUBLIC LIB.	PUBLIC LIB. EST. BY 1923?	REASON	SOURCE
Jan. 19, 1905	No	Yes	Legally unable to support at 10%	M.R. No.67
Dec. 2, 1909	Yes		Council against 10% support	M.R. No.66E
March 8, 1901	Yes		Site problems or controversy	M.R. No.66E
March 21, 1908	No	Yes	Annexation to Cleveland	M.R. No.67
Jan. 22, 1903	No	Yes	Council against 10% support	Questionnaire
May 8, 1914	No	No	World War I and rising building costs	M.R. No.7
June 24, 1911	Yes		Architectural problems	M.R. No.67
Nov. 21, 1911	No	No	Architectural problems	M.R. No.67
Feb. 19, 1901	Yes		Voted down by electorate	M.R. No.67
Dec. 8, 1905	Yes		Voted down twice by electorate	M.R. No.67
Feb. 13, 1906	Yes		Council against 10% support	M.R. No.68
March 21, 1910			World War I and rising building costs	M.R. No.8
March 31, 1916	No	Yes		
Jan. 19, 1905	Yes		Local philanthropist	Questionnaire
Jan. 22, 1903	No	No	Wanted more funds	M.R. No.67
Jan. 10, 1914	Yes		World War I and rising building costs	M.R. No.8
April 11, 1905	No	No	Council against 10% support	M.R. No.67
Feb. 2, 1903	No	No	World War I and rising building costs	M.R. No.67
March 25, 1905	Yes		Site problems or controversy	M.R. No.67
June 28, 1908				
May 8, 1914	Yes		Wanted more funds	M.R. No.9
Jan. 9, 1913	Yes		Voted down by electorate	M.R. No.9
Jan. 29, 1906	Yes		Council against 10% support	Questionnaire

TABLE 13—*continued*

COMMUNITY	STATE	POPULATION	AMOUNT
76. Elizabethtown	Kentucky	1,861 (1900)	$ 7,000
77. Fairport (Perrington School District No. 9)	New York	3,112 (1910)	11,000
78. Fairview	Oklahoma	2,020 (1910)	10,000
79. Farmville	Virginia	2,471 (1900)	10,000
80. Findlay	Ohio	17,613 (1900)	35,000
81. Florence	South Carolina	3,521w(1910)	10,000
82. Frankfort	Kansas	1,167 (1900)	5,000
83. Frankfort	New York	2,664 (1900)	10,000
84. Freeport	New York	2,612 (1900)	10,000
85. Gardner	Illinois	1,036 (1900)	5,000
86. Gatesville	Texas	1,929 (1910)	7,500
87. Georgetown	Delaware	1,658 (1900)	6,000
88. Gibsonburg	Ohio	1,864 (1910)	9,000
89. Gilmer	Texas	1,484 (1910)	7,500
90. Glenville	Ohio	(5,580)	15,000
91. Goldfield	Nevada	(12,000–15,000)	20,000
92. Goldsboro	North Carolina	3,357w(1900)	15,000
93. Goodland	Indiana	1,105 (1910)	8,000
94. Grand Ledge	Michigan	2,893 (1910)	10,000
95. Grand Rapids	Michigan	87,565 (1900)	100,000
96. Granite Falls	Minnesota	1,454 (1910)	6,000
97. Granville	New York	2,700 (1900)	10,000
98. Greenfield	Missouri	1,434 (1910)	8,000
99. Greensboro	Georgia	2,120 (1910)	6,000
100. Greensburg	Pennsylvania	4,202 (1890)	60,000
101. Greenville	Alabama	1,588w(1900)	10,000
102. Greenville	Pennsylvania	4,814 (1900)	16,000
103. Greenville	South Carolina	6,443w(1900)	15,000

TABLE 13—*continued*

DATE OF PROMISE	PREV. PUBLIC LIB.	PUBLIC LIB. EST. BY 1923?	REASON	SOURCE
March 14, 1905	No	Yes	Council against 10% support	Questionnaire
April 13, 1914	Yes		Site problems or controversy	Questionnaire
April 28, 1913	Yes		Financially unable to support at 10%	M.R. No.10
Dec. 24, 1909	No	Yes	Site problems or controversy	M.R. No.67
Jan. 16, 1906	Yes		Unknown	
April 13, 1914	No	No	Wanted more funds	M.R. No.10
Dec. 13, 1907	No	Yes	Financially unable to support at 10%	M.R. No.67
Feb. 12, 1903	No	Yes	Voted down by electorate	M.R. No.67
Nov. 18, 1903	Yes		Unknown	
April 23, 1906	No	No	Unknown	
May 8, 1914	No	No	Unknown	
Feb. 15, 1905	No	Yes	Unknown	
Jan. 17, 1912	No	No	Unknown	
April 3, 1912	No	No	Wanted more funds	M.R. No.12
June 12, 1903	No	Yes	Annexed to Cleveland	M.R. No.67
Feb. 13, 1909	No	No	Unknown	
April 23, 1906	No	Yes	Unknown	
Nov. 21, 1911	Yes		Unknown	
May 17, 1912	No	Yes	Council against 10% support	M.R. No.12
Feb. 9, 1901	Yes		Local philanthropist	M.R. No.67
July 9, 1913	Yes		Wanted more funds	M.R. No.12
Feb. 2, 1903	Yes		Voted down twice by electorate	M.R. No.67
March 31, 1916	No	No	Wanted more funds	M.R. No.12
Sept. 29, 1915	No	No	Financially unable to support at 10%	M.R. No.12
Dec. 7, 1897	No	No	Site problems or controversy	M.R. No.67
Feb. 1, 1909	No	No	Unknown	
Feb. 13, 1901	No	Yes	Unknown	
Jan. 7, 1907	Yes		Architectural problems	M.R. No.13

TABLE 13—*continued*

COMMUNITY	STATE	POPULATION	AMOUNT
104. Greenwood and Pleasant Township	Indiana	1,608 (1910) 1,376 (1910)	$ 10,000
105. Guthrie Center	Iowa	1,193 (1900)	5,000
106. Hampton	New Hampshire	1,209 (1900)	5,000
107. Harlan	Iowa	2,570 (1910)	10,000
108. Harpswell	Maine	1,750 (1900)	5,000
109. Harrisonburg	Virginia	3,938w(1910)	10,000
110. Helena	Montana	10,770 (1900)	30,000
111. High Point	North Carolina	3,235w(1900)	15,000
112. Howard	South Dakota	1,026 (1910)	7,500
113. Hudson Falls	New York	4,473 (1900)	10,000
114. Humansville	Missouri	913 (1910)	5,000
115. Huntington	Pennsylvania	5,729 (1890)	20,000
116. Independence	Missouri	9,859 (1910)	20,000
117. Jackson	Ohio	4,672 (1900)	10,000
118. Kewaunee	Wisconsin	1,773 (1900)	7,000
119. Kingsville	Ohio	(1,690)	8,000
120. Kirksville	Missouri	5,966 (1900)	15,000
121. Knoxville	Pennsylvania	3,511 (1900)	15,000
122. Lancaster	Ohio	8,991 (1900)	17,500
123. Lansdowne	Pennsylvania	2,630 (1900)	10,000
124. Latonia	Kentucky	(1,882)	10,000
125. Laurel	Maryland	2,079 (1900)	10,000
126. Laurel	Mississippi	5,362w(1910)	12,000
127. Lyons	New York	4,460 (1910)	12,500
128. Macon	Georgia	11,722w(1900) 22,515w(1910)	20,000 50,000

TABLE 13 — *continued*

DATE OF PROMISE	PREV. PUBLIC LIB.	PUBLIC LIB. EST. BY 1923?	REASON	SOURCE
May 15, 1916	No	Yes	Site problems or controversy	M.R. No.13
April 11, 1905	No	No	Voted down by electorate	M.R. No.67
March 21, 1908	Yes		Wanted more funds	M.R. No.67
Sept. 29, 1915	No	Yes	Wanted more funds	M.R. No.13
Jan. 8, 1908	No	Yes	Legally unable to support at 10%	M.R. No.67
June 24, 1911	No	No	Financially unable to support at 10%	M.R. No.67
May 2, 1907	Yes		Unknown	
Nov. 27, 1906	No	No	Unknown	
Sept. 25, 1914	Yes		Architectural problems	M.R. No.14
April 26, 1902	No	Yes	Voted down twice by electorate	M.R. No.67
Feb. 26, 1914	No	No	Financially unable to support at 10%	Questionnaire
June 2, 1900	No	No	Financially unable to support at 10%	Questionnaire
March 11, 1914	Yes		Wanted more funds	M.R. No.15
Jan. 2, 1909	Yes		Wanted more funds	M.R. No.67
Jan. 7, 1907	Yes		Financially unable to support at 10%	M.R. No.67
March 18, 1911	Yes		Council against 10% support	M.R. No.67
April 26, 1902	No	No	Site problems or controversy	M.R. No.67
Jan. 25, 1901	No	No	Unknown	
Jan. 27, 1904	Yes		Unknown	
July 22, 1903	Yes		Site problems or controversy	M.R. No.67
Feb. 2, 1903	No	No	Financially unable to support at 10%	M.R. No.67
Dec. 30, 1901	No	No	Legally unable to support at 10%	M.R. No.18
Jan. 31, 1914	No	Yes	Wanted more funds	M.R. No.16
Jan. 9, 1913	Yes		Council against 10% support	M.R. No.18
March 14, 1901	Yes			
Nov. 19, 1916	Yes		Local philanthropist	M.R. No.18

TABLE 13—*continued*

COMMUNITY	STATE	POPULATION	AMOUNT
129. Madera County	California	8,368 (1910)	$ 12,500
130. Madison	Indiana	7,835 (1900)	20,000
131. Mandan	North Dakota	1,658 (1900)	10,000
132. Manson	Iowa	1,424 (1900)	6,000
133. Marine City	Michigan	3,829 (1900)	10,000
134. Martin	Tennessee	2,228 (1910)	9,000
135. Medina	New York	4,716 (1900)	10,000
136. Mentor	Ohio	624 (1900)	10,000
137. Merced	California	1,969 (1900)	10,000
138. Miller	South Dakota	1,202 (1910)	7,500
139. Mobile	Alabama	21,402w(1900)	50,000
140. Modesto	California	4,034 (1910)	12,500
141. Monroe	Wisconsin	3,927 (1910)	12,500
142. Morenci	Michigan	1,334 (1900)	5,000
143. Mound City	Missouri	1,575 (1910)	7,500
144. Nacogdoches	Texas	1,827 (1900)	10,000
145. Neosho	Missouri	2,725 (1900)	10,000
146. Newburgh	New York	27,805 (1910)	42,000
147. New Canaan	Connecticut	1,304 (1900)	
		1,672 (1910)	10,000
148. New Castle	Pennsylvania	28,339 (1900)	40,000
149. New Philadelphia	Ohio	8,542 (1910)	20,000
150. New Richmond	Wisconsin	1,631 (1900)	8,000
			10,000
151. Norcross	Georgia	797 (1900)	5,000
152. Norristown	Pennsylvania	22,265 (1900)	50,000
153. North Andover	Massachusetts	4,243 (1900)	12,000

TABLE 13 — *continued*

DATE OF PROMISE	PREV. PUBLIC LIB.	PUBLIC LIB. EST. BY 1923?	REASON	SOURCE
Jan. 28, 1916	Yes		Architectural problems	M.R. No.18
March 14, 1901	Yes		Voted down twice by electorate	M.R. No.67
June 11, 1904	No	Yes	Site problems or controversy	Questionnaire
March 14, 1905	No	No	Legally unable to support at 10%	M.R. No. 67
Dec. 2, 1909	No	Yes	Voted down twice by electorate	Questionnaire
April 3, 1912	No	No	Architectural problems	M.R. No.19
Jan. 13, 1903	Yes		Unknown	
July 5, 1901	Yes		Legally unable to support at 10%	M.R. No.67
Feb. 10, 1908	No	Yes	Wanted more funds	M.R. No.67
May 15, 1916	Yes		Wanted more funds	M.R. No.67
April 28, 1910	No	Yes	Council against 10% support	Questionnaire
Jan. 6, 1911	Yes		Local philanthropist	M.R. No.67
June 1, 1903	Yes		Local philanthropist	M.R. No.67
Feb. 7, 1905	No	No	Unknown	
April 25, 1911	Yes		Legally unable to support at 10%	M.R. No.67
Jan. 19, 1905	No	Yes	Unknown	
March 27, 1909	No	No	Voted down by electorate	Questionnaire
Feb. 3, 1917	Yes		World War I and rising building costs	M.R. No.21
Dec. 6, 1910	Yes		Architectural problems	M.R. No.67
March 9, 1901	No	Yes	Voted down by electorate	M.R. No.67
Jan. 28, 1916	Yes		World War I and rising building costs	M.R. No.21
April 28, 1910			Financially unable	M.R. No.67
Aug. 8, 1910	Yes		to support at 10%	
March 21, 1908	No	No	Unknown	
March 7, 1901	No	Yes	Site problems or controversy	M.R. No.67
Jan. 14, 1904	Yes		Local philanthropist	M.R. No.86

128   CARNEGIE LIBRARIES

TABLE 13 — *continued*

COMMUNITY	STATE	POPULATION	AMOUNT
154. North East	Pennsylvania	2,068 (1900) $	8,000
155. North Milwaukee	Wisconsin	1,860 (1910)	10,000
156. Norway	Maine	2,034 (1900)	5,000
157. Oakland	Indiana	2,370 (1910)	7,500
158. Oelwein	Iowa	5,142 (1900)	12,500
159. Okmulgee	Oklahoma	4,176 (1910)	15,000
160. Oneida	New York	6,364 (1900)	11,000
			15,000
161. Oregon	Missouri	1,032 (1900)	7,500
162. Palouse	Washington	929 (1900)	9,000
163. Paris	Texas	6,286w(1900)	25,000
164. Parkston	South Dakota	970 (1910)	7,500
165. Paulsboro	New Jersey	(1,717)	10,000
166. Pensacola	Florida	9,182w(1900)	15,000
		12,758w(1910)	25,000
167. Plattsburgh	New York	8,434 (1900)	17,500
168. Port Arthur	Texas	900 (1900)	
		6,170w(1910)	20,000
169. Portage	Wisconsin	5,459 (1900)	12,500
170. Quitman	Georgia	2,114w(1910)	10,000
171. Ravenna	Ohio	4,003 (1900)	10,000
172. Red Bank	New Jersey	5,428 (1900)	10,000
173. Red Bluff	California	2,750 (1900)	10,000
174. Red Cloud	Nebraska	1,684 (1910)	8,000
175. Richmond	Missouri	3,478 (1900)	10,000
176. Richmond	Virginia	52,798w(1900)	100,000
177. Riverhead	New York	(2,017)	5,000
178. Roanoke	Virginia	29,945w(1910)	55,000

TABLE 13 — *continued*

DATE OF PROMISE	PREV. PUBLIC LIB.	PUBLIC LIB. EST. BY 1923?	REASON	SOURCE
June 1, 1903	Yes		Local philanthropist	M.R. No.67
April 3, 1917	Yes		World War I and rising building costs	M.R. No.22
Dec. 30, 1904	Yes		Council against 10% support	M.R. No.67
July 13, 1912	No	Yes	Council against 10% support	M.R. No.22
Jan. 2, 1903	No	Yes	Council against 10% support	M.R. No.67
Nov. 9, 1916	Yes		Wanted more funds	M.R. No.23
Dec. 30, 1901			Wanted more funds	M.R. No.67
Dec. 17, 1902	No	No		
May 8, 1908	No	No	Legally unable to support at 10%	M.R. No.67
March 21, 1910	No	No	Site problems or controversy	M.R. No.67
Feb. 12, 1903	No	Yes	Unknown	
June 1, 1915	No	No	Financially unable to support at 10%	M.R. No.24
March 4, 1904	Yes		Unknown	
July 4, 1901	No		Voted down twice by electorate	M.R. No.67
May 16, 1911	No	Yes		
April 23, 1906	Yes		Financially unable to support at 10%	M.R. No.68
April 17, 1909	No	Yes	Architectural problems	M.R. No.68
March 14, 1905	Yes		Unknown	
Dec. 3, 1915	No	Yes	Architectural problems	M.R. No.68
Jan. 13, 1903	No	Yes	Financially unable to support at 10%	M.R. No.68
Jan. 13, 1903	No	Yes	Financially unable to support at 10%	M.R. No.68
Nov. 24, 1905	Yes		Local philanthropist	Questionnaire
Nov. 9, 1916	No	Yes	Local philanthropist	M.R. No.26
Dec. 8, 1905	No	Yes	Unknown	
Feb. 2, 1901	No	Yes	Financially unable to support at 10%	M.R. No.68
Nov. 27, 1906	Yes		Unknown	
Dec. 7, 1911	No	Yes	Unknown	

TABLE 13 — *continued*

COMMUNITY	STATE	POPULATION	AMOUNT
179. Ruston	Louisiana	1,324 (1900)	$ 10,000
180. St. Clair	Michigan	2,633 (1910)	10,000
181. Saranac Lake	New York	2,594 (1900)	10,000
182. Saratoga	New York	(4,000)	10,000
183. Saratoga Springs	New York	12,409 (1900)	20,000
184. Sea Cliff	New York	1,558 (1900)	6,000
185. Slatington	Pennsylvania	3,773 (1900)	10,000
186. Somersworth	New Hampshire	7,023 (1900)	15,000
187. Southbridge	Massachusetts	10,025 (1900)	20,000
188. South St. Paul	Minnesota	4,510 (1910)	15,000
189. South Whitley	Indiana	1,176 (1910)	10,000
190. Sparta	Georgia	1,150 (1900)	5,000
191. Sparta Village and Township	Tennessee	1,409 (1910)	5,000
192. Spencerville	Ohio	2,794 (1910)	10,000
193. Springvale	Maine	(2,000)	3,000
194. State College	Pennsylvania	1,425 (1910)	7,500
195. Statesville	North Carolina	2,368w(1900)	5,000
196. Steamboat Springs and Franklin Township	Colorado	(1,000)	5,000
197. Strasburg	Ohio	1,885 (1910)	9,000
198. Swampscott	Massachusetts	6,204 (1910)	14,000
199. Tripp	South Dakota	675 (1910)	5,000
200. Twin Falls	Idaho	5,258 (1910)	15,000
201. Tyrone	Pennsylvania	4,705 (1890)	50,000
202. Uniontown	Pennsylvania	6,359 (1890)	50,000
203. Urbana	Illinois	5,728 (1900)	20,000
204. Urbana	Ohio	6,808 (1900)	15,000
205. Waseca	Minnesota	3,054 (1910)	10,000

TABLE 13—*continued*

DATE OF PROMISE	PREV. PUBLIC LIB.	PUBLIC LIB. EST. BY 1923?	REASON	SOURCE
Dec. 24, 1909	No	No	Architectural problems	M.R. No.68
Sept. 29, 1915	No	Yes	Unknown	
Dec. 20, 1903	Yes		Unknown	
March 14, 1902	Yes		Voted down by electorate	M.R. No.68
Dec. 30, 1901	No	Yes	Wanted more funds	M.R. No.68
May 15, 1906	Yes		Local philanthropist	M.R. No.68
Nov. 24, 1905	No	No	Financially unable to support at 10%	M.R. No.68
April 20, 1902	Yes		Unknown	
July 15, 1902	Yes		Local philanthropist	M.R. No.68
Jan. 28, 1916	No	No	Wanted more funds	M.R. No.30
Aug. 11, 1913	No	Yes	Council against 10% support (township)	M.R. No.30
Dec. 26, 1906	No	No	Unknown	
Sept. 29, 1915	No	No	Council against 10% support	Questionnaire
Feb. 6, 1915	No	No	Voted down by electorate	M.R. No.30
March 21, 1910	No	No	Unknown	
Feb. 3, 1917	Yes		World War I and rising building costs	M.R. No.30
Dec. 30, 1904	No	Yes	Unknown	
Dec. 13, 1907	No	Yes	Wanted more funds	M.R. No.68
Nov. 21, 1911	Yes		Unknown	
March 16, 1915	Yes		Local philanthropist	M.R. No.31
July 9, 1913	No	Yes	Financially unable to support at 10%	M.R. No.32
Aug. 11, 1913	Yes		Wanted more funds	M.R. No.32
Oct. 8, 1899	No	No	Council against 10% support	M.R. No.68
Dec. 12, 1899	No	No	Council against 10% support	Questionnaire
March 21, 1908	Yes		Local philanthropist	M.R. No.68
March 27, 1903	No	Yes	Site problems or controversy	M.R. No.68
May 15, 1916	No	Yes	Architectural problems	M.R. No.33

TABLE 13—*continued*

COMMUNITY	STATE	POPULATION	AMOUNT
206. Watervliet	New York	14,321 (1900)	$ 10,000
207. Waynesboro	Georgia	2,030 (1900)	7,500
208. Wellston	Ohio	8,045 (1900)	15,000
209. Wellsville	New York	3,556 (1900)	7,500
210. West Bend	Wisconsin	2,462 (1910)	10,000
211. West Chicago	Illinois	1,877 (1900)	6,500
212. West Orange	New Jersey	6,889 (1900)	15,000
213. West Point	Georgia	1,797 (1900)	5,000
214. Wharton	Texas	1,505 (1910)	8,000
215. Wheeling	West Virginia	33,541w(1890)	75,000
216. Wilkinsburg	Pennsylvania	4,662 (1890) 11,886 (1900)	50,000
217. Williamson	West Virginia	(3,000)	10,000
218. Williamson County (Franklin)	Tennessee	16,385w(1910) 1,507w(1910)	5,000
219. Williamston	Michigan	1,042 (1910)	8,000
220. Williamstown	Massachusetts	5,013 (1900)	10,000
221. Wilmington	North Carolina	10,556w(1900)	25,000
222. Winchendon	Massachusetts	5,001 (1900)	12,500
223. Windsor	Missouri	2,241 (1910)	9,000
224. Wiscasset	Maine	1,273 (1900)	5,000
225. York	Pennsylvania	33,708 (1900)	50,000

*Only the white population (indicated by the letter "w") is given for southern communities of more than 2500, since this was the basis for any Carnegie public library grant. The United States census figures did not provide a breakdown by color for towns with a population of less than 2500. Thus these southern towns are listed with their total (white and Negro) population.

†No population was given in the census figures for some towns. In such instances an estimated population (as recorded in the Carnegie Library Correspondence) is listed in parentheses.

pressed a willingness to meet the conditions in effect for public library gifts. After the Carnegie representatives made

TABLE 13 — *continued*

DATE OF PROMISE	PREV. PUBLIC LIB.	PUBLIC LIB. EST. BY 1923?	REASON	SOURCE
May 15, 1916	No	No	Financially unable to support at 10%	M.R. No.68
March 6, 1903	No	No	Site problems or controversy	M.R. No.68
March 20, 1903	No	No	Unknown	
Feb. 15, 1905	Yes		Financially unable to support at 10%	M.R. No.68
June 6, 1917	Yes		Wanted more funds	M.R. No.34
April 17, 1909	No	No	Voted down by electorate	Questionnaire
Nov. 18, 1903	No	Yes	Unknown	
Jan. 18, 1910	No	Yes	Architectural problems	M.R. No.68
May 8, 1914	Yes		Architectural problems	M.R. No.34
Aug. 12, 1899	Yes		Voted down by electorate	M.R. No.68
June 25, 1900	Yes		Site problems or controversy	Questionnaire
Feb. 13, 1913	Yes		Unknown	
March 9, 1907	No	No	Unknown	
March 31, 1916	No	Yes	Unknown	
Jan. 22, 1903	Yes		Financially unable to support at 10%	M.R. No.68
Jan. 13, 1903	No	Yes	Wanted more funds	M.R. No.68
April 8, 1907	Yes		Local philanthropist	M.R. No.68
Dec. 7, 1911	No	No	Unknown	
April 11, 1902	No	Yes	Financially unable to support at 10%	M.R. No.68
Jan. 16, 1900	No	Yes	Legally unable to support at 10%	M.R. No.68

a tentative offer, something happened to thwart the gift, and the community never did receive a Carnegie library building.

The compilation of town names and locations for this table came from three sources. The most useful was, of course, the microfilmed Carnegie Library Correspondence. Presumably, three of the forty reels were to contain correspondence of the Carnegie grants that had lapsed, but the author found additional towns among the correspondence of those communities which had received gifts. Another source was the *List of* [Carnegie] *Bildings in the United States, Canada, United Kingdom and Other English-speaking Countries, March 31, 1913,* published by the Carnegie Corporation in 1913. This document was found at the University of Michigan General Library together with a letter dated March 2, 1916 from F. M. Coffin to former librarian, William W. Bishop, stating that the list had been brought up to date by penciled notations to December 31, 1915. Additional localities were found by checking the towns in this list (pending as well as completed grants) against an official list of Carnegie library benefactions. Still other communities were traced by checking all the issues of the *Library Journal* during 1916-19 for announcements of towns receiving promises of grants during this period.

After the basic list of communities was obtained, the next task was to complete all the other information deemed necessary. The microfilmed Carnegie Library Correspondence was again a good source if a file of correspondence on the particular town could be found in it. This was especially true for the amount, date of the promise, and the population, although many population figures had to be obtained from the 1890, 1900, and 1910 United States census volumes. It was less true for determining whether the town already had a public library before the Carnegie promise and for discovering the reason for the failure to follow through on the grant. Whenever this information was obtained from the Carnegie Library Correspondence, the actual microfilm reel was noted. The *American Library Directory* (New York: Bowker, 1923) was consulted to check on the number of communities without a public library before the grant application which organized their own and the number still without library service. Whatever information was incomplete was requested in a questionnaire sent to librarians in seventy-eight communities. Fifty-two responses were received, but of these only twenty-two were able to provide the necessary data.

Location

Table 14 shows a breakdown of the 225 communities by state. It is interesting that in certain states a high number of

TABLE 14

UNACCEPTED CARNEGIE LIBRARY OFFERS – BY STATE

STATE	NUMBER OF COMMUNI-TIES NOT RECEIVING A CARNEGIE LIBRARY	NUMBER OF COMMUNI-TIES RECEIVING A CARNEGIE LIBRARY
Alabama	3	12
Arizona	0	4
Arkansas	0	4
California	5	121
Colorado	1	27
Connecticut	3	8
Delaware	1	0
District of Columbia	0	1
Florida	2	10
Georgia	10	20
Idaho	3	10
Illinois	8	105
Indiana	9	155
Iowa	5	99
Kansas	1	58
Kentucky	2	15
Louisiana	1	4
Maine	6	17
Maryland	2	1
Massachusetts	7	35
Michigan	12	53
Minnesota	5	58
Mississippi	2	10
Missouri	13	27
Montana	1	17
Nebraska	3	68
Nevada	1	1
New Hampshire	2	9
New Jersey	5	29
New Mexico	0	3
New York	21	41
North Carolina	5	9
North Dakota	2	8
Ohio	18	77
Oklahoma	5	24
Oregon	0	25
Pennsylvania	20	26
South Carolina	2	14
South Dakota	4	25
Tennessee	5	10

TABLE 14 — *continued*

STATE	NUMBER OF COMMUNI- TIES NOT RECEIVING A CARNEGIE LIBRARY	NUMBER OF COMMUNI- TIES RECEIVING A CARNEGIE LIBRARY
Texas	10	30
Utah	1	23
Vermont	0	4
Virginia	7	2
Washington	1	33
West Virginia	4	3
Wisconsin	6	60
Wyoming	1	16

municipalities did not follow through on the offer of a Carnegie library as compared to the number of those which did. Carnegie's home state, Pennsylvania, with 20 to 26; New York with 21 to 41; Missouri with 13 to 27; and Georgia with 10 to 20, are examples of states with a high percentage of failures. On the other hand, the three states with the highest number of Carnegie grants (California, Illinois, and Indiana) had, in proportion, very few grant failures. The best record was held by Oregon, with no failures and 25 Carnegie library grants. Among the southern states there were 54 grant failures as compared to 132 towns which received Carnegie grants.

Population

The population which would have been served by Carnegie libraries in all the 225 cities not accepting Carnegie library offers totaled 1,362,047. The average population was 6053, but the mean was only 2751. Indeed, Table 15 indicates that 158 of the 225 communities in question had less than 5000 people at the time of their application for a Carnegie library.

The reader may be puzzled at times in comparing a town's population with the amount of financial aid promised, finding the latter too high in relation to the former on the basis of the $2 per capita rate. Three Pennsylvania towns — Beaver

TABLE 15

UNACCEPTED CARNEGIE LIBRARY OFFERS —
BY POPULATION OF COMMUNITY

POPULATION	NUMBER OF COMMUNITIES	POPULATION	NUMBER OF COMMUNITIES
Under 1,000	13	16,000–16,999	2
1,000– 1,999	63	17,000–17,999	1
2,000– 2,999	42	19,000–19,999	2
3,000– 3,999	25	20,000–20,999	1
4,000– 4,999	15	21,000–21,999	2
5,000– 5,999	15	22,000–22,999	2
6,000– 6,999	11	23,000–23,999	1
7,000– 7,999	4	27,000–27,999	1
8,000– 8,999	6	28,000–28,999	1
9,000– 9,999	2	29,000–29,999	1
10,000–10,999	2	33,000–33,999	1
11,000–11,999	1	52,000–52,999	1
12,000–12,999	5	87,000–87,999	1
13,000–13,999	2	94,000–94,999	1
14,000–14,999	1		

(1897), Greensburg (1897), and Tyrone (1899) — if granted gifts, would have fallen into the special Carnegie library-gift category described in Chapter V. They were among the early offers and among the communities in which Carnegie had special interests. It was at Greensburg, for instance, that he had made his start as a telegraph operator. In other cases the grant, in the final analysis, was probably made not only on the basis of the last census figure, but also on the assessed valuation over recent years, as well as by other measures of growth.

Grants

If all grants had been made, $3,493,660 would have been received. With a low of $3000 and a high of $150,000, this would have averaged to $15,458 per town, but the median amount was $10,000. Table 16 shows that this figure was also the most frequently offered amount (to seventy communities).

TABLE 16

UNACCEPTED CARNEGIE LIBRARY OFFERS —
BY AMOUNT

GRANT OFFER	NUMBER OF COMMUNITIES	GRANT OFFER	NUMBER OF COMMUNITIES
$ 3,000	2	16,000	1
4,500	1	16,660	1
5,000	24	17,500	3
6,000	6	20,000	12
6,500	3	22,000	1
7,000	3	25,000	9
7,500	16	30,000	1
8,000	11	35,000	1
8,500	1	40,000	1
9,000	6	42,000	1
10,000	70	50,000	9
11,000	1	55,000	1
12,000	3	60,000	1
12,500	9	75,000	1
13,000	1	100,000	3
14,000	1	150,000	1
15,000	20		

Date

Table 17 reveals that there is no significant relationship between the year the original promise of funds was made and the failure to obtain a grant. Generally the pattern is the same as that in the listing of completed Carnegie public library grants (see Table 3).

Previous Library

Ninety-eight of the 225 communities already had a public library established and in operation, whereas 127 had none, when their first requests for Carnegie funds were made. It is interesting to note that by 1923, 64 of these 127 had public library service established without the aid of Carnegie funds, though many of these libraries were an indirect result of

TABLE 17

UNACCEPTED CARNEGIE LIBRARY OFFERS—
BY YEAR OF OFFER

YEAR	NUMBER	YEAR	NUMBER
1897 or earlier	2	1909	13
1898	0	1910	10
1899	4	1911	16
1900	4	1912	8
1901	18	1913	14
1902	7	1914	11
1903	33	1915	9
1904	6	1916	14
1905	19	1917	5
1906	11	1918	0
1907	9	1919	0
1908	11		

Carnegie giving. For example, civic leaders and town officials of Hudson Falls, New York, decided to build their own library after the Carnegie library was voted down twice by the electorate. A one-week drive for contributions netted $10,000, and labor was also subscribed to help construct the building. The town provided the site, and the same conditions for operation were self-imposed as if it were a Carnegie library. One thousand dollars per year was pledged by city officials for the support of the library.[1]

Reasons for Failure

It was often difficult to discover why a community did not accept a grant. At times the Carnegie Library Correspondence did not divulge the information because of a lack of letters in this regard. At other times the file on a certain community contained many letters from different sources, each citing a different reason for the failure of the offer. The author had hoped to go through the correspondence or the questionnaires and find and define the basic cause for the failures. But quite often there were numerous reasons why the offers were not accepted as one difficulty led to another. Perhaps, at first, there was a problem of obtaining a location. After the site problem was solved, difficulty with building plans sometimes developed. If the final cause proved to be World War I with its rising costs and bans on public building, then this was the reason given for failure listed in Table 13.

The most frequent cause for the grant to lapse or be refused was opposition to the 10 percent annual support pledge. A total of 26 communities failed to obtain funds because of this clause. In most cases it was the city or town council which voted down the maintenance pledge. Twenty-three communities did not take advantage of a grant because a local philanthropist came forward to make a donation for the building. Another 23 did not receive the promised grant because they wanted more money than that allocated by Carnegie officials. Very often this desire was based on the belief that the local population had grown greatly since the last census. At other times it was just a desire for a larger building than the Carnegie funds would have built.

In still another 23 cases the community seemed financially unable to fulfill the 10 percent support pledge. The paving of streets, installation of new sewers, and building of new schools had already placed a heavy financial burden on the locality, and it could not afford the library building. In 21 municipalities a formal vote was held, and the Carnegie library was turned down by the electorate. Normally this kind of election was held specifically for an increase in the tax levy to support the proposed library. There would, also, be a segment of the population which would vote not so much against a rise in taxes as against a "Carnegie" library.

Architectural problems with the projected library building brought about the failure of grants in 16 municipalities. In most instances it was James Bertram who refused to accede to the impractical or overly ambitious desires of local officials and their architects. A site problem or controversy was the basic cause for 15 towns not receiving the promised Carnegie grant. Sometimes the problem was one of buying a site, but most often it was controversy over the location of the library—controversy which raged so long and violently that in the end no Carnegie funds were ever received.

World War I and rising costs served as the cause for 11 communities not obtaining Carnegie library funds. Towns receiving promises of grants before 1916 but not attempting to put up their buildings until later ran into great difficulty as costs began rising.[2] Many communities kept delaying the beginning of building hoping that costs would drop. During World War I most public building was suspended. After the war, building costs continued to be very high, and the Carnegie Corporation was unrelenting in not increasing the original amount.

Nine communities were legally unable to fulfill the 10 percent support pledge, even though they were willing to do so. Most often this was because the tax levy was already at maximum, or the stipulated library tax levy was at such a low level that it would not allow an income sufficient to meet the 10 percent mark. In a few instances legal conflicts of governing bodies or jurisdictional disputes between a school board and a municipality or between a town and a township over a projected Carnegie library resulted in no library at all. In 2 communities, both of these on the outskirts of Cleveland, the original library building offer was rescinded because the communities were eventually annexed to Cleveland.

The reasons for failure remain unknown for 56 communities. The correspondence does not show the cause, and the questionnaires reveal nothing. Quite often the local librarian or city official responding to the questionnaire expressed amazement to learn that his municipality had ever been involved in a Carnegie library request. Others knew of the request but could not supply the answers even after the search of records and old newspaper files. And, of course, by now most of the people involved in the original negotiations were no longer living. In many instances the offer just lapsed. Beginning in 1917, the Carnegie Corporation began to write off its books many of these previous offers after a final letter of inquiry was written to ascertain that no action was being taken to follow through on the original promise.

142   CARNEGIE LIBRARIES

Notes

[1] Clipping from the New York *Herald Tribune*, Feb. 7, 1915, found in Hudson Falls, N.Y., Carnegie Library Correspondence, Microfilm Reel No.67.
[2] Various construction-cost indexes show that costs more than doubled between 1915 and 1920; see p.385–86 of the U.S. Bureau of the Census, *Historical Statistics of the United States, Colonial Times to 1957* (Washington, D.C.: Govt. Print. Off., 1960).

CHAPTER EIGHT

The Alvin Johnson Report and the End of Carnegie Library Giving

THE CONCERN of the Carnegie Corporation about reports of broken pledges and other Carnegie library abuses resulted not only in the sending of questionnaires but also in the hiring of Alvin S. Johnson, an economics professor at Cornell University, to make a study of these libraries. Johnson had received both his B.A. and M.A. degrees at the University of Nebraska. His doctorate in economics was received from Columbia in 1902. From 1906 to 1916 he served as a professor of economics at the universities of Nebraska and Chicago and at Stanford and Cornell. After the writing of the Carnegie report, he later became editor of the *New Republic* (1917–23), director of the New School for Social Research (1923–43), and editor of the *Encyclopedia of Social Sciences.*

In his autobiography[1] Johnson recalled that Henry S. Pritchett, a trustee of the Carnegie Corporation, asked him to go on a sampling tour of the Carnegie libraries throughout the land and take a look at their operations. He answered that a professional librarian might do a better job, but Pritchett did not agree. What the Corporation needed was not a comprehensive report but rather a series of impressions of the libraries and their place in the community. Johnson accepted

143

and took a ten-week winding course through the Middle West to the West Coast, back through the South, up the Middle Atlantic states, and finally through New England, visiting some one hundred Carnegie libraries of various sizes. His report[2] was officially authorized by the Carnegie Corporation's board of trustees on November 18, 1915 and was presented in 1916. But a copy of the report was not privately printed until 1919, and it has never been publicly disseminated. Johnson's incisive and farsighted comments are summarized in the pages that follow.

Alvin Johnson conceived his task to be that of ascertaining whether the policy of establishing free public libraries with the requirement of a definite annual maintenance fund was fulfilling the purpose well enough to justify the outlay involved. He also felt that it was necessary to review and reappraise the Carnegie library benefactions, since more than fifteen years had passed from the time of their inauguration. His report did not present in detail any of the data which he collected or data already in the Corporation archives. He sought rather to discover and present the elusive facts relating to the actual and the potential role of the library in the community. Johnson believed any conclusion regarding the success of Carnegie Corporation library policy should be based primarily on these facts.

Social Significance of the Free Library

In his report Johnson dealt first with the social significance of the free library. He thought that the public library provided a practical and cultural service of great value. A well-organized library offered instruction and entertainment to the whole literate community. Library service was essentially a public service closely related to popular education and equally deserving of public support.

Unfortunately, while the free public library received in a general way almost universal approval, its functions in the modern community were not sufficiently understood. This

lack of understanding frequently resulted in the postpone-
ment of the establishment of library service or in the lack of
adequate appropriations after it was established. But Johnson
had faith in the public library's future development and already saw current tendencies toward the increasing depend-
ence of the community upon the library. He predicted that
the public library would play a significant part in advancing
popular intellectual progress.

Library Philanthropy

Johnson next examined the question of philanthropic initiative in library development. It was a familiar fact, he stated,
that public authorities were slow to recognize new social
needs and still slower to make adequate provisions for their
satisfaction. Another familiar fact was that services provided
at public expense were likely to be administered more or less
mechanically.

Alvin Johnson envisioned the free public library as a relatively new institution. Only during the previous generation
had there been any national development. Thus, it was easy to
understand why this movement had not come to the attention
everywhere of public authorities or gained an important influence over public opinion. Even where public libraries existed, there was often not the least understanding in the community of the role that the library was expected to play. Towns
that were otherwise progressive were still maintaining libraries that did nothing more than circulate books indiffer-
ently suited to community needs. In the course of his travels,
Johnson met numerous library trustees and even librarians.
To many of them it was a novel idea that a library should
actively engage in stimulating and directing the demand for
books and should seek to cooperate with other forces in the
community working for popular education and culture.

Johnson described the free library as a service lying in an
intermediate zone. The public, while recognizing its benefits
in a general way, did not appreciate them sufficiently to compel the civil authorities to make adequate provision for library

service or to control the quality of such service. Such a situation was one in which philanthropic initiative was likely to prove fruitful. What was required was an impetus that would eventually be transmitted to the public authorities.

He also suggested the desirability of adapting to local conditions any philanthropic initiative in establishing library service. Such intervention was less necessary and less justified in the more advanced sections of the United States. It seemed to him that in states like Massachusetts and California library donations should take the form of supplementary grants designed to make possible more adequate library service rather than grants for complete building construction. On the other hand, in states like Texas and Alabama, nothing less than a complete building-construction grant was likely to prove adequate. Indeed, after the unsuccessful experience of the small Carnegie library towns in Texas, Johnson raised the question if better results would not have been obtained here if fewer libraries had been established, and if those actually established had been provided with books and expert librarians to cultivate the library habit through an initial period.

Different cities within the same state might well receive discriminatory treatment. Factors other than population had to be brought into consideration. In the more highly developed states, the smaller cities and towns were less responsive to the modern library movement than the larger ones and, therefore, required preferential treatment. But the South was generally so backward in library service that the large cities offered the best promise for cultivation of libraries. In addition, there was more compelling reason for subsidizing library work in a city with a large foreign-born, unskilled labor population like Scranton, Pennsylvania, than in a town like York, Pennsylvania, where the native-born, skilled element was preponderant. The foreign-born were less familiar with libraries, and collections of books in their native tongues would have to be provided.

The policy of granting donations for library enlargements was also questioned. Johnson felt that after a library was established and was operating so successfully as to become

crowded, then it should be the obligation of the community
to provide for a building expansion. He also thought that the
emphasis in the Carnegie Corporation's total library philosophy might well shift, with the progress of time, to elements
in library service other than the provision of buildings.

Efficient Community Library Service

The second and third chapters of the Johnson report dealt
with his idea of efficient library service and the community
activities of the public library. He felt that no library was properly employing its opportunities if it merely provided reading matter in answer to the requests of the community. An
efficient public library engaged itself actively in creating a demand for reading and in directing existing demand into the
most profitable channels.

One way to do this was to sponsor lectures designed to stimulate the reading of those who attended. Another was to publish lists of newly acquired books in the local newspaper or to
distribute lists of books to selected groups in the community.
The Carnegie Library in Waco, Texas, for example, mailed a
list of available books on child care to every family which reg-
istered the birth of a child. Still another way was the establishment of book collections for special classes of people. At
Leominster, Massachusetts, the library established such deposits in the local industrial plants. Johnson suggested, also,
close contact and cooperation between the library and the various schools in the community.

In order to perform such service, the library staff should
have a systematic knowledge of the occupations and the social
conditions of the community. Johnson found little evidence of
librarians making such surveys or of playing the active role
he espoused. An active library would gradually win the
friendship and support of increasing numbers of the community's population. It would enlist the cooperation of the
schools, the employers and the workingmen's organizations,
and the various other occupational classes. Eventually, it
would establish its title as an important agency of the commu-

nity and would be able to compete successfully with other forms of town improvement in its financial claims. It appeared, therefore, that in determining whether or not a request for a library donation was to be honored, careful consideration ought to be given to the local conditions favoring or hindering the proposed library's activity. An inactive library could easily become dead capital.

In regard to buildings and equipment, Johnson wrote that the principles of architectural control elaborated and put in force by the Corporation met the general requirements quite adequately. It was safe to predict that any relaxation of architectural control would lead to a return of the type of library building characterized by an imposing exterior and a poorly organized, space-wasteful interior. However, a greater degree of flexibility might be permitted depending upon local conditions. A library which was chiefly a center for the circulation of books did not need a large reference room. The proper location and size of the children's room was another factor which could vary from place to place.

Johnson also suggested that local conditions might arise to justify a departure from the rule that money was to be given only for buildings to be used exclusively for library purposes. In some instances combination buildings, financed in a fair proportion by locally raised funds, might be an advantage. For example, as long as the chamber of commerce of a certain town enjoyed a room in the library, its political influence was thrown in favor of the library appropriations. But when a reform librarian expelled the group, financial support almost ended.

It might be wise to attempt to win the support of other influences for the library through the sharing of clubrooms and lecture halls, particularly in areas where the reading habit had not been fully developed (as in the South and in many small towns throughout much of the country). If such a combination building were permitted, the expenses of heating, lighting, and janitor service could be shared and a greater proportion of the library funds applied to books and services. The library could, also, be kept open for longer periods daily and thereby greatly increase its usefulness to the community. In addition, there would be more frequent traffic to the building of persons not attracted by the desire for reading alone. The library's popularity would thus be increased, resulting in more adequate appropriations from the town. It was Johnson's belief that the feeble support of libraries in small towns was a result of the lack of popular interest in the library rather than the consequence of poverty on the part of the municipalities.

Johnson realized that the sharing of facilities would require a personal survey of the local situation by an officer of the Corporation. Abuses would have to be watched so that these shared facilities would not become the preponderant ones in the building plan. A personal survey prior to the authorization of a grant might be a most desirable provision.

Location of Carnegie Library Buildings

The fifth chapter in the report dealt with the location of the Carnegie library buildings. Johnson found that only a small percentage (about one out of ten) of the 100 libraries that he visited enjoyed the best possible location. In a majority of cases, the location appeared to be a distinct handicap to efficient service.

Confirmed readers would find the library wherever it was located. But the library had to attract groups of less eager readers, and one way to accomplish this was to locate it in the center of the business district, which all the inhabitants frequented. The chief disadvantage of a central downtown location in a large city was the likely inconvenience of access for children, but they could be served better in branches in their neighborhoods and near their schools. In fact, in most of the larger cities it seemed evident that better results might have been obtained from a more systematic distribution of funds between central and branch libraries.

Why was the library frequently so poorly located? Often the site was donated, and the community would accept it regardless of its location. At other times the site had to be purchased, and a good central location could not be afforded. In some cases politics with a real estate motive was the influencing factor. But to Johnson the fundamental cause was due to local failure to understand the requirements and potentialities of library service. Marked improvement in this respect could be introduced only if greater stress were laid by the Carnegie Corporation on the importance of the library location.

Library Personnel

Library personnel was the next topic considered in the report. It was Johnson's feeling that the efficiency of the library was largely dependent on the character and training of the librarian and on his or her ability to understand the community and cultivate the reading habit. In the large city libraries, it was the practice for the training and experience of almost the entire staff to be limited to that learned on the job. Johnson felt that this was undesirable as the reading public came into immediate contact, not with the chief librarian, but with his various assistants. In southern towns the librarian was generally found to be a "decayed gentlewoman with the virtues and foibles of her class." She had no special capacity to make good her lack of library experience through a careful study of the technical helps available in printed form to librarians.

In other cases the office of librarian was bestowed upon someone regarded as especially fitted by natural instinct: a local poet, a local authority on Confederate memoirs, or just someone who was popular and liked books. The prevailing view in small towns all over the country was that anyone who was fairly well read, polite, and painstaking would make a satisfactory librarian. Since a community did not know what to expect from a library or its librarian, their shortcomings were often not recognized for a long time.

Johnson recommended that an inquiry should be made regarding the practicability of securing reasonably efficient library service before the Carnegie Corporation granted a donation. The community was to be impressed with the idea that the person selected as librarian should be expected to fulfill certain minimum requirements of training and experience prior to appointment. It seemed inadvisable to donate a library building to a community which neither had a sense of library service nor could be awakened to such a sense. An inactive library was not only a questionable investment of capital. It also encouraged the false notion that it was not necessary to make any financial sacrifices for library purposes. To Johnson nothing contributed more to the certainty of library inactivity than an untrained and unintelligent librarian.

Facilities for Library Education

The seventh chapter was concerned with facilities for library education. Johnson concluded that there was a need for a much larger number of trained librarians than could be provided from existing institutions. There was, also, the need for a broader course of instruction than that offered by most of the existing thirteen schools of library science. The majority of these schools offered one year of technical training. One year might be sufficient after four years of college, but most of these schools required only the completion of high school and the passing of a qualifying entrance examination.

A library school education was needed which would provide a good knowledge of books and their selection for the collection. It would also have to provide a knowledge of reference work so that the library resources could be made really accessible to the community by the librarian. It would have to furnish a training which would give the librarian a grasp of the social and economic conditions in the community. She then would be able to expend the library's finances wisely for the appropriate technical and other practical literature in the proportions necessary for the community. The librarian should obtain the education necessary to enable her to have respect and standing in the community so that she could guide reading and secure the cooperation of the schools, churches, clubs, and other cultural or social agencies.

The evil of underpayment was a serious obstacle to the rapid elevation of the professional library position. But like the old-time barber-surgeon and schoolmaster who received scanty financial support and who hardly deserved more, a considerable proportion of the contemporary low-paid library personnel received quite all they deserved in view of their passivity and inefficiency. Improvement of library training and service would have to come first before an increase in salary at the hands of the public authorities. Such had been the case with the elevation of the medical profession to its current high rank, which did not precede but followed the establishment of extended facilities for professional training. This improvement should be the concern of the Carnegie Corporation, since it was engaged in the work of supplying the permanent plant for a public service whose efficient performance depended upon competent personnel.

Public Library Finances

In regard to public library finances, Alvin Johnson felt that much improvement again was needed. The maintenance appropriations were almost everywhere too meager. Taking a $10,000 building with an annual maintenance appropriation of $1000 as an example, he showed how almost nothing was left for new books, periodicals and newspaper subscriptions. Repairs, alterations, and insurance would take between $100 and $200. A janitor would be paid $100 per year. If the library were located anywhere except in the deep south or lower California and stayed open a minimum of four hours in the afternoons and three hours in the evenings, light and heat would cost $200. The lowest-paid librarian would require an annual salary of $400. If the library had a basic book stock of 4000 volumes, the remaining $100 would be needed for replacing or rebinding older titles.

For a newly established library the small 10 percent maintenance appropriation meant moving into a new building with no books with which to provide service. The erection of a new local library was an event of great importance in a small town. However, when the building opened with nothing in it, the interest soon died. This initial period of stagnation was one of the chief reasons for the highly unsatisfactory condition of the small libraries in Texas. The other cause was the belief that no local legislative body had the power to bind the town to permanent appropriations for services that did not on experience recommend themselves as valuable.

The impression was often created that the Carnegie Corporation judged the 10 percent annual support to be adequate for maintenance. This placed libraries under a serious handicap in their appeals for more liberal appropriations. But Johnson was against changing the annual support clause to a higher level. It would be better, he said, for a town to increase its library appropriation from, say, $1000 to $1500 voluntarily, after satisfying itself of the value of the results to be attained, rather than by a regulatory clause which would make the $1500 per year mandatory. It would, also, be better for the library itself to be forced to prove its right to an adequate income rather than to be placed in a position of claiming such income by formal arrangements.

He further urged that each community seeking a donation should be given all available information as to the meaning of effective library service and its probable cost. Any community unwilling to raise sufficient funds by private subscription or public grant to provide a reasonably satisfactory initial stock of books independent of the stipulated maintenance fund was not worthy of a building offer. If the community were willing but financially unable to do so, then the library donation could well be distributed between building and books.

Specific Recommendations and Suggestions

In the last two chapters, Alvin Johnson gave specific recommendations and suggestions to the Carnegie Corporation. The key to these recommendations lay in the principle that the only justification for investing philanthropic funds in the provision of library buildings was the prospect of efficient library service. A donation was, therefore, to be granted only after it had been made reasonably clear that the beneficiary community would maintain an active and not a passive service.

Johnson was convinced that the library benefactions of the Carnegie Corporation as they had been conducted served an extremely important purpose. Not only had they provided opportunities for reading and study to many people who would otherwise not have had access to good collections of books, but also they had established standards of library architecture and equipment that had influenced even communities not receiving donations. However, experience showed that the fruitfulness of building donations was subject to wide variations.

One of his chief recommendations was for the supplementation of the current mail inquiries being made by the Corporation with the employment of expert field agents. When it appeared probable, as a result of the preliminary mail correspondence, that a donation might advantageously be granted to a community, a field agent could be sent to the petitioning town to prepare a report. The report would cover all relevant points such as available sites and the possibility of library cooperation with schools, churches, women's clubs, and business men's organizations. An agent would be able to form a safe forecast as to the probability of generous support and be in a position to protect the Corporation against unworthy projects. In the course of his investigations, the agent could enter into discussions with the citizens taking part in the library movement and thus have opportunity to spread the correct ideas as to library requirements and possibilities.

Johnson admitted that maintaining such a field staff would add to the complexity of the administration of the library grants as well as to their expense, but it would be well worth while. He estimated quite carefully that the total cost of field supervision by four or five agents would range from 2 to 4 percent of the annual expenditure of $1,500,000 for library buildings. He felt this was not excessive, since no corporation investing funds for social profit in a field where the elements of success were complex should hesitate to devote this small percentage of the capital to a field work designed to determine such elements favorably.

Also, he felt that the assurance of efficient library service by a professionally trained librarian or librarians should be received by the Corporation before an application for a building was finally approved. The Carnegie Corporation simply could not afford to invest its capital in a project that would lie dormant for want of competent personnel. Larger towns receiving $20,000 or more could easily afford the required trained help. The smaller libraries presented a more difficult problem. Their need for efficient service was even more pressing, especially at the outset, yet they could not afford to pay salaries that would attract trained librarians. Johnson thought that the most promising solution would be the provision of properly trained librarians by the Corporation to take charge of each new library through an initial period of operation, ranging from three months in the case of the very small libraries to one year for larger ones.

The benefits of such a scheme would be many. The town would be given immediate experience of the advantages of effective service. The library budget would be relieved of the salary of the librarian for this initial period, and more funds could be used to provide a good stock of books selected by an expert. The prospective librarian would have an opportunity of acquiring knowledge on how to proceed with the work of operating the library. Finally, selfish designs upon the library on the part of local factions would be discouraged by the presence of a librarian in touch with outside opinion and the Carnegie Corporation.

Again, it was admitted that this plan would cost money, but Johnson felt that it, too, would be well worth the additional expense of a maximum of 10 percent of the building outlay. If it were the policy of the Corporation to devote $1,500,000 a year for the establishment of libraries averaging $15,000 in cost, there would have to be fifty to seventy-five of these librarians available each year. Continuous recruitment would be necessary, since many communities would make good salary offers to keep the experts who initiated their library service.

Whether the Carnegie Corporation assumed the responsibility for providing trained personnel to inaugurate the libraries established by it, or whether it preferred to continue the policy of turning the buildings over to the communities as soon as they were completed, Johnson thought the Corporation had to take an interest in and support facilities for library education. The most practicable method of improving the service of the existing Carnegie libraries would be to create one hundred scholarships per year in the established library schools for $500 each, open preferably to college graduates or at least holders of diplomas from high schools who had served not less than one year in library work. Such scholarships would be for two years of schooling. For the very small libraries, pressure from the state library commission on the library trustees to send their librarian to the short courses in library training frequently offered by universities would suffice. The Corporation could well subsidize such courses, as well as extend them to universities which did not currently offer short-term instruction for nonprofessional librarians.

Indeed, it seemed imperative to Johnson that the Carnegie Corporation take the initiative in expanding the facilities for library education by subsidies to existing library schools so that student bodies could be enlarged, or by grants to institutions willing to undertake the organization of library instruction. Such financial help would also enable the Corporation to exert an influence upon the kind of training offered.

Still another suggestion was for the establishment of a certain number of model libraries which would not be financially restricted in regard to personnel or equipment. There was special need for such libraries in the South to demonstrate to a more or less indifferent public the value of library service. Furthermore, these model libraries could assume a position of leadership in elaborating standards of library practice—a need that would persist long after the obligation of providing library buildings had been accepted by the public authorities.

Finally, Johnson felt that the Corporation might well financially assist the American Library Association in projects of mutual interest, such as the collection of statistics and other general information pertaining to library conditions; the preparation of lists of books analyzed and appraised for the use of small libraries as book selection aids; and the coordination of library demand for books with a view to influencing publishers to prepare editions in a paper and binding suitable for library use. Subsidies for library association meetings on a national, regional, and state level would, also, be of advantage to the Corporation's interest in improving library service.

In his autobiography, Alvin Johnson recalled that when he faced the Carnegie Corporation trustees with his recommendations, he also faced the wrath of James Bertram. The secretary declared that the Johnson proposals flew straight into the face of Andrew Carnegie's intentions of no centralized control or expenditure of money on the administration of the gifts. Bertram had managed the whole enterprise with one secretary in one room, but Johnson's suggestions would require twelve secretaries in six rooms. Johnson continued to argue that the protection of the huge investment being made would be worth the expense. But Bertram moved that the report be rejected, and it was so carried. Andrew Carnegie was still living at this time but was no longer taking an active role as an officer in the Corporation activities. There is no record of any reaction from him in regard to the Johnson report.

Later, Elihu Root, who had presided at the above meeting, invited Johnson to tea along with Henry S. Pritchett who was not able to attend the stormy session. They explained to Johnson that the trustees were in general favor of his recommendations but did not wish to offend Bertram since he was very close to Carnegie and would be retiring the following year. Soon after this, they claimed, Johnson would see many of his recommendations go into effect. But here either a change of plans, faulty memory, or attempts by the trustees to smooth over a bad situation cloud the issue, for Bertram was nowhere near retirement age in 1916 and continued to serve the Corporation until his death at the age of sixty-two in 1934.

Johnson went to the Corporation office the day following his report for one of the copies of it, only to be told that Bertram had had all copies destroyed. But Johnson also recalled becoming close friends with Bertram and being invited often to tea by him. If enough "tea" was imbibed, Bertram would admit that there had been much in the report worthy of consideration and that he was sorry to have destroyed it. But it was not destroyed, because the Corporation eventually had some copies privately printed, and Johnson requested and received a copy from Frederick Keppell, then president of the Carnegie Corporation, over the strenuous objections of the latter's secretary. Alvin Johnson claimed this printed copy was highly edited, with some of his strongest criticisms and recommendations left out. Among these were his severe criticism of the Corporation's past policy of granting libraries without a thought about the important factor of efficient library service and his recommendation to set up machinery for obtaining a detailed, yearly report on the operations of all existing Carnegie libraries.[3]

Alvin Johnson's interest in libraries continued, as evidenced in his *The Public Library: A People's University*, published in New York by the American Association for Adult Education in 1938. This was a report of a study of adult education in American libraries. Its object was to discover how libraries functioned in the general adult education movement, what attitudes librarians had on the development of work of this kind, and what the future position of the library seemed to be in this field.

In 1965, in a letter to the author, Johnson added a few more of his Carnegie library survey recollections:

> I visited a library, talked with the librarian and when I could reach him the Chairman of the library board. I looked over the reading room and the stacks. I inquired what classes used the library and what kind of books they read.

In my first interview I produced pencil and pad and took notes. That was a mistake, I realized. Pencil and pad are a barrier to frank conversation.

I hadn't gone far when I began to realize that the making of a library is the librarian. Practically all libraries were handicapped by meagerness of funds. Yet an ardent, energetic librarian could make a good library in spite of handicaps.

Some librarians resented my visits. They felt that I might make public their particular shortcomings. But the great majority were frank and friendly. And the best of them gave meaning to my dream of the library as a People's University.[4]

Although Alvin Johnson was not a librarian or even a person directly associated with libraries, he made many keen and penetrating observations on them. His report deserved wider circulation and, even in this day, merits greater recognition as a landmark in library literature.

End of Carnegie Library Giving

The Carnegie Corporation chose not to make any drastic changes in its library philanthropy in 1916, but less than two years later it terminated library building grants. It did, however, act on many of Johnson's other recommendations, particularly those dealing with setting up model libraries and assistance to library education and the American Library Association (see Chapter X).

Library gifts ended on November 7, 1917, following a resolution adopted by the Carnegie Corporation of New York Trustees. No new applications for the erection of library buildings were to be considered, as wartime demands were being made on money, labor, and materials. Further allotments for the building of new libraries during the war were to be made only in instances where the correspondence had already advanced so far as to imply a decision on the merits of the case.[5] When World War I ended, offers for public library building grants were not resumed by the Corporation. Money, however, continued to be allocated during the 1920's for offers made previously. The twenty-fifth branch of the Philadelphia Free Library (Wyoming Branch) was the last of the Carnegie buildings to receive funds and obtained only one third ($20,000) of its final total cost.[6]

Notes

[1] Alvin S. Johnson, *Pioneer's Progress: An Autobiography* (New York: Viking, 1952), p.235-39.

[2] ———, *A Report to Carnegie Corporation of New York on the Policy of Donations to Free Public Libraries* (New York: Carnegie Corp., 1919).

[3] ———, *Pioneer's Progress: An Autobiography* (New York: Viking, 1952) p.238-39.

[4] Letter from Alvin S. Johnson to the author, Sept. 3, 1965.

[5] "Carnegie Library Grants, February and March, 1918," *Library Journal,* 43:355 (May 1918).

[6] Frank P. Hill, *James Bertram: An Appreciation* (New York: Carnegie Corp., 1936) p.38.

CHAPTER NINE

How Carnegie Libraries Fared

ALVIN JOHNSON's appraisal of Carnegie libraries in 1916 and the results of the questionnaires sent out by the Corporation from 1915 to 20 give a good picture of the library situation at that time. The Carnegie Library Correspondence files provide another source for an evaluation of the success or failure of the Carnegie libraries. These files, which cover the period to 1948, are filled with letters, reports, and clippings sent to the Corporation even after Carnegie library building benefactions ceased. Many of them contained glowing accounts of increased library use and expressed the need for expanded facilities. Others posed local library problems or requested help in various matters.

As Seen through the Correspondence Files

Perhaps the most typical of the enthusiastic comments came from Corsicana, Texas (although for Texas it was an unusual report because of the many broken pledges among Carnegie libraries in that state). The Corsicana Carnegie library book stock rose from 600 to 9000 volumes during eight years of operation. One trained librarian and an assistant operated the building, which was open from 10 A.M. to 9 P.M. Some 60 percent of the 10,000 residents of the town had library cards, and the monthly circulation totaled 35,000 books. The report concluded:

> I am sure if all the libraries which you have built throughout the United States have been as successful as our own and been of such value to the people, and as such [sic] appreciated by the people, as is our own, it will be an increased source of pleasure to you, and a confirmation of your judgment and wisdom in selecting this form of your benefactions for the use and benefit of all classes of people.[1]

Andrew Carnegie responded by writing that he had received many congratulatory letters for gifts of libraries, but Corsicana's report was among the best. Such letters were ample rewards in themselves. He went on to say:

> We have nothing to fear in our great Republic because of our Free School System and the Free Libraries. A reading people are of course an active people, full of new ideas and anxious to test them, which ensures peaceful development. . . .[2]

In contrast, a correspondent from Tampa, Florida, wanted James Bertram and the Carnegie Corporation to send agents to investigate the poor situation in the library there.[3] His letter typifies the negative side, as does one from an irate Huntsville, Alabama, library patron. Norah Davis, a well-known author, reported in 1925 that the city government had shifted all library responsibility to the library board and paid only the salaries of the librarian and janitor plus heat and light bills. As a result, no funds were available for books and magazines. The library rented out books at two cents per day and was open only on weekday afternoons and two hours on Sunday afternoons. Needless to say, the building was little used and then only by a small group of people.

Norah Davis also had a personal complaint. (Hundreds of letters expressing individual grievances are found in the correspondence.) She was upset because she had been expelled from the library for neglecting to give her chauffeur ten cents to pay for a library card renewal. She had always sent her chauffeur into the library because of the antagonistic attitude of the librarian. Her original complaint to the city did little good, as the city officials merely told her to contact the Carnegie Corporation.

James Bertram's reply was that the Corporation could not and would not interfere; instead, the state library commission should be contacted. This the complainant did, only to be informed that they had little power. The commission suggested that she contact the Carnegie Corporation. After writing to the Corporation again, she received a reply from Bertram indicating that the Corporation could not enter into any local library controversy. However, he sent her a copy of the original documents and implied that she could take action as a local citizen, since a library making a charge for regular library service was not really a free library.[4]

The situation at Corbin, Kentucky, in 1922 was no better. The building was constructed in 1913, and shortly thereafter the floors buckled and the walls cracked. Water had been known to stand in the basement for weeks at a time, so that the building was too damp to use. There were no new books except housecleaning castoffs. The majority of the citizens had never been in the library. It was controlled by a small faction of the townspeople, and there was no air of general welcome. In short, according to the correspondent, the library was not fulfilling the role Carnegie had in mind.[5]

Requests for rules, regulations, and bylaws on how to run and operate a Carnegie library also fill the correspondence files. Frequent questions were asked as to the days and hours the library should be open. Another common query was whether nonresidents should be excluded from library use or if they could be charged a fee. Officials at Andrews, North Carolina, wrote to James Bertram asking how to obtain books, record them, and arouse interest in them.[6] The secretary of the Lincoln, Kansas, Library Board was concerned because the librarian allowed large numbers of books to be sent to the high school library for a whole term without the knowledge of the board. She also wanted information on library trustee-ship and on public library management.[7]

Officials at Aurora, Missouri, asked for suggested rules and regulations on the "proper handling of the library."[8] Certain rules had been set up for the Carnegie branch libraries of New York City as to days and hours of operation, but no other attempt had been made by Carnegie or the Corporation to set up guidelines for local management of the gift libraries. To all such requests Bertram had a similar response: Contact the local state library commission, and if no help is obtainable there, then write to the American Library Association. There was only one frequent request upon which James Bertram and the Corporation did make a definite stand. This was the question of paid rental collections. In this regard they strongly felt that the Carnegie library should be entirely free.[9]

Numerous pleas were made for copies of the original agree-ments and correspondence carried on in the early stages of negotiations. Such requests came from city officials, librarians, and library board members. These appeals usually were made because the annual maintenance pledge was not being kept or because of some other action or event that might alter the status of the Carnegie library. The Carnegie Corporation was very obliging in providing such copies (some of them volumi-nous) without any charge.

Some communities wanted to turn over the control and tax support of the Carnegie library to the board of education. The Corporation had no objection as long as there was a legal provision for such a transfer in the state. The board of edu-cation would have to uphold the same resolutions which the municipality had originally voted on. In turn, the city officials had to transfer the control and tax support to the board of education.[10] The Corporation also had no objection to the affiliation of a Carnegie library with a county library system,[11] to the transfer of a municipal library building to the county library,[12] to part of a Carnegie library building being used as headquarters for a county library system,[13] or to the annexa-tion of a town with a Carnegie building by another com-munity with or without a Carnegie library. The crucial point in all such situations was that the Carnegie library be in no way less effective in service or receive less financial support.

According to the correspondence, difficulties frequently arose concerning the status of the librarian. A citizen of Aurora, Missouri, complained that her daughter had been an assistant to the librarian for the two years the building had been open. When the librarian resigned, the mayor appointed someone who was unqualified as political patronage. The writer sent a stamp and hoped for a ruling from the Corporation by return mail. Bertram replied as usual that he could not interfere with local library management and suggested that the matter be brought to the attention of the state library commission.[14] A similar episode was reported from Metropolis, Illinois, where a new mayor appointed a new librarian who had never even used the library in place of one who had served in that capacity for twenty years.[15]

From Guthrie, Oklahoma, came reports that the library board and the librarian were members of the Ku-Klux Klan. They were trying to dispose of the works of Cardinal Newman and the *Catholic Encyclopedia*. These were part of the library collection but were being termed "extra" sets as a justification for their attempted disposal.[16] Still other correspondence regarding librarians contained inquiries about their qualifications for appointment and complaints of low salaries.

The Carnegie Library Correspondence reveals that many of the libraries experienced financial problems in the years following the formal end of Carnegie library philanthropy, particularly during the Depression. Garland, Utah, officials complained that their big Carnegie library building required large expenditures. They felt that the old quarters had served them better, especially since the state had lowered the library levy law by 25 percent.[17] At Ottumwa, Iowa, the city balked at paying the annual maintenance from taxes. The library had received $600,000 in endowment from a local benefactor, and the town wanted to use the income from the gift to support the library. During the 1940's it refused to pay the annual maintenance pledge.[18]

One problem that plagued quite a number of Carnegie library communities was that the annual maintenance did not increase from year to year. When the librarians or library boards complained to the Corporation, James Bertram would answer with a reply similar to the one that follows:

> For the city of Delphos, however, to pay only $1,250 a year for carrying on the library at this time is to fulfill its obligation in the letter and break it in the spirit, because every citizen of Delphos knows that $1,250 in 1911 is not more than $750 today and a few years ago was even less. In other words, if Delphos should do at the present time what it undertook to do, vis., to maintain the library adequately, it should be spending at least $2,000.[19]

Numerous letters described the drastic library budget cuts in the 1930's. When East Jordan, Michigan, officials requested permission to reduce the annual support pledge from $1,000 to $600 in 1933, the Corporation refused.[20] In most cases, however, there was no such request; widespread slashes in the funds for the library were peremptorily made. In answer to the many appeals from librarians and trustees as to what to do, the Corporation sent copies of the original resolutions and agreements and urged local citizens to take measures to ensure that good faith with the original donor was preserved. But this response did little good at a time when financial conditions were bad. In many communities, the library seemed a likely choice to take a cut. Carnegie libraries began to reduce hours, cut back on staffs, and buy fewer books. They also appealed to local friends for support. Phoenixville, Pennsylvania, even made an appeal to the local community chest for funds to support its services.[21]

Alvin Johnson, in his report, made a strong recommendation for the use of library facilities by outside community groups as a means of interesting these groups in the library program and of obtaining their support for its financial needs. Almost all the Carnegie libraries had a lecture room or auditorium that Andrew Carnegie and the Carnegie Corporation specified be used only for library-related activities, such as literary lectures, book reviews, and children's story hours. But as the hundreds of letters in the Carnegie Library Correspondence indicated, every possible organization in the local community wanted to use this facility, and the rule was difficult to define and enforce.

At Etowah, Tennessee, the basement of the Carnegie library almost immediately began to be used for nonlibrary purposes. The city recorder took over one room. High school classes occupied two other rooms. The basement lecture hall served as a study hall for students during the week and doubled as a chapel on Sunday. Protests from the Carnegie Corporation proved to be of no avail.[22] The librarian at Alexandria, Minnesota, sought guidance from the Carnegie Corporation when she faced requests for lecture-room use by the local music club and the Christian Science Church. The reply was a stern reminder that such rooms were only for lectures directly supplementary to library work.[23]

The use of some part of the Carnegie library building for local school functions seemed to be a frequent occurrence. The librarian at Humboldt, Iowa, received a flat "No" from Bertram in reply to a telegram requesting temporary use of the lecture room for classroom instruction because of crowded conditions in the local school.[24] But in most cases no one asked for permission, and the school just encroached on the extra library space. This was especially true whenever the Carnegie library was under the management of the board of education. In Kansas City, Kansas, the superintendent of schools was also the librarian, and all the board of education offices were located on the top floor of the library.[25]

City officials also frequently usurped Carnegie library space for municipal offices. James Bertram contacted the state librarian for assistance in removing city offices from the Upland, California, Carnegie library basement. Library trustees claimed that this was only a temporary measure during the time when the old city hall was being torn down and the new one was being built.[26] The Corporation bluntly informed the library trustees of Bolivar, New York, that not even the town council should be allowed to use the library or any room in it for their meetings.[27] In Lynn, Massachusetts, one of the Carnegie branch libraries was taken over during World War I by the city as an Exemption Board office. In another branch the lecture hall was used continuously as a polling place. The Carnegie library of McCook, Nebraska, in addition to being used as a polling place, also housed the city water commission office, the police court, and all council meetings.[28]

The rest rooms in the Carnegie buildings were another frequent problem area involving outside use. The Anderson, Indiana, library was concerned because its basement rest rooms were being used by downtown shoppers and visiting tourists. There was even some pressure for these rest rooms to be kept open on Sunday and other times when the library was closed.[29] The city council of Anaheim, California, asked the permission of the Carnegie Corporation to install rest rooms in the basement of the Carnegie library for the convenience of auto tourists passing through the city on their way to San Diego or Los Angeles. They assured the Corporation that library patrons would not be disturbed and the rest rooms would be kept clean. Needless to say, Bertram's reply was strongly negative.[30]

Many other letters were found with requests for or complaints about outside infringements on the library's space. It was not uncommon for Sunday schools or even church services to be held in the lecture rooms. At times the chamber of commerce moved into the basement of a Carnegie building, as did the Boy Scouts, Red Cross, GAR, DAR, WPA projects, and even elderly couples who then served as janitor-custodians in the library.

Some libraries used basement space for money-making purposes. The library trustees in Glenwood, Minnesota, wanted permission in 1934 to rent the basement auditorium to the Girl Scouts as an extra source of income.[31] The lecture room of the Sapulpa, Oklahoma, Carnegie library was rented for dances at $10 per evening and was eventually leased to the YMCA on a yearly basis.[32] Carnegie Corporation officials protested to the Jefferson, Texas, library about the use of the upstairs lecture hall as an opera house and moving-picture theater even though the proceeds went toward library support.[33] In these and many other instances the Corporation felt that such rooms were for library-related use only and that library income should come from taxation.

Still another frequent type of problem concerned the condition of the building itself. Numerous requests came for building repairs and replacements. But the Corporation refused to pay for any repairs to Carnegie buildings which were due to normal wear and depreciation or to vandalism. Thus, to the request of Paducah, Kentucky, for $5000 to repair the Carnegie library, Bertram replied:

> You report a building erected so recently as six year ago, with its foundations settled, walls cracked, mural decorations defaced, etc., etc., as if that were quite an ordinary circumstance. It is merely a waste of our time to report such a circumstance without reasons, and your report of action taken to fix the responsibility and obtain compensation.[34]

During the time Carnegie and the Corporation were actively engaged in library building grants, however, they usually paid for the costs of any damage which a Carnegie library building incurred "by an act of God." There were many instances of natural catastrophies. Hayward, California, received an additional $1750 for repairs of earthquake damage sustained during the original building construction in 1906.[35] Fergus Falls, Minnesota, received $5475 in 1919 to restore its building after damage caused by a tornado.[36] The Lincoln, Nebraska, library which was totally destroyed by fire was completely replaced and rebuilt with funds donated by Andrew Carnegie.[37] To Dayton, Ohio, the Corporation gave $15,000 in 1913 for the restocking of two new Carnegie branch libraries. The original book collections of these libraries had been destroyed by a flood in the basement of the main building where they had been placed and readied for the new branches.[38] However, Carnegie libraries destroyed or damaged by earthquakes, tornadoes, floods, or fires after the end of Carnegie library giving had to be replaced or repaired by the local community.

The replacement of Carnegie library buildings began even

before the end of Carnegie public library philanthropy. The library building at Virginia, Minnesota, erected in 1900, was sold for $10,000 in 1912. This amount was applied toward the erection of a new building for $43,092, and the town pledged 10 percent of the total for annual maintenance. A new railroad line and depot had been built near the former Carnegie building, giving it a poor, inconvenient location. James Bertram did not think that more than $22,500 was necessary and had been willing for the Carnegie Corporation to grant $12,500, but the community felt differently.[39] At Needham, Massachusetts, the 1903 Carnegie library was sold in 1915, and a new building erected for $31,000. The Carnegie Corporation's request that a new annual maintenance pledge be made for $3100 was ignored.[40]

But it was not until the 1930's and particularly the postwar 1940's that the real agitation began for Carnegie library enlargement, remodeling, or replacement. In each instance the Carnegie Corporation made no objection to such action. It did, however, make the suggestion that a tablet or plaque be placed somewhere in or on the new library building, stating that it had replaced an earlier structure built with Carnegie funds. The Corporation was no longer interested in the old Carnegie building, and the community was permitted to use it for other activities.

In 1934, Stamford, Texas, reported that its Carnegie library was in bad physical condition. It requested permission to apply for Civil Works Administration funds to have it remodeled or torn down and a new building constructed. The stone library had been built on a filled lot, and when it settled, the walls cracked. The whole structure was leaning dangerously to one side, and the front columns of wood had given way completely. In addition, the belfry was infested with bats, giving the whole building a disagreeable odor.[41] The librarian of Enid, Oklahoma, reported in 1938 that the bond issue toward a new library building had been defeated and closed her letter with, "How we wish for Andrew Carnegie!"[42] But despite hundreds of such requests from Carnegie library towns, the Corporation refused to donate money for enlargement, remodeling, or replacement of buildings after 1917. These were now the responsibility of each community.

Current Status

In order to obtain up-to-date information on the present-day status of Carnegie libraries, the author sent a questionnaire in the spring of 1967 to the head librarians of the 1412 communities which had received Carnegie funds for one or more public library buildings. After a second, reminder questionnaire the total responses received on the status of 1619 buildings came from 1362 towns, a 96.5 percent return.

The questionnaire requested the following information: Was the public library building in the community, erected with funds from Andrew Carnegie or the Carnegie Corporation, still in use as a library? If so, had it been extensively remodeled or enlarged, and when and how did this occur? If not, were there any plans for remodeling, expansion, or replacement, and, if so, what was being planned, and when was the project to be completed? If the Carnegie building was no longer in use as a library, the following queries were made: When was it replaced by a new building? When was the old building demolished, or, if not destroyed, what use was being made of it?

Table 18 summarizes the results of the questionnaire and gives a detailed breakdown by state and region. The data show that a large number (1348) of the Carnegie buildings are still in use as libraries, and of these, 1137 have substantially the same exteriors as when they were first built. Many librarians wrote in glowing terms of the good appearance and upkeep of the buildings, sent pictures, and listed, often with painstaking care and detail, all the improvements that had been made over the years.

The questionnaire also reveals that at least half of the 1137 buildings have been extensively repaired or remodeled on the interior. The most common of these renovations has been the conversion of the basement to a children's department. Seventy-one Carnegie libraries have done this, and 10 others

TABLE 18

CURRENT STATUS OF CARNEGIE PUBLIC LIBRARY BUILDINGS (1967)

BY STATE

STATE	NUMBER OF CARNEGIE BUILDINGS	STILL USED AS PUBLIC LIBRARY	ORIGINAL STRUCTURE IN USE	ORIGINAL BUILDING EXPANDED	NOT IN USE AS PUBLIC LIBRARY	DEMOLISHED	STANDING BUT BEING USED FOR OTHER PURPOSES	NO REPORT
Alabama	14	6	6	0	8	4	4	—
Arizona	4	2	1	1	2	1	1	—
Arkansas	4	4	3	1	0	0	0	—
California	142	86	67	19	54	37	17	2
Colorado	35	26	22	4	9	6	3	—
Connecticut	11	10	5	5	0	0	0	1
Florida	10	8	5	3	2	1	1	—
Georgia	24	16	12	4	5	1	4	3
Idaho	10	8	6	2	2	0	2	—
Illinois	106	96	82	14	7	5	2	3
Indiana	164	151	136	15	8	5	3	5
Iowa	101	96	83	13	2	1	1	3
Kansas	59	49	44	5	7	3	4	3
Kentucky	23	21	21	0	1	0	1	1
Louisiana	9	2	2	0	6	2	4	1
Maine	17	16	12	4	0	0	0	1
Maryland	14	7	4	3	7	1	6	—
Massachusetts	43	41	29	12	1	0	1	1
Michigan	61	45	40	5	13	4	9	3
Minnesota	65	52	45	7	10	8	2	3
Mississippi	11	7	5	2	3	2	1	1
Missouri	33	29	27	2	4	1	3	—
Montana	17	14	12	2	2	2	0	1
Nebraska	69	61	53	8	7	4	3	1

Nevada	1	0	0	1	0	1	0	—
New Hampshire	9	9	7	0	2	0	0	—
New Jersey	35	29	16	4	15	2	2	2
New Mexico	3	3	3	0	0	0	0	—
New York	106	93	83	10	10	5	5	3
North Carolina	10	4	2	5	2	2	3	1
North Dakota	8	6	4	2	2	0	2	—
Ohio	105	91	70	12	21	4	8	2
Oklahoma	24	15	13	8	2	4	4	1
Oregon	31	24	21	5	3	1	4	2
Pennsylvania	58	49	48	6	1	2	4	3
South Carolina	14	11	7	3	4	1	2	—
South Dakota	25	23	21	2	2	2	0	—
Tennessee	13	8	8	5	0	2	3	—
Texas	32	14	13	13	1	10	3	5
Utah	23	16	15	5	1	2	3	2
Vermont	4	4	3	0	1	0	0	—
Virginia	3	2	2	1	0	0	1	—
Washington	43	25	21	17	4	7	10	1
West Virginia	3	2	2	0	0	0	0	1
Wisconsin	63	55	47	8	8	5	3	—
Wyoming	16	12	9	4	3	3	1	—

BY REGION

Midwest	698	615	530	64	85	33	31	19
Northeast	300	260	209	28	51	10	18	12
Northwest	262	215	186	40	29	22	18	7
Far West	217	135	109	77	26	46	31	5
Southeast	135	89	73	39	16	15	24	7
Southwest	63	34	30	23	4	15	8	6
District of Columbia	4	0	0	0	0	0	0	4
TOTAL	1679	1348	1137	271	211	141	130	60

are planning to do so in the immediate future. Other popular refurbishing activities most often cited have been: construction of a new entrance; lowering the ceilings; the addition of a mezzanine or another floor within the original structure; rearrangement of interiors; purchase of new furniture, lighting, or heating; and the installation of carpeting, elevators, or air conditioners. In addition, interior walls and ceilings have been painted or paneled, outside walls have been sandblasted or tucked, and new roofs and floors have been installed. All this renovation seems to be an ongoing activity, as a number of librarians indicated future plans for repairs or remodeling. In many branch libraries in large cities, particularly, extensive and systematic rehabilitation programs are under way or are being planned.

Of the 1348 Carnegie buildings still in use as libraries, 211 have been expanded. Indeed, 29 of them have been expanded twice, 4 have had three additions, and 1 has been expanded four times. All these additions occurred during the following periods:

No date given	16
1910–19	3
1920–29	27
1930–39	63
1940–49	17
1950–59	50
1960–67	95

Reports from 73 libraries indicated that additions are being planned, while 23 others stated that either an enlargement or a new building was being contemplated.

In the building of an addition, an attempt was often made to preserve the "charm," as many librarians termed it, of the old building by blending the addition into the old structure. Most expansions have been conventional ones — building onto the back or sides of the original building. But, in some cases, the old Carnegie library has been almost hidden by the expansion. This is true, for example, at Lakewood, Ohio, where the Carnegie building has been so extensively enlarged and remodeled that few people are aware it is still there. At Athol, Massachusetts, two thirds of the old Carnegie structure was razed, and a new building was added to the remaining portion. In still other communities, the old building has been hidden by a wing of a much larger new building, or, in a few cases, it has become enveloped on two or three sides by a new structure.

Another interesting development occurred in 8 communities. When the old Carnegie libraries which had been built as main buildings in these cities became overcrowded, they were not enlarged but rather were converted for use as branches. Then, larger main libraries were put up in other locations.

Library expansion or the construction of new library buildings during the 1930's was often the result of the sponsorship of the Civilian Works Administration, the Works Progress Administration, or the Public Works Administration. In recent years this expansion and construction have been spurred by urban renewal projects, civic center developments, and funds from the Library Services and Construction Act.

The sentiment for preserving Carnegie library buildings seems to be strong. "The community loves the building," wrote one librarian, "and it will probably be kept even when it is replaced." Another librarian reported that a patron declared the destruction of the building would deeply hurt her feeling for the community, "since she was first kissed by a boy, later her husband on the steps of the old Carnegie building."

These buildings, however, *are* being replaced, and their number will continue to diminish in the future. By early 1967, 271 Carnegie buildings were reported as no longer in use as libraries. Less than half of them (130) are still standing but are being used for nonlibrary purposes, while 141 have been demolished during the following periods:

No date given	8
1910–19	1
1920–29	2
1930–39	11
1940–49	9
1950–59	40
1960–67	70

Some 68 new library buildings are either under construction or scheduled for completion by the end of 1968. It is already known that 11 of these old Carnegie buildings will be demolished and 9 will be sold or used for other purposes. The fate of the others was not known or not recorded in the questionnaire. In addition, 171 new buildings are in early planning stages but with no definite indication of the time when they will be completed.

A number of the public libraries in Carnegie buildings adopted new quarters but not new buildings. Evansville, Indiana, for example, sold its branch Carnegie library building to the Boy Scouts of America and used the money to buy a bookmobile. Four Carnegie libraries have moved into former post-office buildings, while 4 others have gone into various types of rented quarters. Other libraries formerly located in Carnegie buildings have moved into various places, such as a county garage building, housing development, remodeled bank, and a county welfare building.

But most libraries vacating Carnegie buildings have moved into new buildings built for library purposes. Reno, Nevada, has had two new buildings since its original Carnegie structure: one in 1929 and another in 1966.

Behind some of the Carnegie library demolishments are interesting stories. Buildings were destroyed by fire at Remington, Indiana (1961); Galesburg, Illinois (1958); and Temple, Texas (1918). One branch building each in Brooklyn and Cleveland were also destroyed by conflagration. Three of the New Orleans, Louisiana, branches were either destroyed or so damaged by fires and hurricanes that they are not being used. The Carnegie building at Coatesville, Indiana, was blown away by a tornado on Good Friday of 1948. At Dewitt, Nebraska, the library moved out of the Carnegie building just in time before the foundation gave way and the walls fell in. One branch each at the Detroit and New York public libraries was demolished for street widening and another in New York City to make way for the Mid-Town Tunnel. At San Jose, California, the Carnegie building was sold to San Jose State College in 1936, and the money used to purchase an old post-office building which was remodeled as a library. The old Carnegie building became a student union but was then demolished to make space for the enlargement of the college library.

Twenty-five branch libraries in Baltimore, Cincinnati, Cleveland, Detroit, Nashville, New York City, Portland (Oregon), Philadelphia, and St. Louis have been demolished or closed down and not replaced with either a new building or other quarters. This fate was usually due to changes in the neighborhoods of the branches, which made it no longer necessary to provide library service from the old location. There is also evidence that in 4 communities (one each in New Jersey, Pennsylvania, Texas, and Utah) the Carnegie building was demolished and the library was not reopened elsewhere, although in two of these communities library service was eventually restored in later years.

It is interesting to trace the status of the 130 Carnegie buildings still standing but no longer used as libraries. Of these 4 have just been sold, and 12 are standing vacant but are scheduled to be demolished within a short time.

Various city or county bureaus and offices are using 31 Carnegie buildings. Recreation departments or centers are located in 9 of them, while a welfare office, police station, and police court occupy 3 other former Carnegie structures.

The number of Carnegie buildings used for commercial purposes totals 20, of which 6 were merely described as office buildings. Other specific uses included: a radio station, telephone company, bank, savings and loan association, law office, insurance agency, realty office, printing company, dress shop, antique store, mortuary, and warehouse.

Educational institutions are occupying 19 buildings. Local school boards use 10, one of which is now a technical processing center for school libraries, while yet another is a practice area for a high school wrestling team. Colleges and universities make use of 8, and 1 has been converted into a dance school.

Social and welfare groups occupy 13 buildings. Of these, 3 have become senior citizen centers, and 2 are now YMCA buildings. Others in this category include: a social settlement house, Boy Scout office, Junior Achievement center, Red Cross office, and USO. Still another 10 buildings are now museums, most of them historical ones. But 3 are combination museums and headquarters for the local chamber of commerce.

Seven are utilized as halls or meeting places: 2 for garden clubs, 2 for musical or chorus groups, 2 as lodge halls, and 1 as a labor hall. Churches use 6 Carnegie buildings. Of these 2 are serving as places of worship, while 4 others are for church-related activities. One Carnegie building has been made into an apartment dwelling. Another was reported as simply a "Memorial Building." Three others were shown as still standing, but no details were given on current use.

The questionnaire also gave evidence of continuing outside use of Carnegie public library buildings. As an extreme example, one Pennyslvania public librarian described the local library as providing its second floor for an auditorium, reception room, and kitchen for the DAR and another women's club, while its basement held a kitchen and dining room for the Kiwanis Club. A report from a North Carolina community showed that an addition had been built in the rear of the Carnegie building to house the fire truck in the basement and library office rooms on the ground floor. However, the responses also indicated a decline in nonlibrary use. As collections and services have grown, outside use has decreased under the pressure of library space needs.

The use of the name "Carnegie" to identify the public libraries built with Carnegie funds has diminished. A check of the twenty-fifth edition of the *American Library Directory,* published in 1967, reveals that only 179 of the 1320 Carnegie communities listed make use of the benefactor's name. This is only 13.5 percent compared to the 27 percent with the Carnegie name in the survey made by Learned in 1923.[43]

Most of the buildings no longer named for Carnegie carry the name of the community coupled with the words "Free," "City," or usually "Public" Library. But 7 of the libraries have the Carnegie name in combination with another, most frequently that of a donor who shared the cost of the original building or gave funds for an addition. Twenty-two Carnegie libraries are now named for other people. Most of these buildings replace structures built with Carnegie funds and are named after the new donor.

It was noted above that 1320 Carnegie library towns (of a total of 1412) are listed in the *American Library Directory*. The Directory, however, does not include small public libraries with annual incomes of less than $2000 or book funds of less than $500. In examining the listings in this Directory, it is evident that a great number of Carnegie public libraries are still small, but many of them are now parts of county and regional library systems and can draw upon their resources.

Librarians responded not only to the specific questions on the questionnaire but also provided a wealth of additional comments which reflected their opinions on the current status of these Carnegie buildings. A few notes were critical. One small-town librarian said, "It is my considered opinion, after struggling with this old, outmoded building for four years, that your A. Carnegie set back the Public Library Movement at least fifty years. Not only does the general public wait to be given library service, but these buildings with steps prevent people from coming to the library who can use it most. Then there are the nuts who are too enamoured with the past to move out of the building and insist on preserving what must have been a monstrosity when the thing was new." Another Oklahoma librarian, in describing the extensive remodeling of a Carnegie building, lamented over the financial inability to remove the "Carnegie" from the front of the building, since this would have cost more than $200.

For the most part, however, comments were favorable and enthusiastic. The librarian of an Iowa community described the Carnegie library as a focal point of the town. Located centrally on a triangular island surrounded by streets, its front steps had been the scene of an address by William Jennings Bryan as well as the arrival of Santa Claus and Christmas carolers. The basement had been the home of the district court until it was made into a children's library. A typical remark was, "It's old—but we love it!" "We are justifiably

proud of our 'old Carnegie' building. It is still very much in
use and will be for a long time, I hope" was another common
sentiment expressed. These two words, "love" and "pride,"
appeared repeatedly in the responses regarding the Carnegie
library. Many expressed their gratitude for Carnegie benefactions. "Carnegie was farsighted and no one can really
estimate how much good he did," wrote the librarian from a
community in Minnesota. Another from a Massachusetts
town exclaimed, "The people of . . . will always be grateful
to Andrew Carnegie."

Notes

[1] Charles H. Allyn, Board of Trustees, to Andrew Carnegie, May 15, 1914
(Corsicana, Texas, Carnegie Library Correspondence, Microfilm Reel No.7).
[2] Andrew Carnegie to Charles H. Allyn, May 20, 1914 (Corsicana, Texas,
Carnegie Library Correspondence, Microfilm Reel No.7).
[3] Edward P. Moses to James Bertram, Feb. 1, 1929 (Tampa, Fla., Carnegie
Library Correspondence, Microfilm Reel No.31).
[4] Huntsville, Ala., Carnegie Library Correspondence, Microfilm Reel
No.14.
[5] Mrs. S. H. Kash to Carnegie Corporation of New York, Feb. 14, 1922
(Corbin, Ky., Carnegie Library Correspondence, Microfilm Reel No.7).
[6] Andrews, N.C., Carnegie Library Correspondence, Microfilm Reel No.1.
[7] Mrs. T. W. Baker to Carnegie Corporation of New York, July 5, 1924
(Lincoln, Kans., Carnegie Library Correspondence, Microfilm Reel No. 17).
[8] M. V. H. Walker, secretary of the Board of Trustees, to James Bertram,
Oct. 29, 1918 (Aurora, Mo., Carnegie Library Correspondence, Microfilm
Reel No.2).
[9] Enterprise, Ore., Carnegie Library Correspondence, Microfilm Reel
No.10.
[10] This procedure was spelled out in a letter from James Bertram to Miss
Della Weiser, librarian, June 4, 1924 (Delaware, Ohio, Carnegie Library
Correspondence, Microfilm Reel No.8).
[11] Colusa, Calif., Carnegie Library Correspondence, Microfilm Reel No.7.
[12] Bellefontaine, Ohio, Carnegie Library Correspondence, Microfilm Reel
No.3.
[13] Bryan, Texas, Carnegie Library Correspondence, Microfilm Reel No.4.
[14] J. C. Gardner to Carnegie Corporation of New York, April 20, 1921;
James Bertram to J. C. Gardner, April 25, 1921 (Aurora, Mo., Carnegie
Library Correspondence, Microfilm Reel No.2).
[15] Metropolis, Ill., Carnegie Library Correspondence, Microfilm Reel
No.19.
[16] John Adams, attorney, to James Bertram, May 10, 1924 (Guthrie, Okla.,
Carnegie Library Correspondence, Microfilm Reel No.13).

[17] Garland, Utah, Carnegie Library Correspondence, Microfilm Reel No.11.

[18] Ottumwa, Iowa, Carnegie Library Correspondence, Microfilm Reel No.23.

[19] James Bertram to A. S. Perkins, president of the Library Board, Feb. 19, 1924 (Delphos, Ohio, Carnegie Library Correspondence, Microfilm Reel No.8).

[20] East Jordan, Mich., Carnegie Library Correspondence, Microfilm Reel No.9.

[21] Phoenixville, Pa., Carnegie Library Correspondence, Microfilm Reel No.25.

[22] Etowah, Tenn., Carnegie Library Correspondence, Microfilm Reel No.10.

[23] Alexandria, Minn., Carnegie Library Correspondence, Microfilm Reel No.1.

[24] James Bertram to T. C. Ferreby, Library Board secretary, Jan. 17, 1916 (Humboldt, Iowa, Carnegie Library Correspondence, Microfilm Reel No.14).

[25] Kansas City, Kans., Carnegie Library Correspondence, Microfilm Reel No.15.

[26] Upland, Calif., Carnegie Library Correspondence, Microfilm Reel No.32.

[27] James Bertram to E. W. Cowles, Library Board president, Jan. 12, 1911 (Bolivar, N.Y., Carnegie Library Correspondence, Microfilm Reel No.3).

[28] McCook, Nebr., Carnegie Library Correspondence, Microfilm Reel No.18.

[29] Anderson, Ind., Carnegie Library Correspondence, Microfilm Reel No.1.

[30] Anaheim, Calif., Carnegie Library Correspondence, Microfilm Reel No.1

[31] Glenwood, Minn., Carnegie Library Correspondence, Microfilm Reel No.12.

[32] Sapulpa, Okla., Carnegie Library Correspondence, Microfilm Reel No.28.

[33] Jefferson, Texas, Carnegie Library Correspondence, Microfilm Reel No.15.

[34] James Bertram to E. W. Bagby, Library Board of Trustees president, July 29, 1908 (Paducah, Ky., Carnegie Library Correspondence, Microfilm Reel No.24).

[35] Hayward, Calif., Carnegie Library Correspondence, Microfilm Reel No.13 and 86.

[36] Fergus Falls, Minn., Carnegie Library Correspondence, Microfilm Reel No.86.

[37] Lincoln, Nebr., Carnegie Library Correspondence, Microfilm Reel No.17.

[38] Dayton, Ohio, Carnegie Library Correspondence, Microfilm Reel No.86.

[39] Virginia, Minn., Carnegie Library Correspondence, Microfilm Reel No.33.

[40] Needham, Mass., Carnegie Library Correspondence, Microfilm Reel No.21.

[41] Lois K. Green, Chamber of Commerce secretary, to Carnegie Corporation of New York, Jan. 2, 1934 (Stamford, Texas, Carnegie Library Correspondence, Microfilm Reel No.20).

[42] Mabel B. McClure, librarian, to Robert M. Lester, secretary of the Carnegie Corporation of New York, Oct. 12, 1938 (Enid, Okla., Carnegie Library Correspondence, Microfilm Reel No.10).

[43] William S. Learned, *The American Public Library and the Diffusion of Knowledge* (New York: Harcourt, 1924), p.74.

CHAPTER TEN

Impact of Carnegie Philanthropy on American Public Library Development

CONTEMPORARY PUBLIC OPINION on Andrew Carnegie's library philanthropy was depicted in Chapter VI. Later biographers, historians, and commentators have written relatively little on the evaluation of Andrew Carnegie's library gifts and their effect on American public library development. Their comments have been brief, sketchy, and for the most part full of praise. Almost no mention is found of the accusation frequently made by contemporaries that Carnegie libraries were merely expressions of Carnegie's exalted egotism and monuments of himself for posterity.

Published Views

Burton J. Hendrick, who might be called Carnegie's official and most exhaustive biographer, was the most laudatory. According to him, Andrew Carnegie believed that public libraries were as essential to the development of citizens as elementary education. This idea, however, was not generally accepted and needed momentum to survive. Carnegie gave the concept impetus when he donated money for buildings in which libraries could be established and operated. Hendrick wrote that Carnegie's library benefactions were a carefully conceived campaign to induce the states to establish free libraries as part of the regular educational system and represented the "Gospel of Wealth" in its highest and best meaning. Writing in the early 1930's, Hendrick declared that the free public library was then as much a part of life in the United States as the public school and the church. The American community could not function without it. Funds for libraries were no longer being given by the Carnegie Corporation because America had learned its lesson. Hendrick felt that the free public library had this permanent standing in American society largely because of the influence of Carnegie.[1]

Samuel Morison and Henry Commager concluded that the most effective impetus to the public library movement did not come from official sources or from public demand but from Carnegie's generosity. This generosity was, in turn, the result of Carnegie's genuine passion for education, his persuasion that the public library was the most democratic of all roads to learning, and a mindfulness of his own debt to and love of books. Morison and Commager termed Carnegie's library philanthropy as "not only munificent but wise, for by requiring a guarantee of adequate support to the libraries which he built, he laid the foundations for healthy growth of library facilities after his own gifts had served their immediate purpose."[2] Harold Underwood Faulkner concurred with Morison and Commager. He credited Andrew Carnegie with being the greatest single incentive to library growth in the United States.[3]

Sidney Ditzion, in his study of public libraries in New England and the Middle West from 1850 to 1900, characterized Carnegie's role in the library movement as not that of an initiator but rather as that of a "stimulant to an organism which might have rested long on a plateau had it not been spurred on to greater heights." Ditzion believed that the free library movement began on a firm foundation in New England and probably would have grown and gained acceptance

throughout the rest of the country without Carnegie's help.
However, it would have taken a much longer time, because
many local officials and politicians were shirking municipal
responsibility while waiting for some local, wealthy patron to
establish and support a library. Carnegie's novel scheme of
helping only those who helped themselves was a deterrent
to such evasion.[4]

In the late thirties, William Munthe, a distinguished European observer of the American library scene, stated that
Andrew Carnegie's gifts to public libraries in the United
States were the evidence of an individual man's faith in the
significance of books to society and as aids to the individual
in his struggle with life. Munthe lamented the lack of a library
philanthropist such as Carnegie in European countries. He
felt that new buildings resulted in the increased understanding of library significance by all classes of society. The old
baronial European buildings hindered the attainment of
library service on the American level.[5]

In the postwar 1940's, the historian Dwight Dumond wrote
that Carnegie and the other capitalists of the new industrial
empire believed

> . . . that they had a moral obligation to dispense their wealth
> for the benefit of humanity, and they did so in generous fashion.
> Their philosophy, that superior intelligence had given them
> wealth and the same superior intelligence enabled them to spend
> it more wisely than their less fortunate brethren, belonged to a
> passing age, but their benefactions were for the most part wisely
> chosen and hastened the progress of sweeping reforms.[6]

Stuart Sherman stated that Americans would not have ac-
complished what Carnegie did, even if he had charged less
per ton of steel. Instead, we "would have apportioned our
little 'surplus' to our tobacco fund and our soft drink for the
tranquilization of our nerves and the alleviation of our
thirst." [7]

At the beginning of the 1930 decade, Mark Sullivan wrote
that it was still too early to estimate the results of Carnegie
munificence. But he did think that these benefactions had
the effect of democratizing culture. Sullivan concluded, how-

ever, that to a generation of Americans who had enjoyed the fruits of Carnegie's gifts Carnegie, himself, was little more than a name over a library door.[8]

Writing more recently, Ralph Munn, formerly director of the Carnegie Library in Pittsburgh, called Andrew Carnegie a great library patron and a stimulator of library development. He credited the benefactor for emphasizing the library as a responsibility of the local government, spurring education for librarianship, and bringing about improvements in library architecture. Furthermore, he felt that the generous and widely publicized gifts gave prominence to the entire library movement. But he also criticized the philanthropist, declaring that Carnegie's gifts to hundreds of small towns throughout the land were, in one sense, a hindrance to public library development. According to Munn, many millions of Americans have known only these small village and town Carnegie libraries and have formed their entire concept of the public library from them. These libraries, too small to provide even the minimum essentials of good service, have been in part responsible for the attitude of benevolent apathy with which so many people regard public libraries.[9]

James Truslow Adams was almost alone in his disdain for Carnegie, the man "who had fought his workingmen's reasonable demands for better living conditions and had replaced native American labor by foreign immigrants for the sake of more complete control over their destinies, [and] had begun to distribute millions for his libraries, buying cheap notoriety on terms so onerous that more than one city, including the one in which I happened to live, declined to accept the money in accordance with them." [10]

A Personal Appraisal of Carnegie's Philanthropy

It seems unnecessary now to consider the question of how Carnegie made his money and whether it was morally right for communities to accept it as library philanthropy. Andrew Carnegie was no worse, and perhaps even better, than the other capitalists and industrial leaders of his time in respect to wages and working conditions. The effects of his surplus wealth on public library development are the only concern here.

Also, little attention need be given the question of whether or not Carnegie gave money for library buildings so that they would serve as monuments to posterity. This may have been one of his motivations, but a far more important one was his belief in the value of books and libraries as a means for self-improvement. It must be remembered that Carnegie did not require his name to be used on the buildings. Indeed, he preferred otherwise. Furthermore, he did not suggest that pictures or busts of him appear in the libraries. Communities wanting to place such objects in their Carnegie buildings had to buy them from commercial sources.

But if immortality *were* a Carnegie motivation, then it has been achieved. While it is true that fewer of the library buildings now officially bear his name and many are being demolished, nevertheless, the Carnegie name has not been forgotten. It has long been associated with libraries, and still is. In fact, many of Carnegie's other activities, and those of the trusts which he established, have been overshadowed in the public mind by his contributions to public libraries. Even at this date, library buildings are still being requested from the Carnegie Corporation. The author, in his research and writing during the last few years, has been impressed by the awareness and appreciation of Carnegie public library philanthropy voiced by the general public.

Carnegie had no master design in mind when he began giving gifts of libraries. A study of Table 3, Chapter I, on the years in which communities were promised buildings reveals a pattern beginning with a few donated libraries in the early years from 1886 to 1896; then a sharp rise from 1898 to a peak in 1903; with a gradual leveling off thereafter to the end of giving in 1919. Carnegie's early gifts of buildings attracted attention and requests for similar benefactions. With faith in this type of philanthropy, Carnegie acceded to the appeals as they continued to increase. Gradually a plan did evolve. The amount given was based on the population. The

10 percent support clause became mandatory for all communities. Application forms were developed and revised through the years. Eventually, even library architecture was regulated. Improvements were made throughout the life of the program as experience taught its lessons.

With the help of hindsight, it is now easy to look back and suggest what Andrew Carnegie could or should have done. It is probably true that Carnegie's gifts to small communities have made it difficult to break away from this pattern of local municipal control for more efficient and economical regional library service crossing city and county lines. It is now recognized that small localities cannot operate successful public libraries, even if they tax themselves heroically. In order to succeed they must pool their resources and services into a county or regional system. Although there has been great progress in this direction, more than two thirds of all public libraries today serve an area with a population of 10,000 or less. Almost 42 percent of all public libraries serve localities with less than 3000 people.[11] About 2700 public libraries still have an annual income of less than $2000 or book funds of less than $500 per year.[12]

But Carnegie's emphasis on municipal government seemed the most logical at the time. This was the common way in which public libraries were being founded. After all, the appeals did come to Carnegie from the local community. People were not as mobile then, and communities were not able to provide efficient library service on a wide area basis. When Carnegie began giving, there were no county libraries. The county library movement had its beginnings only during the period of Carnegie library philanthropy. In 1903 small, horse-drawn book wagons were serving some sixty-six stations throughout Washington County out of a headquarters library in Hagerstown, Maryland. Carnegie donated $25,000 in that same year toward the support of this library extension service.[13] Funds were contributed for county library buildings as the systems were formed, particularly in the South and West. The terms were the same as those for municipal libraries.

Vol XLV
No 2310

10 Cents a Copy
$4 00 a Year

HARPER'S
WEEKLY

A JOURNAL OF CIVILIZATION

NEW YORK   MARCH 30, 1901

BUILDING A VERY SOLID TEMPLE OF FAME
Harper's Weekly, March 30, 1901

Carnegie's solid temples of fame

The autonomous, municipal libraries were not only a logical development but perhaps a necessary one. The large number of local libraries scattered all over the United States helped to bring about a public willing to vote local, state, and federal funds for the improvement of public library service.

It is also easy to assert now that Carnegie should have provided each building with books and librarians. But he and his officials felt, and rightfully so, that this was the responsibility of each community. These problems were not peculiar to Carnegie libraries. All libraries needed librarians and larger, better collections. The time was a period of rapid public library growth. The momentum of the establishment of new public libraries was ahead of the development of library service and training.

It was a wise decision on the part of the Carnegie Corporation to stop giving library buildings when it did. For more than twenty years this philanthropy had helped sell the value of libraries, and there were now other needs, as suggested by Alvin Johnson, which were more important and needed early solution in order to gain further support for public library service everywhere, not just for Carnegie libraries.

The program of Carnegie benefactions had been generally very successful. Relatively few of the 1679 buildings in 1412 communities were failures as libraries. Even the percentage of those not acceding to the 10 percent support clause was not great. There were even fewer failures and broken pledges among the large cities and in states with strong library associations and commissions. Communities in such strong library states (as, for instance, California and Indiana) did well in all respects. They received the most building grants, had the fewest grant request failures, and were represented by the most communities obtaining Carnegie funds.

Obviously, the provision of more than $40,000,000 for Carnegie buildings all over the United States had a great impact on public library development. In terms of 1968 purchasing power, Carnegie's public library building benefactions would probably be equal to more than $150,000,000.[14] Public libraries in the United States are currently going through a similar wave of building expansion under the Library Services and Construction Act.

The importance of Carnegie library philanthropy lies in its perfect timing. It came in the best possible period — during the height of library expansion in the United States. Beginning in the 1890's, states began to play active roles in organizing public libraries in each community. The need for library buildings was desperate, and Carnegie's gifts helped to fill the void. The provision of new buildings created an avid interest in and enthusiasm for libraries in their early, crucial years of development.

An important factor in further stimulating public library development was the publicity and advertising resulting from these beneficences. Although the public library, by the beginning of the twentieth century, was generally accepted and approved as a worthy agency, it was, nevertheless, often confronted with lack of understanding, little appreciation, and even with indifference. Carnegie dramatized the value of libraries. Here was a famous millionaire who believed that libraries were important and who gave millions for their support. Carnegie and the Carnegie Corporation provided the incentive for each community to obtain a library for its populace. The rivalry among some towns to outdo each other was still another factor. In the long run Carnegie made more libraries and books available to more people and helped speed the momentum of the public library movement.

Carnegie's initiative also stimulated other library benefactions. During the 1890's, more than $10,000,000 were donated for libraries by philanthropists. From 1900 to 1906, 3099 individual contributions were made to libraries totaling more than $24,000,000. Almost half of this amount was expended for buildings and sites.[15]

But, more importantly, Carnegie's philanthropy widened the acceptance of the principle of local government responsibility for the public library. The method of giving was not perfect. Poor sites were often selected. The 10 percent support pledge was sometimes broken or more often not surpassed. Nevertheless, it was a wise provision. It placed indirect pressure on government bodies and the public to accept the organization and maintenance of the public library as a governmental service.

In library architecture, too, Carnegie provided a stimulus. Derogatory comments are often heard about Carnegie library architecture. These remarks, however, usually refer to the older libraries built before Carnegie and the Corporation became involved in architectural control. The short architectural memorandum in simplified spelling, issued by James Bertram in 1911, was composed of the best library opinion of the time on the subject. It decried architectural elaboration and offered basic principles and outline sketches, all of which led to a more open, flexible, and less expensive structure. But it still left every community with a great deal of freedom to plan its own library interior as it liked, within these few reasonable bounds, and to design the exterior as it pleased, as long as it refrained from expensive columns, portals, stairways, and domes. The memorandum was the beginning of modern library architecture, and many of the principles are still in effect.

But one must be careful not to give Carnegie philanthropy all the credit for the growth of the public library. At times some commentators imply that Carnegie practically founded the entire public library movement, or that it would long have rested on a plateau with little further development. On the contrary, as shown in Chapter I, the public library system of the United States was expanding under its own power before Carnegie's generosity started on a "wholesale" basis in 1898. In just twenty years the number of public libraries had grown from 188 in 1876 to 971 with 1000 volumes or more in 1896.[16]

By 1923, 3873 towns with populations of 1000 or more had public libraries serving a total population of 56,782,000 (or 53.5 percent of the entire United States population, then listed as 105,710,000). Of these 1408 Carnegie library towns were serving 32,956,500 people (31 percent), and 2462 communities with non-Carnegie libraries were serving 23,823,500 (22 percent). Two additional facts must immediately be presented as further interpretation: (1) a few Carnegie libraries were located in towns with less than 1000 population, and (2) almost all the larger cities were represented on the Carnegie library listing of 1408 towns, but many of these had buildings in their library systems which were not built with Carnegie funds.[17]

William Learned intimates that not all the 1408 Carnegie library communities had organized their libraries as a result of the Carnegie offer, but he gives no breakdown of the number not doing so. This is unfortunate since the usual implication is that every Carnegie gift was a newly established library. A careful analysis of the microfilmed Carnegie Library Correspondence files and the questionnaires which were sent to libraries for which the files lacked sufficient information revealed that about two thirds of these communities already had a free public library or were in the process of organizing one when the Carnegie gift was made. To be sure, many had just been organized or were being organized as a result of the stimulation of Carnegie benefactions and with the hope of obtaining new buildings. Table 19 gives a detailed breakdown and analysis of the Learned and Carnegie Library Correspondence files findings.

It is interesting to observe that only in the southern and southwestern states did Carnegie's benefactions actually bring about more newly established public libraries and not just new buildings for already established libraries. All 14 of the Carnegie grants in Alabama were newly established libraries, as were 19 out of 20 in Georgia. On the other hand, all 35 of the Carnegie grants in Massachusetts were to already established public libraries, as were 57 out of 60 in Wisconsin. It can be seen that the incentive of Carnegie's gifts was enough to accelerate the library movement to a stampede. Some 188 public libraries in 1876 jumped to 3873 by 1923. By 1967, according to the *American Library Directory*, the total had reached almost 7000.

Recognition must also be given to James Bertram and Alvin Johnson as two important figures in Carnegie library history and in American public library development. Bertram was the

TABLE 19

ANALYSIS OF UNITED STATES PUBLIC LIBRARIES, 1896–1923*

I: Communities possessing public libraries of 1000 volumes or more in 1896.
II: Communities obtaining one or more Carnegie library buildings by 1923.
II A: Number already having (or organizing) a public library before the Carnegie grant.
II B: Number not having a public library at time of Carnegie grant.
III: Communities of 1000 population or more in 1923 possessing public libraries unaided by Carnegie funds.

| STATE | ANALYSIS BY STATE | | | | |
	I	II	II A	II B	III
Alabama	0	14	0	14	13
Arizona	1	4	2	2	6
Arkansas	0	4	0	4	22
California	28	121	91	30	50
Colorado	6	27	19	8	18
Connecticut	61	8	7	1	135
Delaware	2	0	0	0	10
District of Columbia	0	1	1	0	0
Florida	2	10	1	9	27
Georgia	1	20	1	19	20
Idaho	0	10	6	4	12
Illinois	62	105	81	24	110
Indiana	23	155	100	55	37
Iowa	23	99	61	38	51
Kansas	10	58	31	27	56
Kentucky	1	15	4	11	28
Louisiana	1	4	2	2	6
Maine	31	17	14	3	131
Maryland	3	1	1	0	20
Massachusetts	271	35	35	0	257
Michigan	40	53	33	20	116
Minnesota	14	58	41	17	54
Mississippi	1	10	1	9	11
Missouri	6	26	7	19	30
Montana	7	17	12	5	21
Nebraska	11	68	42	26	42
Nevada	0	1	0	1	1
New Hampshire	76	9	6	3	75
New Jersey	19	29	24	5	150
New Mexico	0	3	0	3	8
New York	106	41	35	6	218

STATE	ANALYSIS BY STATE				
	I	II	II A	II B	III
North Carolina	2	9	2	7	42
North Dakota	1	8	6	2	22
Ohio	29	77	53	24	80
Oklahoma	0	24	12	12	44
Oregon	0	25	17	8	16
Pennsylvania	23	26	10	16	137
Rhode Island	41	0	0	0	43
South Carolina	2	14	7	7	9
South Dakota	1	25	12	13	17
Tennessee	2	10	1	9	6
Texas	1	30	7	23	61
Utah	0	23	16	7	15
Vermont	24	4	4	0	106
Virginia	0	2	2	0	27
Washington	3	33	19	14	20
West Virginia	1	3	1	2	10
Wisconsin	34	60	57	3	74
Wyoming	1	16	7	9	1
Total	971	1,412	891	521	2,465
REGION	ANALYSIS BY REGION				
	I	II	II A	II B	III
Northeast	658	173	137	36	1,292
Southeast	12	112	21	91	211
Midwest	231	633	433	200	552
Southwest	2	61	21	40	119
Northwest	37	252	151	101	204
Far West	31	180	127	53	87
District of Columbia	0	1	1	0	0
Total	971	1,412	891	521	2,465

*Sources: William S. Learned, *The American Public Library and the Diffusion of Knowledge* (New York: Harcourt, 1924), p.84, citing the U.S. Bureau of Education, *Statistics of Libraries and Library Legislation in the United States, 1895-1896* (Washington, D.C.: Govt. Print. Off., 1897) for Column I; Carnegie Library Microfilmed Correspondence for Column II, II A, II B; and William S. Learned, p.84, citing the *American Library Directory, 1923* (New York: Bowker, 1923) for Column III.

real power behind Carnegie public library building grants. Alvin Johnson's sagacious and penetrating report on Carnegie libraries led to broader support by the Carnegie Corporation to public libraries in the United States.

Continuing Activities of the Carnegie Corporation in Public Library Development

The Carnegie Corporation, it will be recalled, was organized in 1911 by Andrew Carnegie in order to ". . . promote the advancement and diffusion of knowledge and understanding among the people of the United States." It was to accomplish this purpose through grants to schools, libraries, research, and publications. Carnegie had personally distributed $29,452,853 for library buildings up to 1911. Then the public library giving was turned over to the Corporation, which distributed $11,781,000 for this purpose up to 1917. After that time the Carnegie Corporation did not consider any new requests for buildings, but it did make grants as late as 1919 for requests which had been made before 1917.

The Corporation has never ceased receiving requests for library buildings, although the tempo of such appeals has diminished. At the end of 1924, James Bertram reported that 1500 meritorious applications were on file for library buildings.[18] An accurate record kept from 1923 to 1953 reveals a total number of 1631 requests for funds by libraries of all kinds for establishment, buildings, books, equipment, renovation, and expansion, with the following breakdown:[19]

1923–45	1149	1950	92
1946	16	1951	41
1947	77	1952	57
1948	81	1953	40
1949	78		

The secretary of the Corporation reported in 1965 that requests were still being received for library buildings, as well as for repairs and expansion of old libraries and for information regarding the disposal of old structures that had been or were being replaced.[20]

Andrew Carnegie's philanthropy continued to benefit public libraries long after the formal termination of building grants. This extended library philanthropy is still in evidence to this day, and in many ways is even more important than the orginal bequest of Carnegie buildings. Indeed, the Carnegie Corporation, which took over Carnegie's philanthropy program, has been so identified with libraries that many people have assumed it was operating solely for the benefit and control of libraries and librarians.

During the Corporation's first fifty years of operation, from 1911 to 1961, it spent $33,457,142 to improve library service. Although this expenditure represents only about 11 percent of the total of all its grants during the first fifty years, the Corporation has been associated with every major development in library service in the United States. A brief review of these library involvements will show their importance and also demonstrate that the Carnegie Corporation did follow through on many of Alvin Johnson's recommendations. The Corporation has given support to all types of libraries, but only those grants involving or greatly affecting public libraries are noted here.[21]

Following World War I, Corporation trustees did not resume gifts of money for buildings. Instead, during the period 1917–25, they organized a series of conferences to determine the manner and means by which the Corporation might be of assistance in improving library services and training.

In 1918 the Corporation asked Charles C. Williamson to make a study of library training. His report[22] recommended that librarians should receive their education in a university rather than in a training school sponsored by a public library. Williamson also recommended the establishment of a graduate library school for advanced study, a national accrediting and certification system for library schools, and numerous fellowships. His study was a monumental work which resulted in a complete revision of the curriculum in library schools.

A Carnegie Corporation–sponsored study in 1924 by William S. Learned[23] centered on the role of the library as a medium for spreading information. It called for expanded services to be provided by the American Library Association, and for local and regional experiments and demonstrations leading to better ways of getting books to the people.

In 1926 the Corporation embarked on a ten-year "Library Service Program" for which the trustees approved $5,000,000 in financial support. The aim of this program was to strengthen the library profession by supporting the activities of the American Library Association, by improving training opportunities, and by support for certain centralized library services and projects.

Andrew Carnegie had already provided $100,000 in endowment funds to the American Library Association in 1902, and the Corporation gave $549,500 for the general support of the Association from 1924 to 1926. In 1926 it added $2,000,000 in endowment funds. During this period the Corporation also provided financial assistance to the Library of Congress and to bibliographic centers and regional catalogs, such as those at the Denver and Philadelphia public libraries.

Gifts for the endowment and support of library schools and the establishment of the first graduate library school at the University of Chicago totaled $3,359,550. Fellowships for library training and the sponsorship of conferences, studies, and publications were also provided. Among the latter was a book on public library architecture by Joseph L. Wheeler and Alfred M. Githens.[24] This volume came to be the indispensable handbook for the planning and design of public libraries.

The Corporation provided funds for several demonstrations of methods and techniques for bringing books to people of all ages who were living in rural areas far from the major population centers. In 1925 the first of these was started in Louisiana with a grant to the League of Library Commissioners. A central lending library was begun, several parishes (counties) were encouraged to establish libraries with initial book collections provided by the commission, and summer library training courses were provided for the first time by a university in the state. Shortly after the demonstration began, the Louisiana state legislature voted money to supplement the funds of the commission during the demonstration period, and later continued its financial support of statewide library service. Other such experiments and demonstrations were to follow throughout the United States.

Following World War II, during which the Corporation's library philanthropy was for the most part in a state of suspension, the trustees and officers evolved a new Corporation grant program in which library interests no longer had a major emphasis, although library grants were not excluded. In fact, although the number of grants and the amount expended may have decreased, those which were made were of great importance.

The Corporation provided $212,170 to the Social Science Research Council for the Public Library Inquiry. The idea of a study of the library's actual and potential contribution to American society was suggested by the American Library Association. The appraisal was made in sociological, cultural, and human terms with the investigators asking and answering such questions as:

Who uses the library and why?
Who are the librarians and how well qualified are they for the job?
Where does the money come from and is it adequate?
What services does and should the library perform?

The overall report was published in 1950.[25] Specific studies were issued in twelve volumes between 1949 and 1951. The most significant finding was the poor status of the American public library outside the major cities. There was a superabundance of small, poorly financed, independent local libraries with inadequate book stocks and reference services. The Public Library Inquiry discovered that 65 percent of all libraries were in small towns of less than 5000 and spent less than $4000 per year. The survey suggested the organization of larger library systems and the concentration of state and federal library aid for the encouragement of such systems. The small libraries could and should continue to serve the communities that organized them. But they should also be related to other surrounding libraries in order to form regional systems with common pools of books and other materials, specialized personnel available for guidance, and centralized reference and processing services.

Again, financial assistance from the Carnegie Corporation helped the American Library Association, in 1956, to formulate and publish what popularly became known as the Public Library Standards.[26] The Public Library Inquiry discovered the failings of the public libraries, and the Standards presented what they should be doing by setting up minimum guidelines of good service. Public libraries were urged to cooperate, federate, or consolidate into library systems for better library service.

In 1956 a grant of $50,000 was made to the School of Library Science at Western Reserve University for the study of a new curriculum in library training in the light of modern cultural and technological developments. A statement was to be formulated on the nature of librarianship and on the kinds of knowledge librarians should have in order to fulfill their professional functions.

The Corporation's financial support of demonstration centers for extension of library service in rural areas, of the Public Library Inquiry, and of the Standards was an important factor in bringing about federal aid for public libraries. The Library Services Act (P.L. 597, 84th Congress), signed into law in 1956, was designed as a five-year program to demonstrate improved public library services in areas of less than 10,000 people which had nonexistent or inadequate library service. The Act was extended in 1960 for five additional years. In 1964 the Library Services Act was amended and renamed the Library Services and Construction Act (P.L. 88-269). Benefits were extended to urban as well as to rural areas, and for the first time these funds were not limited to operation and maintenance but could be expended for construction. An amendment in 1966 included money for strengthening cooperation among libraries. Federal aid has always been based on matching funds from states and in many cases from local government.

In signing the Library Services and Construction Act on February 11, 1964, President Johnson declared:

> . . . chances are that the public libraries are among the oldest buildings in any community. Only four per cent of our public

libraries have been built since 1940. Many of them were built through the wise generosity of Andrew Carnegie forty years ago. This Nation needs a larger and more diversified collection of books. We need better housing for these books. We sorely need libraries closer to the people, whether through more centrally located libraries or through bookmobiles and branch locations. The central fact of our times is this: Books and ideas are the most effective weapons against intolerance and ignorance.[27]

Thus, the rural areas which were somewhat neglected by the original Carnegie library benefactions were the first to receive federal aid. More recently, all kinds of public libraries—rural, suburban, and urban—have found a new library benefactor on the scale of Andrew Carnegie.

Building on the foundation laid by the social libraries, public libraries in the United States have had four important phases of growth. The public library enabling laws, beginning in the 1850's, were the first stimulus. Carnegie's gifts to public libraries were the second. A third major stimulus could well be attributed to the library activities of the Carnegie Corporation. We are now experiencing the fourth—that of the stimulus of federal support. This latest development has come about, to some extent at least, as the result of the influence of Andrew Carnegie and the Carnegie Corporation's library activities. Carnegie's benefactions have, in truth, played a major role in American public library development.

Notes

[1] Burton J. Hendrick, *The Benefactions of Andrew Carnegie* (New York: Carnegie Corp., 1935), p.13-15.

[2] Samuel Eliot Morison and Henry Steele Commager, *The Growth of the American Republic* (New York: Oxford Univ. Pr., 1950), II: 312-13.

[3] Harold Underwood Faulkner, *The Quest for Social Justice, 1898-1914* (New York: Macmillan, 1931), p.279.

[4] Sidney Ditzion, *Arsenals of a Democratic Culture* (Chicago: American Library Assn., 1947), p.150.

[5] William Munthe, *American Librarianship from a European Angle* (Chicago: American Library Assn., 1939), p.18.

[6] Dwight L. Dumond, *America in Our Time, 1896-1946* (New York: Holt, 1947), p.19-20.

[7] Stuart P. Sherman, *Americans* (New York: Scribner, 1922), p.254-55.

[8] Mark Sullivan, *Our Times: The United States, 1900-1925* (6 vols.; New York: Scribner, 1932), IV:159, 163.

[9] Ralph Munn, "Hindsight on the Gifts of Carnegie," *Library Journal*, 76: 1967-70 (Dec. 1, 1951).

[10] James Truslow Adams, *The Epic of America* (Boston: Little, 1931), p.345.

[11] Henry T. Drennan, "The Public Library Service Gap," in *National Inventory of Library Needs* (Chicago: American Library Assn., 1965), p.40-41.

[12] *Bowker Annual of Library and Book Trade Information, 1968* (New York: Bowker, 1968), p.6.

[13] Hagerstown, Md., Carnegie Library Correspondence, Microfilm Reel No.13.

[14] Based on the U.S. Dept. of Labor, Bureau of Labor Statistics, *Consumer Price Index*, with $1957-59 = 100$: $1900 = 29.3$, $1910 = 33.3$, July, $1968 = 121.5$.

[15] "Gifts to Libraries," *Library Journal*, Vols. 15-31 (1890-1906).

[16] Samuel S. Green, *The Public Library Movement in the United States, 1853-1893* (Boston: Boston Book Co., 1913), p.152-53; U.S. Bureau of Education, *Statistics of Libraries and Library Legislation in the United States, 1895-1896* (Washington, D.C.: Govt. Print. Off., 1897); William S. Learned, *The American Public Library and the Diffusion of Knowledge* (New York: Harcourt, 1924), p.73.

[17] William S. Learned, *op. cit.*, p.71-73. (Learned listed 1408 communities receiving Carnegie grants; later listings by the Carnegie Corporation reveal 1412.)

[18] James Bertram to Mrs. Charles Scheuber, librarian, Dec. 30, 1924 (Fort Worth, Texas, Carnegie Library Correspondence, Microfilm Reel No.11).

[19] Information obtained from Carnegie Corporation files in New York City.

[20] Letter from Miss Florence Anderson, secretary of the Carnegie Corporation, to the author, Oct. 12, 1965.

[21] Most of the following review was obtained from the Carnegie Corporation of New York, *Carnegie Corporation Library Program, 1911-1961* (New York: Carnegie Corp., 1963), p.3-24.

[22] Charles C. Williamson, *Training for Library Service* (New York: Carnegie Corp., 1923).

[23] William S. Learned, *op. cit.*

[24] Joseph L. Wheeler, and Alfred M. Githens, *The American Public Library Building: Its Planning and Design with Special Reference to Its Administration and Service* (New York: Scribner, 1941).

[25] Robert D. Leigh, *The Public Library in the United States: The General Report of the Public Library Inquiry* (New York: Columbia Univ. Pr., 1950).

[26] American Library Association, *Public Library Service: A Guide to Evaluation, with Minimum Standards* (Chicago: A.L.A., 1956).

[27] Germaine Krettek and Eileen D. Cooke, "Federal Legislation," *Bowker Annual of Library and Book Trade Information, 1965* (New York: Bowker, 1965), p.155.

Appendix A

Samples of Standard Letters and Forms as Found in the Carnegie Library Correspondence

1. Standard reply to a request for a Carnegie grant when it came from a person other than the mayor or the municipal council

MY DEAR SIR:

Your favor has been duly received. If (town) has not adequate library accomodation and desires the assistance of Carnegie Corporation of New York in obtaining a bilding, those interested should have the Mayor or Council (or the officials which correspond to them in your community) rite an official letter of application, stating what the community is willing to do for its part in levying a tax for revenue and in providing a site.

2. The three versions of the questionnaire sent to each community requesting a Carnegie gift

The earliest, basic form was as follows:

FREE PUBLIC LIBRARY

1. Town?
2. Population?

3. Has it a Library at present?
4. How Housed?
5. Amount Taxes Paid by Community, Yearly for Support
6. Amount Guaranteed from Taxes Yearly if Building Obtained
7. Is Requisite Site Available?
8. Amount Now Collected toward Building

To facilitate Mr. Carnegie's consideration of your appeal, will you oblige by filling in the above, and return with statement of any particulars likely to assist in making decision?

Respectfully

JAS. BERTRAM *Secretary*

A second, later version was expanded thus:

FREE PUBLIC LIBRARY

1. Town
2. Population
3. Has it a Library at present?
4. Number of Books (excluding Government Reports)?
5. Circulation for past year?
6. How is Library Housed?
7. Number and measurements of Rooms, and their uses?
8. Finances according to last Yearly report

Receipts		Expenditures	
City Appropriation	$. . . .	Rent	$. . . .
Bequests	. . . .	Salaries	. . . .
Miscell. Receipts	. . . .	Books	. . . .
. . . .	. . . .	Miscell.	. . . .
Total Revenue for year	. . . .	Total Expenditures	. . . .

9. Rate at which Councils will pledge support of Library yearly (levying tax for purpose) if building obtained
10. Is requisite Site Available?
11. Amount now Collected toward Building?

To facilitate Mr. Carnegie's consideration of your appeal, will you oblige by filling in the above, and return with statement of any particulars likely to assist in making decision?

It is necessary to give explicit answer to each question, as in the absence of such, there is no basis for action, and the matter will be delayed pending further communication.

In the third version two questions were merely added as follows:

> 9A. What is the highest rate of levy allowed by law for support of the library. (State anser, if possible in mills in the dollar).
>
> 9B. What income would this rate of levy hav yielded during each of the last five years.

3. Typical letters of promise sent to a community favored with a Carnegie library grant.

> *President F. S. Thompson*
> *Public Library*
> *Albion, Neb.*
>
> DEAR SIR,
>
> Responding to your communication on behalf of Albion, — If the City agree by resolution of Council to maintain a Free Public Library at a cost of not less than Six Hundred Dollars a year, and provides a suitable site for the building, Mr. Carnegie will be glad to give Six Thousand dollars to erect a Free Public Library Building for Albion.
>
> Respectfully yours
>
> *P. Secretary*

Correspondence of later years shows that the following two paragraphs were added:

> It should be noted that the amount indicated is to cover the cost of the library building complete, redy for occupancy and for the purpose intended.
>
> Before any expenditure on bilding or plans is incurd, the approval of proposed plans by Carnegie Corporation

of New York must be secured, to obtain which pleaz send
tentativ plans for inspection.

Very truly yours

CARNEGIE CORPORATION OF
NEW YORK

By Secretary

*4. Copy of standard pledge drawn up by Carnegie officials for
use by communities accepting a library grant*

A RESOLUTION
TO ACCEPT THE DONATION OF ANDREW CARNEGIE

Whereas, Andrew Carnegie has agreed to furnish
_____ Dollars to the _____
to erect a FREE PUBLIC LIBRARY BUILDING, on condition
that said _____ shall pledge itself by RESOLUTION
OF COUNCIL, to support a FREE PUBLIC LIBRARY, at cost of
not less than _____ Dollars a year, and PROVIDE A
SUITABLE SITE for said building; now therefore_____
Be it Resolved by the Council of the _____
of _____ that said _____ accept
said DONATION, and it does hereby pledge itself to comply with the requirements of said ANDREW CARNEGIE.

Resolved that it will furnish a suitable SITE for said
BUILDING when erected, at a cost of not less than _____
Dollars a year.

Resolved, that an ANNUAL LEVY shall hereafter be made
upon the taxable property of said_____
_____ sufficient in amount to comply with the above
requirements.

*Clerk*_____ *Mayor*_____

I,_____Clerk of the_____
do hereby certify that the foregoing is a full and complete
copy and transcript of a RESOLUTION passed by the COUN-
CIL of said_____at their regular session on_____
Witness my hand and the seal of said _____
this _____

Clerk _____

Appendix B

List of Communities in the United States Receiving Carnegie Grants for Public Library Buildings*

LOCATION	WAS A PUBLIC LIBRARY ESTABLISHED BEFORE THE CARNEGIE GRANT?	AMOUNT OF CARNEGIE GRANT	DATE
Aberdeen, S.D.	Yes	$ 15,000	Mar. 14, 1901
Aberdeen, Wash.	No	15,000	Jan. 18, 1907
Abilene, Kan.	No	12,500	Dec. 8, 1905
Abilene, Tex.	No	17,500	Mar. 9, 1907
Adrian, Mich.	Yes	27,500	Dec. 20, 1904
Aitkin, Minn.	Yes	6,500	Apr. 23, 1908
Akron, Ind.	No	12,500	May 21, 1913
Akron, Ohio	Yes	82,000	Dec. 24, 1901

*The list of towns and the date and amount of each grant were obtained from the Carnegie Corporation's *Carnegie Grants for Library Buildings, 1890–1917* (New York: Carnegie Corp., 1943) and from *Carnegie Corporation Library Program, 1911–1961* (New York: Carnegie Corp., 1963). The information as to whether a community had a public library established or not at the time of the Carnegie gift was obtained from a careful examination of the microfilmed correspondence of each community. If this information was not found here, then various old library directories were consulted, or, most often, a questionnaire was sent to the librarian of the community.

Some of the towns in this list are no longer in existence but have been incorporated with other communities; often their Carnegie buildings are now branch libraries. The libraries of many other communities have now joined with county and regional library systems.

The number in parentheses following the names of some communities indicates the number of library buildings erected with Carnegie funds if more than one.

207

208 APPENDIX B

LOCATION	WAS A PUBLIC LIBRARY ESTABLISHED BEFORE THE CARNEGIE GRANT?	AMOUNT OF CARNEGIE GRANT	DATE
Alameda, Cal.	Yes	$ 35,000	Oct. 3, 1899
Alamosa, Colo.	Yes	6,000	Mar. 21, 1908
Albany, Ga.	No	10,700	Jan. 9, 1905
Albany, Mo.	No	12,500	June 2, 1903
Albany, Ore.	No	12,500	Apr. 8, 1911
Albert Lea, Minn.	Yes	13,000	Apr. 11, 1902
Albia, Iowa	Yes	10,000	Apr. 11, 1905
Albion, Ind.	Yes	10,000	Jan. 28, 1916
Albion, Mich.	No	17,500	Jan. 2, 1903
Albion, Neb.	Yes	6,000	Apr. 8, 1907
Alden, Iowa	Yes	9,000	Nov. 3, 1913
Aledo, Ill.	No	10,000	May 21, 1913
Alexandria, Ind.	Yes	14,000	Apr. 26, 1902
Alexandria, La.	Yes	10,000	Apr. 8, 1907
Alexandria, Minn.	Yes	12,000	Feb. 2, 1903
Algona, Iowa	Yes	10,000	Mar. 27, 1903
Allegan, Mich.	Yes	10,000	Feb. 13, 1913
Allegheny, Pa.	No	481,012	1886
Alliance, Neb.	Yes	10,000	Dec. 2, 1909
Alliance, Ohio	Yes	25,000	Jan. 13, 1903
Alma, Neb.	No	10,000	Dec. 13, 1907
Alturas, Cal.	Yes	10,000	Nov. 20, 1908
American Fork, Utah	Yes	10,000	Sept. 26, 1919
Americus, Ga.	No	20,000	Apr. 23, 1908
Ames, Iowa	No	16,000	Feb. 2, 1903
Amherst, Ohio	No	10,000	Mar. 8, 1904
Amsterdam, N.Y.	Yes	25,000	Feb. 4, 1902
Anacortes, Wash.	No	10,000	Dec. 14, 1908
Anaheim, Cal.	Yes	10,000	Feb. 6, 1907
Anderson, Ind.	Yes	50,000	Apr. 11, 1902
Anderson, S.C.	Yes	18,700	Mar. 14, 1905
Andover, N.Y.	Yes	5,000	Nov. 21, 1911
Andrews, N.C.	No	5,000	Apr. 13, 1914
Angola, Ind.	No	10,000	Mar. 27, 1909
Ann Arbor, Mich.	No	30,000	Jan. 13, 1903
Anniston, Ala.	No	20,000	May 15, 1916
Anoka, Minn.	Yes	12,500	Mar. 27, 1903
Anthony, Kan.	Yes	10,000	Dec. 14, 1908
Antigo, Wis.	Yes	15,000	Mar. 20, 1903
Antioch, Cal.	No	2,500	June 1, 1915
Arcadia, Neb.	No	7,000	Mar. 31, 1916
Arcadia, Wis.	Yes	5,000	Mar. 14, 1905

LOCATION	WAS A PUBLIC LIBRARY ESTABLISHED BEFORE THE CARNEGIE GRANT?	AMOUNT OF CARNEGIE GRANT	DATE
Arcola, Ill.	No	$ 10,000	Mar. 27, 1903
Ardmore, Okla.	No	15,000	Mar. 20, 1903
Arkansas City, Kan.	No	18,400	Apr. 10, 1906
Armada, Mich.	Yes	8,000	Dec. 8, 1913
Armour, S.D.	Yes	7,500	Feb. 26, 1914
Ashland, Mass.	Yes	10,000	Feb. 20, 1903
Ashland, Neb.	Yes	5,500	Mar. 18, 1911
Ashland, Ore.	Yes	15,000	June 25, 1909
Ashtabula, Ohio	Yes	15,000	Mar. 6, 1901
Athens, Ohio	No	30,000	Dec. 16, 1903
Athol, Mass.	Yes	22,000	Mar. 14, 1902
Atlanta, Ga. (4)	No	202,000	Oct. 3, 1898
Atlanta, Ind.	Yes	10,000	May 15, 1916
Atlantic, Iowa	No	12,500	Mar. 14, 1902
Atlantic City, N.J.	Yes	71,075	Jan. 22, 1903
Attica, Ind.	Yes	10,000	Jan. 13, 1903
Auburn, Cal.	Yes	10,000	Mar. 9, 1907
Auburn, Me.	Yes	25,000	Jan. 13, 1903
Auburn, Wash.	Yes	9,000	May 17, 1912
Audubon, Iowa	No	9,000	Mar. 29, 1911
Aurora, Ill.	Yes	50,000	Jan. 16, 1901
Aurora, Mo.	No	9,000	Mar. 14, 1913
Aurora, Neb.	Yes	10,000	Dec. 2, 1909
Austin, Minn.	No	15,000	Oct. 3, 1901
Avon, N.J.	Yes	5,000	May 15, 1916
Avondale, Ala.	No	10,000	Dec. 13, 1907
Azusa, Cal.	Yes	10,000	Dec. 24, 1908
Baker City, Ore.	Yes	25,000	Dec. 13, 1907
Ballard, Wash.	No	15,000	Mar. 27, 1903
Ballinger, Tex.	No	17,500	Feb. 10, 1908
Baltimore, Md. (14)	Yes	500,000	Nov. 10, 1906
Baraboo, Wis.	Yes	15,000	Mar. 14, 1902
Barnesville, Ga.	No	10,000	Apr. 28, 1909
Barron, Wis.	Yes	7,000	May 17, 1912
Bartlesville, Okla.	No	12,500	Apr. 23, 1908
Bartow, Fla.	No	8,000	Mar. 18, 1911
Basin, Wyo.	Yes	17,500	June 29, 1908
Bay City, Mich.	Yes	35,000	May 15, 1916
Bayfield, Wis.	Yes	10,000	Feb. 2, 1903
Bayliss District, Cal.	Yes	4,000	Jan. 5, 1916
Bayonne, N.J.	Yes	83,000	Apr. 13, 1903

210 APPENDIX B

LOCATION	WAS A PUBLIC LIBRARY ESTABLISHED BEFORE THE CARNEGIE GRANT?	AMOUNT OF CARNEGIE GRANT	DATE
Beardstown, Ill.	Yes	$ 10,000	Jan. 22, 1903
Beatrice, Neb.	Yes	23,000	Mar. 14, 1902
Beaufort, S.C.	No	7,500	Sept. 25, 1914
Beaumont, Cal.	Yes	10,000	Apr. 28, 1913
Beaver, Utah	No	10,000	Dec. 8, 1913
Beaver Falls, Pa.	No	50,000	Aug. 15, 1899
Bedford, Ind.	Yes	20,000	Jan. 9, 1902
Bedford, Iowa	No	10,000	Apr. 8, 1907
Bellefontaine, Ohio	Yes	14,000	Jan. 6, 1903
Belleville, Ill.	Yes	45,000	Aug. 11, 1913
Belleville, N.J.	Yes	20,000	Apr. 28, 1909
Bellevue, Ohio	No	13,600	Jan. 13, 1903
Bellingham, Wash. (2)	Yes	36,000	Mar. 27, 1903
Belmar, N.J.	Yes	13,000	Jan. 14, 1914
Beloit, Wis.	Yes	25,000	July 16, 1901
Belton, Tex.	No	10,000	Feb. 2, 1903
Belvidere, Ill.	Yes	17,500	Apr. 8, 1910
Bemidji, Minn.	Yes	12,500	Feb. 10, 1908
Benson, Minn.	Yes	7,500	Apr. 3, 1912
Benton Harbor, Mich.	Yes	20,000	Mar. 14, 1902
Berkeley, Cal.	Yes	40,000	Feb. 12, 1903
Berkley, Mass.	Yes	5,000	Feb. 6, 1915
Berlin, N.H.	Yes	17,000	Dec. 27, 1902
Berlin, Wis.	Yes	12,250	Feb. 2, 1903
Bessemer, Ala.	No	10,000	Feb. 13, 1906
Biggs, Cal.	No	5,000	Apr. 23, 1906
Big Timber, Mont.	Yes	7,500	May 16, 1911
Binghamton, N.Y.	Yes	75,000	Apr. 26, 1902
Bismarck, N.D.	No	25,000	Jan. 28, 1916
Black River Falls, Wis.	Yes	10,000	Mar. 11, 1914
Blair, Neb.	No	10,000	Mar. 31, 1916
Bloomfield, Ind.	Yes	12,000	July 22, 1908
Bloomfield, Iowa	No	10,000	Nov. 21, 1911
Bloomfield, Neb.	Yes	5,000	Jan. 2, 1913
Bloomington, Ind.	Yes	31,000	Oct. 21, 1901
Blue Island, Ill.	Yes	15,000	Mar. 14, 1902
Bluffton, Ind.	Yes	13,000	Jan. 13, 1903
Boise, Ida.	Yes	40,000	Feb. 12, 1903
Bolivar, Mo.	No	8,000	Nov. 3, 1913
Bolivar, N.Y.	Yes	5,000	Apr. 10, 1909
Boonville, Ind.	Yes	12,000	Nov. 3, 1913
Boston, Ga.	Yes	6,000	Dec. 3, 1912

LOCATION	WAS A PUBLIC LIBRARY ESTABLISHED BEFORE THE CARNEGIE GRANT?	AMOUNT OF CARNEGIE GRANT	DATE
Boswell, Ind.	Yes	$ 8,000	Nov. 30, 1910
Boulder, Colo.	Yes	15,000	Feb. 20, 1904
Boyne City, Mich.	Yes	15,000	Mar. 31, 1916
Bozeman, Mont.	Yes	15,000	Mar. 14, 1902
Braddock, Pa.	No	357,782	Dec. 31, 1895
Bradentown, Fla.	No	10,000	Feb. 3, 1917
Bradford, Pa.	Yes	40,000	Jan. 19, 1900
Brainerd, Minn.	Yes	12,000	Jan. 6, 1903
Brazil, Ind.	Yes	20,000	Mar. 14, 1902
Bridgeport, Conn. (2)	Yes	50,000	Apr. 13, 1914
Brigham City, Utah	Yes	12,500	June 11, 1914
Bristolville, Ohio	No	6,000	Apr. 25, 1911
Britt, Iowa	No	8,000	Mar. 31, 1916
Britton, S.D.	No	7,500	May 8, 1914
Brockton, Mass.	Yes	110,000	Apr. 16, 1910
Broken Bow, Neb.	Yes	10,000	July 23, 1914
Bronson, Mich.	Yes	8,500	July 15, 1910
Brook, Ind.	Yes	7,000	May 21, 1913
Brookfield, Ill.	Yes	10,000	Apr. 3, 1912
Brookfield, Mo.	No	12,000	Nov. 9, 1916
Brookings, S.D.	Yes	10,000	Dec. 13, 1907
Brookston, Ind.	Yes	10,000	Sept. 29, 1915
Brookville, Ind.	Yes	10,000	Nov. 30, 1910
Brownsburg, Ind.	No	12,500	Apr. 3, 1912
Browns Valley, Minn.	Yes	5,500	Jan. 31, 1914
Brownsville, Tenn.	No	7,500	Dec. 2, 1909
Brownwood, Tex.	No	15,000	Mar. 27, 1903
Brush, Colo.	No	6,000	June 11, 1914
Bryan, Ohio	No	10,000	Feb. 12, 1903
Bryan, Tex.	No	10,000	Apr. 11, 1902
Bucyrus, Ohio	Yes	15,000	June 1, 1903
Buffalo, Wyo.	No	12,500	Jan. 14, 1909
Burlington, Kan.	Yes	9,656	Apr. 25, 1911
Burlington, Vt.	Yes	50,000	July 25, 1901
Burlington, Wash.	No	5,000	Apr. 13, 1914
Burwell, Neb.	Yes	5,000	May 21, 1913
Butler, Ind.	Yes	10,000	Dec. 8, 1913
Butler, Pa.	Yes	37,000	May 3, 1917
Cadillac, Mich.	No	15,000	Mar. 20, 1903
Caldwell, Ida.	Yes	12,500	Apr. 3, 1912
Caldwell, Kan.	No	7,000	Dec. 2, 1909

LOCATION	WAS A PUBLIC LIBRARY ESTABLISHED BEFORE THE CARNEGIE GRANT?	AMOUNT OF CARNEGIE GRANT	DATE
Caldwell, N. J.	Yes	$ 10,000	Jan. 8, 1908
Calexico, Cal.	Yes	10,000	Mar. 16, 1915
Cambridge, Ohio	Yes	21,000	Jan. 22, 1902
Camden, N. J. (3)	Yes	120,000	Jan. 2, 1903
Camden, S.C.	Yes	5,000	Nov. 17, 1914
Canastota, N.Y.	Yes	10,000	Jan. 10, 1902
Canon City, Colo.	Yes	13,000	Dec. 14, 1901
Canton, Kan.	No	6,000	Nov. 9, 1916
Canton, Ohio	Yes	60,000	Apr. 15, 1901
Canton, S.D.	No	10,000	Dec. 2, 1904
Cape Girardeau, Mo.	No	25,000	Nov. 9, 1916
Carey, Ohio	No	8,000	Dec. 30, 1904
Caribou, Me.	Yes	10,000	Mar. 21, 1910
Carlisle, Ind.	Yes	10,000	Feb. 6, 1915
Carmel, Ind.	Yes	11,000	Mar. 14, 1913
Carmi, Ill.	Yes	10,000	Jan. 14, 1914
Carnegie, Pa.	No	310,000	Apr. 26, 1898
Carroll, Iowa	Yes	10,000	Feb. 12, 1903
Carrollton, Ill.	Yes	10,000	Oct. 3, 1901
Carthage, Mo.	Yes	25,000	Apr. 26, 1902
Casper, Wyo.	No	13,000	Feb. 13, 1906
Cassopolis, Mich.	No	10,000	Apr. 23, 1908
Catskill, N.Y.	Yes	20,000	Feb. 2, 1901
Cedar City, Utah	Yes	10,000	Apr. 3, 1912
Cedar Falls, Iowa	Yes	15,000	Mar. 14, 1902
Cedar Rapids, Iowa	Yes	75,000	Feb. 19, 1901
Celina, Ohio	Yes	12,000	Dec. 30, 1904
Centralia, Ill.	Yes	20,000	Feb. 14, 1901
Centralia, Wash.	No	15,000	Jan. 6, 1911
Chadron, Neb.	Yes	5,788	Apr. 16, 1910
Chanute, Kan.	Yes	14,500	Dec. 30, 1904
Chariton, Iowa	Yes	11,000	Jan. 13, 1903
Charles City, Iowa	Yes	12,500	Jan. 2, 1903
Charleston, Ill.	Yes	15,000	Oct. 3, 1901
Charleston, S.C.	No	5,000	Feb. 26, 1914
Charlevoix, Mich.	Yes	10,000	Feb. 21, 1907
Charlotte, Mich.	Yes	12,000	Mar. 14, 1902
Charlotte, N.C.	No	40,000	Mar. 12, 1901
Chatfield, Minn.	No	6,000	July 9, 1913
Chatham, N.Y.	Yes	15,000	Aug. 16, 1901
Chattanooga, Tenn.	No	50,000	Dec. 27, 1900
Cheboygan, Mich.	Yes	15,000	Feb. 10, 1908

LOCATION	WAS A PUBLIC LIBRARY ESTABLISHED BEFORE THE CARNEGIE GRANT?	AMOUNT OF CARNEGIE GRANT	DATE
Chehalis, Wash.	No	$ 10,000	May 8, 1908
Chelsea, Mass.	Yes	60,000	July 20, 1908
Cherokee, Iowa	Yes	12,000	Jan. 6, 1903
Cherryvale, Kan.	No	10,000	Apr. 30, 1912
Cheyenne, Wyo.	Yes	50,000	Dec. 27, 1899
Chicago Heights, Ill.	Yes	15,000	Mar. 14, 1902
Chickasha, Okla.	No	10,000	Feb. 12, 1903
Chico, Cal.	Yes	10,000	Jan. 7, 1904
Chillicothe, Ill.	No	10,000	Apr. 19, 1915
Chillicothe, Ohio	Yes	30,000	Apr. 13, 1903
Chinook, Mont.	No	15,000	Oct. 29, 1918
Chippewa Falls, Wis.	Yes	20,000	Feb. 15, 1902
Chula Vista, Cal.	Yes	10,000	Mar. 31, 1916
Cincinnati, Ohio (9)	Yes	286,000	Apr. 9, 1902
Claremont, N.H.	No	15,000	Jan. 13, 1903
Clarinda, Iowa	Yes	15,000	Feb. 21, 1907
Clarks, Neb.	No	7,500	May 3, 1917
Clarksdale, Miss.	No	10,000	Nov. 21, 1911
Clarkston, Wash.	Yes	10,000	Jan. 17, 1912
Clarksville, Tex.	Yes	10,000	Sept. 5, 1902
Clay Center, Kan.	No	10,000	Dec. 2, 1909
Clay Center, Neb.	Yes	7,000	Jan. 6, 1915
Clear Lake, Iowa	Yes	8,500	Mar. 31, 1916
Clearwater, Fla.	No	10,000	Mar. 16, 1915
Cleburne, Tex.	No	20,000	Apr. 13, 1903
Cleveland, Ohio (14)	Yes	590,000	Apr. 4, 1903
Clinton, Ind.	No	12,500	Feb. 25, 1908
Clinton, Iowa	Yes	45,000	Aug. 24, 1901
Clinton, Mass.	Yes	25,000	Mar. 8, 1901
Clintonville, Wis.	Yes	9,000	Apr. 19, 1915
Clovis, Cal.	Yes	7,000	Mar. 11, 1914
Clyde, Ohio	Yes	12,500	Dec. 2, 1904
Coalinga, Cal.	Yes	20,000	Jan. 27, 1912
Coatesville, Ind.	Yes	8,000	Apr. 13, 1914
Cody, Wyo.	Yes	15,000	Apr. 13, 1914
Coffeyville, Kan.	Yes	25,000	Jan. 6, 1911
Coleraine, Minn.	No	15,000	Dec. 16, 1908
Colfax, Ind.	Yes	9,000	Sept. 29, 1915
Colfax, Iowa	Yes	6,500	Dec. 2, 1904
College View, Neb.	Yes	7,500	Sept. 25, 1914
Collingswood, N.J.	Yes	15,000	Jan. 5, 1916
Collinsville, Okla.	No	7,500	June 1, 1915

214 APPENDIX B

LOCATION	WAS A PUBLIC LIBRARY ESTABLISHED BEFORE THE CARNEGIE GRANT?	AMOUNT OF CARNEGIE GRANT	DATE
Colorado City, Colo.	Yes	$ 10,000	Mar. 20, 1903
Colorado Springs, Colo.	Yes	60,000	Jan. 2, 1903
Colton, Cal.	No	10,000	Apr. 10, 1906
Columbus, Ga.	No	30,000	Apr. 26, 1902
Columbus, Ind.	Yes	15,000	Dec. 30, 1901
Columbus, Kan.	Yes	10,000	July 13, 1912
Columbus, Neb.	Yes	13,000	Aug. 11, 1913
Columbus, Ohio	Yes	200,000	Dec. 30, 1901
Columbus, Wis.	Yes	10,000	Mar. 27, 1903
Colusa, Cal.	Yes	10,000	Jan. 19, 1905
Concord, Cal.	Yes	2,500	June 1, 1915
Concordia, Kan.	No	10,000	Dec. 13, 1907
Conneaut, Ohio	No	25,000	Dec. 2, 1904
Connellsville, Pa.	No	75,000	Apr. 22, 1899
Connersville, Ind.	Yes	20,000	Dec. 13, 1907
Converse, Ind.	No	9,000	Nov. 9, 1916
Corbin, Ky.	No	6,000	Apr. 13, 1914
Cordele, Ga.	No	17,556	Jan. 13, 1903
Cordell, Okla.	Yes	9,000	Jan. 6, 1911
Corning, Cal.	Yes	10,000	Aug. 11, 1913
Corona, Cal.	Yes	11,500	Mar. 25, 1905
Corry, Pa.	Yes	15,000	Nov. 9, 1916
Corsicana, Tex.	No	25,000	Mar. 16, 1904
Corydon, Ind.	Yes	7,500	Sept. 27, 1912
Corydon, Iowa	No	8,000	Nov. 7, 1917
Coshocton, Ohio	Yes	17,000	Dec. 27, 1902
Council Bluffs, Iowa	Yes	70,000	Jan. 6, 1903
Council Grove, Kan.	No	10,000	Mar. 27, 1903
Covina, Cal.	Yes	9,000	Apr. 11, 1905
Covington, Ind.	Yes	10,000	Mar. 14, 1913
Covington, Ky.	Yes	85,000	Jan. 15, 1900
Cozad, Neb.	Yes	6,000	Sept. 14, 1917
Cranford, N. J.	No	10,000	Jan. 20, 1908
Crawfordsville, Ind.	Yes	25,000	Mar. 8, 1901
Cresco, Iowa	Yes	17,500	Feb. 13, 1913
Crete, Neb.	Yes	10,000	Aug. 11, 1913
Crookston, Minn.	No	17,500	Nov. 25, 1903
Crown Point, Ind.	No	12,000	Feb. 28, 1906
Culver, Ind.	Yes	10,000	Jan. 6, 1915
Cumberland, Wis.	Yes	10,000	Jan. 19, 1905
Cuthbert, Ga.	No	7,000	May 17, 1912

LOCATION	WAS A PUBLIC LIBRARY ESTABLISHED BEFORE THE CARNEGIE GRANT?	AMOUNT OF CARNEGIE GRANT	DATE
Dallas, Ore.	Yes	$ 10,000	Dec. 7, 1911
Dallas, S.D.	No	5,000	Apr. 28, 1913
Dallas, Tex. (2)	No	76,000	Aug. 23, 1899
Danville, Ill. (2)	Yes	65,000	Dec. 21, 1901
Danville, Ind.	No	10,000	Mar. 14, 1902
Darlington, Ind.	Yes	10,000	Feb. 6, 1915
Darlington, S.C.	Yes	10,000	May 15, 1916
Darlington, Wis.	Yes	10,000	Feb. 5, 1904
Davenport, Iowa	No	75,000	Dec. 2, 1899
David City, Neb.	Yes	10,000	Nov. 9, 1916
Dawson, Ga.	No	10,000	Mar. 14, 1913
Dawson, Minn.	No	9,000	Mar. 31, 1916
Dayton, Ohio (2)	Yes	65,000	Jan. 6, 1911
Deadwood, S.D.	Yes	15,000	Apr. 11, 1902
Decatur, Ala.	No	12,000	Feb. 12, 1903
Decatur, Ill.	Yes	60,000	Feb. 6, 1901
Decatur, Ind.	No	12,000	Mar. 8, 1904
Defiance, Ohio	Yes	22,000	Nov. 25, 1903
DeLand, Ill	No	8,000	Apr. 25, 1911
Delavan, Ill.	Yes	10,000	Apr. 28, 1913
Delaware, Ohio	Yes	21,500	Dec. 27, 1902
Dell Rapids, S.D.	Yes	6,000	Nov. 20, 1908
Delphi, Ind.	Yes	10,000	Dec. 30, 1904
Delphos, Ohio	No	12,500	May 2, 1911
Delta, Colo.	No	6,500	Feb. 20, 1911
Denison, Iowa	Yes	12,500	Mar. 14, 1902
Denver, Colo. (9)	Yes	360,000	Mar. 14, 1902
Derby Neck, Conn.	Yes	3,400	Mar. 12, 1906
Des Plaines, Ill.	No	5,000	Apr. 10, 1906
Detroit, Mich. (9)	Yes	750,000	June 23, 1901
Detroit, Minn.	Yes	10,000	Dec. 23, 1911
Devils Lake, N.D.	Yes	12,500	Apr. 23, 1908
DeWitt, Iowa	Yes	7,116	Apr. 8, 1907
DeWitt, Neb.	Yes	3,000	Nov. 14, 1906
Dickinson, N.D.	No	12,500	Mar. 21, 1908
Dighton, Mass.	Yes	6,000	Feb. 15, 1905
Dillon, Mont.	Yes	7,500	Jan. 22, 1902
Dinuba, Cal.	No	8,000	Mar. 16, 1915
Dixon, Cal.	No	10,000	Nov. 21, 1911
Dodge City, Kan.	No	8,500	Feb. 1, 1905
Douglas, Wyo.	No	10,000	July 20, 1908

LOCATION	WAS A PUBLIC LIBRARY ESTABLISHED BEFORE THE CARNEGIE GRANT?	AMOUNT OF CARNEGIE GRANT	DATE
Dover, N.H.	Yes	$ 30,000	Apr. 26, 1902
Dowagiac, Mich.	No	12,500	Jan. 13, 1903
Downers Grove, Ill.	Yes	8,500	Feb. 13, 1906
Downs, Kan.	Yes	6,140	Jan. 19, 1905
Dublin, Ga.	No	10,000	Mar. 27, 1903
Dubuque, Iowa	No	71,500	Jan. 12, 1901
Duluth, Minn. (3)	Yes	125,000	Oct. 7, 1899
Dunkirk, N.Y.	Yes	25,000	Feb. 20, 1904
Dunlap, Iowa	No	10,000	May 2, 1911
Duquesne, Pa.	No	310,000	Jan. 23, 1901
Durand, Wis.	Yes	7,500	Dec. 23, 1905
Durango, Colo.	Yes	15,000	Jan. 16, 1906
Durham, N.C.	Yes	32,000	Sept. 14, 1917
Eagle Grove, Iowa	Yes	10,000	Apr. 26, 1902
Eagle Rock, Cal.	No	7,500	Mar. 11, 1914
Earl Park, Ind.	Yes	7,500	Nov. 21, 1911
East Chicago, Ind. (2)	No	40,000	Jan. 13, 1903
East Cleveland, Ohio	No	35,000	Dec. 20, 1904
East Jordan, Mich.	No	10,000	Feb. 6, 1915
East Liverpool, Ohio	No	50,000	June 30, 1899
Easton, Pa.	No	57,500	July 4, 1901
East Orange, N.J. (3)	No	116,000	Jan. 18, 1900
East San Diego, Cal.	No	10,000	June 1, 1915
Eatonton, Ga.	No	6,000	June 11, 1914
Eau Claire, Wis.	Yes	40,000	Feb. 4, 1902
Edgartown, Mass.	Yes	4,000	Apr. 26, 1902
Edgerton, Wis.	Yes	10,000	Mar. 14, 1905
Edgewater, N.J.	Yes	15,000	Mar. 16, 1915
Edgewood, Pa.	No	12,500	May 8, 1914
Edmonds, Wash.	Yes	5,000	Jan. 31, 1910
Edwardsville, Ill.	No	12,500	Feb. 12, 1903
El Centro, Cal.	No	10,000	Feb. 13, 1909
Eldon, Iowa	Yes	7,500	Mar. 18, 1911
Eldora, Iowa	Yes	10,000	Dec. 30, 1901
El Dorado, Kan.	Yes	10,000	Nov. 30, 1910
Elizabeth, N.J. (2)	Yes	130,810	Feb. 3, 1910
Elk City, Okla.	Yes	10,000	Apr. 13, 1914
Elkhart, Ind.	No	35,000	Mar. 6, 1901
Ellensburg, Wash.	No	10,000	Jan. 8, 1908
Elmira, N.Y.	Yes	70,000	Jan. 28, 1916
El Paso, Ill.	No	6,000	Sept. 1, 1905

LOCATION	WAS A PUBLIC LIBRARY ESTABLISHED BEFORE THE CARNEGIE GRANT?	AMOUNT OF CARNEGIE GRANT	DATE
El Paso, Tex.	Yes	$ 37,500	Jan. 9, 1902
El Reno, Okla.	Yes	12,500	Nov. 25, 1903
El Roy, Wis.	No	10,000	Nov. 24, 1905
Elwood, Ind.	Yes	30,000	Oct. 3, 1901
Emmetsburg, Iowa	Yes	10,000	Feb. 20, 1911
Emporia, Kan.	Yes	22,000	Apr. 26, 1902
Enfield, Conn.	Yes	20,000	Nov. 9, 1910
Englewood, N.J.	Yes	25,000	July 9, 1913
Enid, Okla.	Yes	25,000	Feb. 20, 1904
Ensley, Ala.	No	10,000	Mar. 25, 1905
Enterprise, Ore.	Yes	5,000	Jan. 31, 1913
Ephraim City, Utah	Yes	10,000	Jan. 14, 1914
Escanaba, Mich.	No	21,200	Apr. 11, 1902
Escondido, Cal.	Yes	7,500	June 29, 1908
Estherville, Iowa	Yes	10,000	Feb. 15, 1902
Etowah, Tenn.	No	8,000	Sept. 29, 1915
Eufaula, Ala.	No	10,000	Feb. 2, 1903
Eugene, Ore.	Yes	10,000	Dec. 14, 1903
Eureka, Cal.	Yes	20,000	Oct. 3, 1901
Eureka, Kan.	No	9,000	May 21, 1913
Eureka City, Utah	No	11,000	Dec. 24, 1907
Eureka Springs, Ark.	No	15,500	Apr. 23, 1906
Evanston, Ill.	Yes	50,000	Dec. 14, 1903
Evanston, Wyo.	No	11,000	Feb. 20, 1903
Evansville, Ind. (3)	Yes	60,000	Jan. 6, 1911
Eveleth, Minn.	No	15,000	Feb. 20, 1911
Everett, Wash.	Yes	25,000	Jan. 6, 1903
Excelsior Springs, Mo.	No	10,000	Apr. 28, 1913
Exeter, Cal.	No	5,000	May 8, 1914
Fairbury, Neb.	Yes	12,500	Dec. 24, 1907
Fairfield, Iowa	No	30,000	Jan. 15, 1892
Fairfield, Neb.	No	6,000	Jan. 9, 1913
Fairhaven, Vt.	Yes	8,000	Jan. 19, 1905
Fairmont, Minn.	Yes	10,000	Feb. 12, 1903
Fargo, N.D.	Yes	20,000	Mar. 6, 1901
Farmington, Ill.	Yes	5,600	Jan. 29, 1906
Fayette, Mo.	No	10,000	May 21, 1913
Fergus Falls, Minn.	Yes	21,475	Feb. 20, 1904
Ferndale, Cal.	Yes	8,000	Mar. 21, 1908
Fitzgerald, Ga.	No	12,500	Apr. 13, 1914
Flint, Mich.	Yes	25,000	Dec. 27, 1902

LOCATION	WAS A PUBLIC LIBRARY ESTABLISHED BEFORE THE CARNEGIE GRANT?	AMOUNT OF CARNEGIE GRANT	DATE
Flora, Ill.	Yes	$ 10,000	Feb. 20, 1903
Flora, Ind.	No	10,000	Feb. 3, 1917
Florence, Colo.	Yes	10,000	Feb. 3, 1917
Fond du Lac, Wis.	Yes	30,000	Feb. 4, 1902
Fort Benton, Mont.	No	15,000	Mar. 31, 1916
Fort Branch, Ind.	No	10,000	May 15, 1916
Fort Collins, Colo.	Yes	12,500	Jan. 22, 1903
Fort Dodge, Iowa	Yes	30,000	Jan. 10, 1901
Fort Fairfield, Me.	Yes	10,000	Feb. 20, 1911
Fort Morgan, Colo.	Yes	10,000	Nov. 17, 1914
Fort Scott, Kan.	Yes	18,000	Mar. 14, 1901
Fort Smith, Ark.	No	25,000	Mar. 24, 1906
Fortville, Ind.	No	10,000	Mar. 31, 1916
Fort Wayne, Ind.	Yes	90,000	Mar. 14, 1901
Fort Worth, Tex.	No	50,000	June 30, 1899
Fostoria, Ohio	Yes	20,000	Mar. 20, 1903
Fowler, Ind.	Yes	7,500	Apr. 11, 1906
Francesville, Ind.	No	9,000	Apr. 19, 1915
Frankfort, Ind.	Yes	22,500	Nov. 24, 1905
Franklin, Ind.	Yes	17,500	Apr. 28, 1913
Franklin, Neb.	No	5,000	Sept. 29, 1915
Franklin, N.H.	No	15,000	Nov. 25, 1903
Franklin, Tex.	No	7,500	Apr. 2, 1913
Franklinville, N.Y.	Yes	2,200	May 8, 1914
Frederick, Okla.	No	10,000	Sept. 25, 1914
Freehold, N.J.	No	11,000	Mar. 27, 1903
Freeport, Ill.	Yes	30,000	Feb. 21, 1901
Freeport, Me.	Yes	6,500	Mar. 14, 1905
Fremont, Neb.	Yes	15,000	Dec. 30, 1901
Fresno, Cal.	Yes	30,000	Feb. 14, 1901
Fullerton, Cal.	No	10,000	Dec. 8, 1905
Fullerton, Neb.	No	6,000	July 13, 1912
Fulton, Ill.	Yes	5,000	Dec. 14, 1908
Fulton, Mo.	Yes	12,000	Apr. 8, 1911
Fulton, N.Y.	Yes	15,000	Mar. 14, 1902
Gadsden, Ala.	No	10,000	Nov. 18, 1903
Gaffney, S.C.	Yes	7,500	Apr. 2, 1913
Gainesville, Fla.	No	10,000	Mar. 31, 1916
Gainesville, Tex.	Yes	15,000	Apr. 3, 1912
Galena, Ill.	Yes	12,500	Apr. 20, 1905
Galesburg, Ill.	Yes	50,000	Feb. 14, 1901

LOCATION	WAS A PUBLIC LIBRARY ESTABLISHED BEFORE THE CARNEGIE GRANT?	AMOUNT OF CARNEGIE GRANT	DATE
Galion, Ohio	No	$ 15,000	Apr. 11, 1902
Gallipolis, Ohio	Yes	12,500	Dec. 27, 1902
Galva, Ill.	No	8,000	Feb. 10, 1908
Garden City, Kan.	No	10,000	Apr. 17, 1909
Garland, Utah	Yes	8,000	Jan. 17, 1912
Garner, Iowa	Yes	6,500	June 11, 1914
Garrett, Ind.	Yes	10,000	Mar. 14, 1913
Gary, Ind. (2)	Yes	90,000	Apr. 28, 1910
Gas City, Ind.	No	12,500	Jan. 2, 1913
Geneva, Ill.	Yes	7,500	Jan. 23, 1907
Geneva, Neb.	Yes	8,000	Jan. 31, 1911
Geneva, Ohio	Yes	10,000	Dec. 14, 1908
Germantown, Ohio	Yes	10,000	Dec. 20, 1904
Gibbon, Neb.	No	6,000	May 17, 1912
Gilman, Ill.	Yes	10,000	Sept. 29, 1915
Gilroy, Cal.	No	10,000	Mar. 12, 1906
Girard, Kan.	Yes	8,000	Nov. 24, 1905
Glasgow, Mont.	Yes	7,500	Apr. 8, 1907
Glendale, Cal.	Yes	12,500	Aug. 11, 1911
Glen Ellyn, Ill.	No	10,000	May 17, 1912
Glenwood, Iowa	No	7,000	July 27, 1903
Glenwood, Minn.	No	10,000	May 2, 1907
Gloversville, N.Y.	Yes	50,000	Mar. 8, 1901
Goldendale, Wash.	Yes	8,000	Nov. 3, 1913
Goodland, Kan.	No	10,000	Dec. 14, 1908
Goshen, Ind.	No	25,000	Jan. 15, 1901
Gothenburg, Neb.	No	8,000	Jan. 14, 1914
Graceville, Minn.	Yes	7,000	May 21, 1913
Grafton, N.D.	Yes	10,000	Feb. 2, 1903
Granby, Mass.	Yes	5,000	Mar. 31, 1916
Grand Forks, N.D.	Yes	22,700	July 4, 1901
Grand Haven, Mich.	Yes	12,500	Feb. 12, 1903
Grand Island, Neb.	Yes	20,000	Apr. 26, 1902
Grand Junction, Colo.	No	8,000	Dec. 21, 1899
Grand Rapids, Minn.	Yes	10,000	Jan. 19, 1905
Grandview, Ind.	Yes	8,000	Sept. 14, 1917
Grants Pass, Ore.	No	12,500	Nov. 18, 1903
Grass Valley, Cal.	Yes	15,000	Jan. 6, 1915
Grayville, Ill.	Yes	6,000	May 16, 1911
Great Bend, Kan.	No	12,500	Nov. 14, 1906
Great Falls, Mont.	Yes	31,700	June 21, 1901
Green Bay, Wis.	Yes	45,000	Feb. 13, 1901

220   APPENDIX B

LOCATION	WAS A PUBLIC LIBRARY ESTABLISHED BEFORE THE CARNEGIE GRANT?	AMOUNT OF CARNEGIE GRANT	DATE
Greencastle, Ind.	Yes	$ 20,165	Jan. 22, 1902
Greeneville, Tenn.	No	10,000	Nov. 3, 1913
Greenfield, Ind.	Yes	10,000	Mar. 8, 1904
Greenfield, Iowa	No	7,500	Sept. 29, 1915
Green River, Wyo.	No	20,000	Dec. 8, 1905
Greensboro, N.C. (2)	No	40,446	Apr. 26, 1902
Greensburg, Ind.	No	15,000	Mar. 14, 1902
Greenup, Ill.	Yes	8,000	Jan. 27, 1904
Greenville, Ill.	No	11,000	Apr. 23, 1903
Greenville, Ohio	Yes	25,000	Mar. 7, 1901
Greenville, Tex.	No	15,000	Apr. 13, 1903
Greenwood, Miss.	No	10,000	Sept. 29, 1911
Greenwood, S.C.	Yes	12,500	May 15, 1916
Gridley, Cal.	No	7,000	Jan. 2, 1913
Griggsville, Ill.	Yes	5,000	Apr. 19, 1915
Grundy Center, Iowa	No	6,000	Apr. 8, 1910
Guilford, Me.	Yes	5,750	Mar. 21, 1908
Gulfport, Miss.	Yes	10,000	May 15, 1916
Guthrie, Okla.	Yes	26,000	Oct. 17, 1901
Halstead, Kan.	Yes	7,500	Jan. 23, 1909
Hamburg, Iowa	No	9,000	Dec. 3, 1915
Hamburg, N.Y.	No	5,000	July 23, 1914
Hamburg, Pa.	No	10,000	Feb. 20, 1903
Hamilton, Mont.	Yes	9,000	July 23, 1914
Hammond, Ind.	Yes	27,000	Jan. 14, 1904
Hampton, Iowa	Yes	10,000	Mar. 14, 1902
Hanford, Cal.	Yes	12,500	Mar. 20, 1903
Hardin, Mont.	Yes	7,500	Mar. 31, 1916
Harriman, Tenn.	No	10,000	Nov. 20, 1908
Harrisburg, Ill.	Yes	12,500	Mar. 21, 1908
Hartford City, Ind.	Yes	16,000	Jan. 22, 1902
Hartington, Neb.	Yes	8,000	Mar. 11, 1914
Harvard, Neb.	No	6,000	June 11, 1914
Harvey, Ill.	Yes	13,500	Feb. 1, 1905
Hastings, Neb.	No	15,000	Dec. 27, 1902
Havana, Ill.	Yes	8,000	Oct. 3, 1900
Havelock, Neb.	Yes	7,000	Mar. 24, 1906
Havre, Mont.	Yes	12,000	Mar. 14, 1913
Hawarden, Iowa	Yes	5,000	Oct. 3, 1901
Hays, Kan.	No	8,000	Apr. 28, 1910
Hayward, Cal.	Yes	11,750	Feb. 20, 1906

LOCATION	WAS A PUBLIC LIBRARY ESTABLISHED BEFORE THE CARNEGIE GRANT?	AMOUNT OF CARNEGIE GRANT	DATE
Hayward, Wis.	Yes	$ 10,000	Dec. 14, 1903
Healdsburg, Cal.	Yes	10,000	Aug. 31, 1909
Hebron, Ind.	No	10,000	Sept. 14, 1917
Hemet, Cal.	Yes	10,000	Nov. 30, 1910
Henderson, Ky.	No	25,000	July 3, 1901
Hendersonville, N.C.	No	10,000	May 2, 1911
Herington, Kan.	No	10,000	July 9, 1913
Hermiston, Ore.	No	5,000	Jan. 6, 1915
Hiawatha, Kan.	Yes	10,000	Apr. 10, 1906
Hibbing, Minn.	No	25,000	Apr. 23, 1906
Hickman, Ky.	No	10,000	Nov. 27, 1906
Hickory, N.C.	Yes	13,250	May 3, 1917
Highland Park, Ill.	Yes	12,000	Mar. 27, 1903
Hillsboro, Ill.	Yes	11,000	Nov. 25, 1903
Hillsboro, Ore.	No	10,000	Nov. 3, 1913
Hinton, W.Va.	No	12,500	Apr. 8, 1907
Hobart, Ind.	No	16,000	Jan. 14, 1914
Hobart, Okla.	No	10,000	May 2, 1911
Holdredge, Neb.	No	8,500	Nov. 16, 1904
Hollister, Cal.	Yes	10,000	Apr. 16, 1910
Holliston, Mass.	Yes	10,000	Jan. 6, 1903
Hollywood, Cal.	No	10,000	Feb. 28, 1906
Homestead, Pa.	No	322,067	Nov. 27, 1896
Honea Path, S.C.	No	5,000	Mar. 7, 1907
Hood River, Ore.	No	17,500	Dec. 3, 1912
Hoopeston, Ill.	Yes	12,500	Feb. 12, 1903
Hopkinsville, Ky.	No	15,000	Dec. 3, 1912
Hoquiam, Wash.	Yes	20,000	Dec. 2, 1909
Hornell, N.Y.	Yes	25,000	Jan. 22, 1903
Hot Springs, S.D.	No	10,000	Mar. 9, 1907
Houghton, Mich.	Yes	15,000	Apr. 23, 1908
Houlton, Me.	No	10,000	Jan. 13, 1903
Houston, Miss.	No	6,000	Feb. 25, 1908
Houston, Tex. (2)	Yes	65,000	Oct. 28, 1899
Howell, Mich.	No	15,000	Jan. 9, 1902
Hudson, Mass.	Yes	12,500	Jan. 6, 1903
Hudson, Mich.	No	10,000	Mar. 27, 1903
Hudson, Wis.	No	12,000	Mar. 20, 1903
Humboldt, Iowa	No	10,000	Dec. 13, 1906
Huntington, Ind.	Yes	25,000	Dec. 21, 1901
Huntington, W.Va.	No	35,000	Dec. 30, 1901
Huntington Beach, Cal.	Yes	10,000	Feb. 13, 1913

LOCATION	WAS A PUBLIC LIBRARY ESTABLISHED BEFORE THE CARNEGIE GRANT?	AMOUNT OF CARNEGIE GRANT	DATE
Huntsville, Ala.	No	$ 12,500	May 8, 1914
Huntsville, Mo.	No	10,000	Apr. 13, 1914
Huron, S.D.	No	10,000	Dec. 13, 1907
Hutchinson, Kan.	Yes	32,000	Apr. 11, 1902
Hutchinson, Minn.	Yes	12,500	Apr. 13, 1903
Idaho Falls, Ida.	No	15,000	Mar. 13, 1909
Idaho Springs, Colo.	No	10,443	June 1, 1903
Imperial, Cal.	Yes	10,000	Jan. 23, 1909
Independence, Kan.	No	22,500	Nov. 24, 1905
Indianapolis, Ind. (5)	Yes	100,000	Jan. 19, 1909
Indianola, Iowa	Yes	12,000	Jan. 13, 1903
Inglewood, Cal.	Yes	10,000	Nov. 9, 1916
Iola, Kan.	No	15,000	Dec. 20, 1904
Iowa City, Iowa	Yes	35,000	Mar. 14, 1902
Iowa Falls, Iowa	Yes	10,000	Mar. 20, 1903
Iron Mountain, Mich.	No	17,500	Mar. 12, 1901
Ironwood, Mich.	No	17,000	Apr. 21, 1900
Ishpeming, Mich.	No	25,000	Mar. 12, 1901
Jackson, Mich.	Yes	70,000	Mar. 14, 1901
Jackson, Miss.	No	25,000	Jan. 31, 1911
Jackson, Tenn.	No	30,000	Feb. 13, 1901
Jacksonville, Fla.	No	55,000	Feb. 13, 1902
Jacksonville, Ill.	Yes	40,000	Feb. 6, 1901
Janesville, Minn.	Yes	5,000	May 2, 1911
Janesville, Wis.	Yes	30,000	Mar. 7, 1901
Jefferson, Iowa	Yes	10,000	Feb. 2, 1903
Jefferson, Tex.	No	10,000	May 15, 1906
Jefferson, Wis.	Yes	10,000	Jan. 23, 1911
Jefferson City, Mo.	No	25,000	Jan. 15, 1900
Jeffersonville, Ind.	Yes	16,000	Feb. 15, 1902
Jennings, La.	No	10,000	Mar. 9, 1907
Jerseyville, Ill.	Yes	12,000	Apr. 11, 1902
Johnson City, Tenn.	No	25,000	Dec. 23, 1902
Johnstown, N.Y.	No	25,000	Mar. 6, 1901
Johnstown, Pa.	No	55,332	May 9, 1890
Joplin, Mo.	No	60,000	July 16, 1901
Kalispell, Mont.	Yes	10,000	Dec. 21, 1901
Kansas City, Kan. (2)	No	100,000	July 4, 1901
Kaukauna, Wis.	Yes	12,000	Dec. 27, 1902

LOCATION	WAS A PUBLIC LIBRARY ESTABLISHED BEFORE THE CARNEGIE GRANT?	AMOUNT OF CARNEGIE GRANT	DATE
Kearney, Neb.	Yes	$ 12,000	Jan. 13, 1903
Kearny, N.J.	No	27,600	Jan. 16, 1906
Kendallville, Ind.	Yes	12,500	July 13, 1912
Kent, Ohio	Yes	11,500	Aug. 16, 1901
Kentland, Ind.	No	10,000	Dec. 2, 1909
Kenton, Ohio	Yes	20,000	Jan. 22, 1902
Kewanee, Ill.	Yes	25,000	Mar. 14, 1901
Kewanna, Ind.	Yes	8,000	May 21, 1913
Kilbourn, Wis.	Yes	6,000	Feb. 15, 1912
Kingman, Ind.	No	8,000	July 9, 1913
Kingman, Kan.	Yes	10,000	May 21, 1913
Kingston, N.Y.	Yes	30,000	Apr. 26, 1902
Kingstree, S.C.	No	6,000	Apr. 19, 1915
Kinsman, Ohio	Yes	7,000	Mar. 29, 1911
Kirklin, Ind.	Yes	7,500	May 8, 1914
Klamath Falls, Ore.	No	20,000	Mar. 14, 1913
Knightstown, Ind.	Yes	10,000	Apr. 25, 1911
Knoxville, Iowa	No	10,000	Nov. 30, 1910
Knoxville, Tenn.	No	10,000	May 15, 1916
Kokomo, Ind.	Yes	25,000	Mar. 14, 1902
Lackawanna, N.Y.	No	30,000	May 3, 1917
Ladysmith, Wis.	Yes	10,000	Feb. 6, 1907
LaGrande, Ore.	Yes	12,500	Apr. 2, 1913
LaGrange, Ill.	No	12,500	Mar. 27, 1903
LaGrange, Ind.	Yes	12,500	Nov. 9, 1916
LaHarpe, Ill.	Yes	5,000	Dec. 20, 1904
Lake Andes, S.D.	No	5,000	Nov. 21, 1911
Lake Charles, La.	No	10,000	Oct. 17, 1901
Lake City, Iowa	Yes	7,500	May 8, 1908
Lake City, Minn.	No	13,000	Nov. 7, 1917
Lakeport, Cal.	Yes	8,000	Nov. 17, 1914
Lakeville, Mass.	Yes	5,000	July 13, 1912
Lakewood, Ohio	No	44,600	May 2, 1907
Lakewood, N.J.	Yes	12,500	Feb. 3, 1917
Lamar, Colo.	No	12,000	Feb. 6, 1907
Lander, Wyo.	No	15,000	Nov. 27, 1906
Lansing, Mich.	Yes	35,000	Jan. 9, 1902
Lapeer, Mich.	No	13,750	Apr. 3, 1917
LaPorte, Ind.	Yes	27,500	Mar. 31, 1916
Laramie, Wyo.	Yes	20,000	Jan. 2, 1903

LOCATION	WAS A PUBLIC LIBRARY ESTABLISHED BEFORE THE CARNEGIE GRANT?	AMOUNT OF CARNEGIE GRANT	DATE
LaSalle, Ill.	No	$ 25,000	June 2, 1904
Las Vegas, N.M.	No	10,000	Mar. 14, 1902
Latta, S.C.	No	5,000	Apr. 3, 1912
Laurens, Iowa	Yes	3,800	Feb. 6, 1907
Lavonia, Ga.	No	5,000	Feb. 12, 1910
Lawrence, Kan.	Yes	27,500	May 31, 1902
Lawrenceburg, Ind.	Yes	11,000	Apr. 13, 1914
Lawrenceburg, Ky.	No	5,800	Apr. 6, 1908
Lawton, Okla.	Yes	20,000	Mar. 31, 1916
Leadville, Colo.	Yes	20,000	June 21, 1901
Leavenworth, Kan.	Yes	30,000	Jan. 16, 1900
Lebanon, Ind.	No	15,000	Jan. 6, 1903
Lebanon, N.H.	No	12,500	Dec. 13, 1907
Lebanon, Ohio	No	10,000	Feb. 20, 1903
Lee, Mass.	Yes	12,000	Nov. 25, 1903
Lehi, Utah	Yes	10,000	Nov. 7, 1917
LeMars, Iowa	Yes	12,500	Jan. 22, 1903
Leominster, Mass.	Yes	27,500	Dec. 24, 1906
Leon, Iowa	Yes	6,000	Apr. 20, 1905
Lewiston, Ida.	Yes	10,000	Mar. 27, 1903
Lewiston, Me.	No	60,000	Jan. 15, 1901
Lewistown, Ill.	Yes	5,400	Dec. 16, 1905
Lewistown, Mont.	Yes	10,000	Jan. 19, 1905
Lexington, Ky.	Yes	60,000	Jan. 16, 1902
Lexington, Neb.	No	10,000	Nov. 9, 1916
Liberty, Ind.	No	10,000	Jan. 6, 1915
Ligonier, Ind.	No	10,000	Apr. 8, 1907
Lima, Ohio	No	34,000	June 21, 1901
Lincoln, Cal.	Yes	6,000	Dec. 13, 1907
Lincoln, Ill.	Yes	25,000	Mar. 6, 1901
Lincoln, Kan.	Yes	6,000	Mar. 14, 1913
Lincoln, Neb. (2)	Yes	87,000	Dec. 20, 1899
Linden, Ind.	Yes	7,500	Jan. 28, 1916
Linton, Ind.	No	15,000	Dec. 24, 1907
Litchfield, Ill.	Yes	15,000	Jan. 6, 1903
Litchfield, Minn.	No	10,000	Feb. 12, 1903
Little Falls, Minn.	Yes	10,000	Mar. 14, 1902
Little Falls, N.J.	Yes	10,000	Apr. 3, 1917
Little Rock, Ark.	No	88,100	Mar. 24, 1906
Littleton, Colo.	Yes	8,000	Jan. 6, 1915
Littleton, N.H.	Yes	15,000	Mar. 14, 1902
Livermore, Cal.	Yes	10,000	Aug. 5, 1909

LOCATION	WAS A PUBLIC LIBRARY ESTABLISHED BEFORE THE CARNEGIE GRANT?	AMOUNT OF CARNEGIE GRANT	DATE
Livingston, Mont.	Yes	$ 10,000	Mar. 20, 1903
Lodi, Cal.	Yes	9,000	Dec. 13, 1907
Logan, Iowa	Yes	10,000	Dec. 3, 1915
Logansport, Ind.	Yes	35,000	Apr. 26, 1902
Lompoc, Cal.	Yes	10,000	Dec. 13, 1909
London, Ohio	Yes	10,000	Mar. 14, 1902
Long Beach, Cal.	Yes	30,000	Jan. 19, 1905
Long Branch, N. J.	Yes	30,000	Feb. 3, 1917
Longmont, Colo.	Yes	12,500	Dec. 13, 1907
Lorain, Ohio	Yes	30,000	July 8, 1902
Los Angeles, Cal. (6)	Yes	210,000	Jan. 31, 1911
Los Gatos, Cal.	No	10,400	Oct. 17, 1901
Louisiana, Mo.	No	10,000	Apr. 11, 1902
Louisville, Ky. (9)	No	450,000	Nov. 11, 1899
Loup City, Neb.	No	8,000	Mar. 31, 1916
Loveland, Colo.	Yes	10,000	May 2, 1907
Lowell, Ind.	No	12,500	Mar. 11, 1918
Ludington, Mich.	No	15,000	June 5, 1903
Lusk, Wyo.	Yes	11,000	May 8, 1914
Lu Verne, Minn.	Yes	10,000	Mar. 27, 1903
Lyndon, Kan.	No	8,000	Dec. 2, 1909
Lynn, Mass. (2)	Yes	50,000	Mar. 16, 1915
Lyons, Kan.	No	6,000	Jan. 5, 1909
McAlester, Okla.	Yes	25,000	Mar. 24, 1906
McCook, Neb.	Yes	11,000	Dec. 8, 1905
McKeesport, Pa.	No	50,000	Apr. 2, 1899
McMinnville, Ore.	Yes	10,000	Jan. 6, 1912
McPherson, Kan.	Yes	12,500	Mar. 16, 1915
Macomb, Ill.	Yes	15,000	Apr. 13, 1903
Madison, Me.	Yes	8,000	June 2, 1904
Madison, Minn.	No	8,000	Feb. 1, 1905
Madison, Neb.	Yes	6,000	Jan. 31, 1911
Madison, Ohio	No	10,000	June 1, 1915
Madison, S.D.	No	10,000	Jan. 16, 1906
Madison, Wis. (2)	Yes	90,000	Aug. 16, 1901
Malta, Mont.	No	15,000	Feb. 3, 1917
Malvern, Iowa	No	8,000	Sept. 29, 1915
Mancelona, Mich.	Yes	10,000	Jan. 5, 1916
Manchester, Iowa	Yes	10,000	Apr. 11, 1902
Manhattan, Kan.	No	10,000	Jan. 22, 1903
Manistee, Mich.	No	35,000	Apr. 26, 1902

226   APPENDIX B

LOCATION	WAS A PUBLIC LIBRARY ESTABLISHED BEFORE THE CARNEGIE GRANT?	AMOUNT OF CARNEGIE GRANT	DATE
Manitou, Colo.	No	$ 6,500	Dec. 13, 1909
Manitowoc, Wis.	Yes	25,000	Dec. 27, 1902
Mankato, Minn.	Yes	40,000	Feb. 6, 1901
Mansfield, Ohio	Yes	37,000	Mar. 27, 1903
Mansfield, Pa.	Yes	5,000	Mar. 29, 1911
Manti City, Utah	No	11,470	Mar. 21, 1910
Mapleton, Minn.	Yes	5,000	Mar. 25, 1905
Maquoketa, Iowa	No	12,500	Mar. 14, 1902
Marceline, Mo.	No	12,500	May 3, 1917
Marengo, Iowa	No	10,000	Mar. 27, 1903
Marietta, Ohio	Yes	30,000	Jan. 2, 1913
Marion, Ill.	No	18,000	Feb. 13, 1909
Marion, Ind.	Yes	50,000	Feb. 18, 1901
Marion, Iowa	No	11,500	Jan. 22, 1903
Marion, Ohio	Yes	30,000	Dec. 27, 1902
Marion, S.C.	Yes	7,500	Nov. 16, 1904
Marlboro, Mass.	Yes	30,000	Apr. 26, 1902
Marlette, Mich.	Yes	7,500	Apr. 16, 1918
Marseilles, Ill.	No	10,000	June 2, 1904
Marshall, Minn.	Yes	10,000	Feb. 12, 1903
Marshalltown, Iowa	Yes	30,000	Dec. 30, 1901
Marshfield, Mo.	No	5,000	Apr. 8, 1910
Marshfield, Ore.	Yes	12,500	Apr. 28, 1913
Martinsville, Ind.	No	12,500	Feb. 13, 1906
Marysville, Ohio	No	10,000	Nov. 27, 1906
Maryville, Mo.	No	14,000	Dec. 29, 1903
Mason City, Iowa	Yes	20,000	Apr. 11, 1902
Mattoon, Ill.	Yes	25,000	June 21, 1901
Maumee, Ohio	No	10,000	Sept. 29, 1915
Maywood, Ill.	Yes	12,500	Aug. 19, 1904
Medford, Ore.	Yes	20,000	Jan. 6, 1911
Medford, Wis.	Yes	6,000	May 21, 1913
Melrose, Mass.	Yes	25,000	Dec. 30, 1901
Memphis, Tex.	No	10,000	Jan. 27, 1912
Mendon, Mich.	Yes	10,000	Apr. 11, 1905
Mendota, Ill.	Yes	10,000	Jan. 14, 1904
Meridian, Miss. (2)	No	38,000	Dec. 2, 1904
Merom, Ind.	No	10,000	Nov. 9, 1916
Merrill, Wis.	Yes	17,500	Dec. 13, 1907
Metropolis, Ill.	Yes	9,000	Jan. 27, 1912
Mexico, Mo.	No	12,500	Apr. 30, 1912
Miami, Okla.	No	10,000	May 15, 1916

LOCATION	WAS A PUBLIC LIBRARY ESTABLISHED BEFORE THE CARNEGIE GRANT?	AMOUNT OF CARNEGIE GRANT	DATE
Miamisburg, Ohio	No	$ 12,500	Dec. 24, 1908
Middleport, Ohio	Yes	8,100	Jan. 31, 1911
Middlesboro, Ky.	No	15,000	Nov. 20, 1908
Middletown, Ohio	No	25,000	Apr. 26, 1902
Midland, Mich.	Yes	12,500	Feb. 3, 1917
Midland, Pa.	No	20,000	May 8, 1914
Milan, Ohio	Yes	8,000	Jan. 6, 1911
Milbank, S.D.	Yes	7,000	Apr. 11, 1905
Miles City, Mont.	No	10,000	July 16, 1901
Milford, Ill.	Yes	7,000	Dec. 30, 1904
Milford Junction, Ind.	Yes	10,000	Dec. 3, 1915
Millbury, Mass.	Yes	12,500	Mar. 16, 1915
Mill Valley, Cal.	Yes	10,000	Jan. 18, 1910
Milo, Me.	Yes	8,500	Sept. 30, 1908
Milton, Ore.	No	7,500	Jan. 6, 1915
Minneapolis, Minn. (4)	Yes	125,000	Apr. 3, 1912
Minot, N.D.	Yes	15,000	Aug. 29, 1908
Mishawaka, Ind.	Yes	30,000	Jan. 6, 1915
Misscula, Mont.	Yes	21,500	Jan. 13, 1903
Missouri Valley, Iowa	Yes	10,000	Feb. 1, 1909
Mitchell, Ind.	No	15,000	May 8, 1914
Mitchell, S.D.	No	12,000	Jan. 10, 1902
Moberly, Mo.	Yes	20,000	Apr. 26, 1902
Moline, Ill.	Yes	40,000	Aug. 16, 1901
Monon, Ind.	No	10,000	Dec. 8, 1913
Monroe City, Mo.	No	7,500	May 15, 1916
Monrovia, Cal.	Yes	10,000	Jan. 19, 1905
Montclair, N.J. (2)	Yes	60,000	Mar. 8, 1901
Monterey, Cal.	Yes	10,000	Dec. 24, 1907
Monterey, Ind.	No	5,000	Apr. 3, 1917
Montevideo, Minn.	Yes	10,000	Dec. 16, 1905
Monte Vista, Colo.	No	10,000	May 15, 1916
Montezuma, Ga.	No	10,000	Mar. 24, 1906
Montezuma, Iowa	No	8,000	May 3, 1917
Montgomery, Ala.	No	50,000	Feb. 13, 1901
Monticello, Ind.	Yes	10,000	Jan. 16, 1906
Monticello, Iowa	No	10,500	Feb. 12, 1903
Montpelier, Ind.	Yes	10,000	Feb. 21, 1907
Mooresville, Ind.	No	10,000	Jan. 2, 1913
Moorhead, Minn.	No	12,000	Feb. 20, 1904
Morrilton, Ark.	No	10,000	Sept. 29, 1915
Morris, Ill.	No	12,500	Jan. 6, 1912

LOCATION	WAS A PUBLIC LIBRARY ESTABLISHED BEFORE THE CARNEGIE GRANT?	AMOUNT OF CARNEGIE GRANT	DATE
Morris, Minn.	Yes	$ 10,000	Dec. 4, 1903
Morristown, Vt.	Yes	7,000	Mar. 18, 1911
Moscow, Ida.	No	10,000	June 2, 1904
Moultrie, Ga.	No	10,000	Dec. 3, 1906
Mound Bayou, Miss.	No	4,000	Feb. 13, 1909
Mountain Home, Ida.	Yes	6,000	Dec. 13, 1907
Mountain Iron, Minn.	No	8,000	Jan. 14, 1914
Mount Ayr, Iowa	No	8,000	Sept. 29, 1915
Mount Carmel, Ill.	No	15,000	Apr. 10, 1909
Mount Carroll, Ill.	No	11,000	Jan. 19, 1905
Mount Clemens, Mich.	Yes	17,000	Mar. 14, 1902
Mount Pleasant, Iowa	Yes	12,500	Jan. 13, 1903
Mount Pleasant, Utah	Yes	10,000	May 15, 1916
Mount Sterling, Ohio	No	10,000	Jan. 23, 1911
Mount Vernon, Ill.	Yes	15,000	Mar. 27, 1903
Mount Vernon, Ind.	No	14,000	Dec. 27, 1902
Mount Vernon, N.Y.	Yes	72,000	Feb. 19, 1901
Muncie, Ind.	No	55,000	Mar. 8, 1901
Murphy, N.C.	No	7,500	May 15, 1916
Murray City, Utah	Yes	10,000	Jan. 6, 1911
Muskogee, Okla.	Yes	60,000	Aug. 30, 1910
Nampa, Ida.	Yes	10,500	Jan. 18, 1907
Napoleon, Ohio	Yes	10,000	Mar. 29, 1911
Nashua, Iowa	Yes	5,690	Jan. 19, 1905
Nashville, Tenn. (4)	Yes	175,000	July 23, 1901
National City, Cal.	Yes	10,000	Feb. 13, 1909
Needham, Mass.	Yes	10,000	Jan. 13, 1903
Neenah, Wis.	Yes	12,500	Oct. 3, 1901
Neillsville, Wis.	Yes	10,000	Nov. 3, 1913
Neligh, Neb.	Yes	5,000	Dec. 14, 1908
Nevada, Mo.	No	17,500	June 1, 1915
Nevada City, Cal.	Yes	10,000	Mar. 20, 1904
New Albany, Ind.	Yes	40,000	Mar. 14, 1902
Newaygo, Mich.	No	5,000	Dec. 8, 1913
Newberg, Ore.	Yes	10,000	Mar. 18, 1911
New Brunswick, N.J.	Yes	52,500	Mar. 14, 1902
Newburgh, Ind.	Yes	10,000	May 15, 1916
New Carlisle, Ind.	No	9,000	Sept. 14, 1917
New Castle, Ind.	Yes	20,000	July 9, 1913
Newcastle, Wyo.	No	12,500	Feb. 20, 1911
New Hampton, Iowa	No	10,000	Aug. 15, 1908

LOCATION	WAS A PUBLIC LIBRARY ESTABLISHED BEFORE THE CARNEGIE GRANT?	AMOUNT OF CARNEGIE GRANT	DATE
New Haven, Conn. (3)	Yes	$ 60,000	Mar. 14, 1913
New London, Ohio	No	10,000	June 11, 1914
New London, Wis.	Yes	10,000	Nov. 25, 1903
Newman, Cal.	No	8,000	Nov. 17, 1914
New Marlboro, Mass.	Yes	5,000	Feb. 3, 1917
Newnan, Ga.	No	10,000	Dec. 30, 1901
New Orleans, La. (6)	Yes	350,000	Dec. 29, 1902
Newport, Ky.	Yes	26,500	Oct. 30, 1899
New Rochelle, N.Y.	Yes	60,000	Mar. 14, 1901
Newton, Iowa	Yes	10,000	Jan. 22, 1902
Newton, Kan.	Yes	16,000	Mar. 14, 1902
New York, N.Y. (66)	Yes	5,202,621	Dec. 8, 1899
Niagara Falls, N.Y.	Yes	50,000	Mar. 8, 1901
Niles, Mich.	No	15,000	Jan. 22, 1903
Noblesville, Ind.	Yes	12,500	Dec. 29, 1903
Norfolk, Neb.	Yes	10,000	Dec. 13, 1907
Norfolk, Va. (2)	Yes	70,000	Mar. 8, 1901
North Bend, Neb.	Yes	7,500	Dec. 7, 1911
North Bessemer, Pa.	No	20,600	May 1, 1901
Northfield, Minn.	Yes	10,000	Jan. 8, 1908
North Judson, Ind.	No	10,000	Sept. 14, 1917
North Manchester, Ind.	Yes	10,000	Apr. 8, 1910
North Platte, Neb.	No	12,000	Apr. 8, 1910
Northport, N.Y.	Yes	10,000	May 21, 1913
North Tonawanda, N.Y.	Yes	20,000	Dec. 27, 1902
North Vernon, Ind.	No	20,000	Feb. 8, 1918
North Yakima, Wash.	Yes	15,000	Dec. 14, 1903
Norwalk, Conn.	Yes	20,000	Aug. 16, 1901
Norwalk, Ohio	No	15,000	Feb. 2, 1903
Norwood, Ohio	No	23,000	Nov. 3, 1904
Nutley, N.J.	Yes	20,000	Feb. 13, 1913
Nyack, N.Y.	Yes	15,000	Dec. 21, 1901
Oakdale, Cal.	Yes	7,000	May 15, 1916
Oakland, Cal. (5)	Yes	190,000	Aug. 23, 1899
Oakland, Me.	Yes	10,000	Feb. 15, 1912
Oakmont, Pa.	No	25,000	Jan. 24, 1899
Ocala, Fla.	No	10,000	Feb. 21, 1907
Odebolt, Iowa	Yes	4,000	Mar. 8, 1904
Ogden, Utah	Yes	25,000	Mar. 9, 1901
Oil City, Pa.	No	44,000	Apr. 12, 1900
Oklahoma City, Okla.	No	60,000	Oct. 27, 1899

LOCATION	WAS A PUBLIC LIBRARY ESTABLISHED BEFORE THE CARNEGIE GRANT?	AMOUNT OF CARNEGIE GRANT	DATE
Okolona, Miss.	No	$ 7,500	Mar. 11, 1914
Olathe, Kan.	Yes	10,000	Dec. 24, 1909
Old Town, Me.	Yes	10,000	Feb. 12, 1903
Olean, N.Y.	No	40,000	Nov. 27, 1906
Olney, Ill.	Yes	11,500	Jan. 6, 1903
Olympia, Wash.	No	25,000	Mar. 20, 1903
Onarga, Ill.	Yes	5,000	Dec. 13, 1906
Onawa, Iowa	Yes	10,000	Dec. 13, 1907
O'Neill, Neb.	No	10,000	May 17, 1912
Ontario, Cal.	Yes	12,000	June 8, 1905
Ontario, Ore.	Yes	7,500	Dec. 3, 1912
Orange, Cal.	Yes	10,000	Mar. 9, 1907
Oregon, Ill.	Yes	10,000	Apr. 20, 1905
Oregon City, Ore.	Yes	12,500	Dec. 23, 1911
Orland, Cal.	No	8,000	Nov. 3, 1913
Orleans, Ind.	Yes	10,000	Jan. 6, 1915
Orosi, Cal.	No	3,000	Sept. 14, 1917
Oroville, Cal.	Yes	10,000	May 2, 1911
Ortonville, Minn.	Yes	10,000	Aug. 11, 1913
Osage, Iowa	Yes	10,000	Mar. 27, 1905
Osawatomie, Kan.	Yes	7,500	Apr. 16, 1910
Osborne, Kan.	No	6,000	Jan. 27, 1912
Osceola, Iowa	Yes	11,000	Dec. 14, 1908
Osgood, Ind.	Yes	9,000	Jan. 9, 1913
Oskaloosa, Iowa	Yes	22,000	Mar. 14, 1902
Ossining, N.Y.	Yes	26,000	Dec. 23, 1911
Oswego, Kan.	Yes	5,000	Dec. 2, 1909
Ottawa, Kan.	Yes	15,000	Jan. 9, 1902
Ottumwa, Iowa	Yes	50,000	Feb. 16, 1900
Owensboro, Ky.	No	30,000	Nov. 18, 1903
Owensville, Ind.	No	12,500	Dec. 3, 1915
Owosso, Mich.	Yes	20,000	Apr. 2, 1913
Oxford, Ind.	No	8,000	Jan. 14, 1914
Oxnard, Cal.	No	12,000	Feb. 13, 1906
Pacific Grove, Cal.	Yes	10,000	Mar. 12, 1906
Paducah, Ky.	No	35,000	Oct. 13, 1901
Palestine, Tex.	Yes	15,000	Sept. 27, 1912
Palmetto, Fla.	No	10,000	Jan. 14, 1914
Palo Alto, Cal.	Yes	10,000	Feb. 20, 1903
Pana, Ill.	Yes	14,000	Jan. 31, 1911
Panguitch, Utah	Yes	6,000	Dec. 3, 1915

LOCATION	WAS A PUBLIC LIBRARY ESTABLISHED BEFORE THE CARNEGIE GRANT?	AMOUNT OF CARNEGIE GRANT	DATE
Paoli, Ind.	Yes	$ 8,000	Jan. 31, 1913
Paris, Ill.	Yes	18,000	Mar. 14, 1902
Paris, Ky.	No	12,000	Jan. 2, 1903
Parkersburg, W.Va.	Yes	34,000	Dec. 29, 1903
Park Rapids, Minn.	Yes	5,000	May 8, 1908
Park Ridge, Ill.	No	7,500	Dec. 2, 1909
Parowan, Utah	Yes	6,000	Jan. 31, 1913
Parsons, Kan.	Yes	22,500	Nov. 14, 1907
Pasco, Wash.	No	10,000	Dec. 13, 1909
Paso Robles, Cal.	Yes	10,000	Dec. 13, 1906
Patchogue, N.Y.	Yes	15,000	Jan. 8, 1905
Paterson, Cal.	No	3,000	June 6, 1917
Paulding, Ohio	Yes	40,000	July 13, 1912
Pawnee City, Neb.	No	7,000	Dec. 30, 1904
Paw Paw, Mich.	No	10,000	Apr. 3, 1917
Paxton, Ill.	No	10,000	Mar. 20, 1903
Peabody, Kan.	Yes	10,000	Mar. 20, 1903
Pecos, Tex.	No	9,000	June 25, 1911
Pekin, Ill.	Yes	17,500	Oct. 8, 1900
Pelham, Ga.	No	10,000	Dec. 13, 1906
Pella, Iowa	No	11,000	Nov. 24, 1905
Pendleton, Ind.	No	8,000	Apr. 25, 1911
Pendleton, Ore.	Yes	25,000	Jan. 6, 1915
Penn Yan, N.Y.	Yes	10,000	Jan. 6, 1903
Peoria, Ill.	Yes	20,000	Dec. 13, 1909
Perry, Iowa	No	10,600	Jan. 13, 1903
Perry, N.Y.	No	12,000	July 13, 1912
Perry, Okla.	Yes	10,000	Feb. 13, 1909
Perth Amboy, N.J.	Yes	50,450	Mar. 8, 1901
Peru, Ill.	No	15,000	Apr. 8, 1910
Peru, Ind.	Yes	25,000	Mar. 8, 1901
Petaluma, Cal.	Yes	12,500	Jan. 13, 1903
Petersburg, Ill.	Yes	8,000	Dec. 13, 1906
Petosky, Mich.	Yes	12,500	Apr. 8, 1907
Philadelphia, Pa. (25)	Yes	1,500,000	Jan. 5, 1903
Phoenix, Ariz.	Yes	25,000	Apr. 26, 1902
Phoenixville, Pa.	Yes	20,000	Mar. 9, 1901
Pickerington, Ohio	Yes	10,000	Jan. 27, 1912
Pierce, Neb.	No	4,000	Mar. 29, 1911
Pierceton, Ind.	No	10,000	Dec. 3, 1915
Pierre, S.D.	No	12,500	Mar. 20, 1903
Pipestone, Minn.	Yes	10,000	Mar. 22, 1903

LOCATION	WAS A PUBLIC LIBRARY ESTABLISHED BEFORE THE CARNEGIE GRANT?	AMOUNT OF CARNEGIE GRANT	DATE
Pittsburg, Kan.	Yes	$ 40,000	June 25, 1909
Pittsburg, Tex.	No	5,000	Apr. 30, 1898
Pittsburgh, Pa. (9)	Yes	1,160,614	Feb. 6, 1890
Pittsfield, Ill.	Yes	7,500	Nov. 24, 1905
Pittsfield, Me.	Yes	10,000	Mar. 20, 1903
Plainfield, Ind.	Yes	9,000	Nov. 21, 1911
Plainfield, N.J.	Yes	50,000	Feb. 7, 1911
Plainview, Neb.	Yes	6,000	Dec. 3, 1915
Plainville, Kan.	No	5,000	Feb. 20, 1911
Plano, Ill.	Yes	10,250	Dec. 20, 1904
Platteville, Wis.	Yes	12,500	Jan. 14, 1914
Plattsmouth, Neb.	Yes	12,500	June 1, 1915
Plymouth, Ind.	Yes	15,000	Jan. 6, 1911
Plymouth, Wis.	Yes	10,000	Apr. 6, 1908
Pocatello, Ida.	No	12,000	Nov. 14, 1906
Polo, Ill.	Yes	10,000	Apr. 13, 1903
Pomeroy, Ohio	Yes	10,000	Jan. 27, 1912
Pomona, Cal.	Yes	25,000	Jan. 23, 1902
Ponca, Neb.	Yes	4,500	Apr. 25, 1911
Ponca City, Okla.	No	6,500	Aug. 29, 1908
Port Angeles, Wash.	No	12,500	Nov. 9, 1916
Porterville, Cal.	Yes	10,000	Feb. 6, 1907
Port Huron, Mich.	Yes	45,000	Feb. 4, 1902
Port Jervis, N.Y.	Yes	30,000	Feb. 21, 1901
Portland, Ind.	Yes	15,000	Mar. 12, 1901
Portland, Mich.	Yes	10,000	Mar. 25, 1905
Portland, Ore. (7)	Yes	165,000	Feb. 21, 1901
Portsmouth, Ohio	Yes	50,000	July 8, 1901
Port Townsend, Wash.	Yes	12,500	July 13, 1912
Poseyville, Ind.	Yes	5,500	Jan. 2, 1904
Pottsville, Pa.	Yes	45,000	Jan. 28, 1916
Prescott, Ariz.	No	4,000	July 4, 1899
Presque Isle, Me.	Yes	10,000	May 15, 1906
Preston, Ida.	No	10,000	Mar. 11, 1914
Preston, Minn.	Yes	8,000	Dec. 2, 1909
Price, Utah	Yes	10,000	Jan. 2, 1913
Princeton, Ind.	Yes	15,000	Jan. 22, 1903
Prosser, Wash.	Yes	5,000	Apr. 28, 1909
Provo City, Utah	Yes	17,500	Apr. 8, 1907
Pueblo, Colo.	Yes	70,000	Feb. 4, 1902
Puyallup, Wash.	Yes	12,500	Feb. 15, 1912

LOCATION	WAS A PUBLIC LIBRARY ESTABLISHED BEFORE THE CARNEGIE GRANT?	AMOUNT OF CARNEGIE GRANT	DATE
Racine, Wis. (2)	Yes	$ 60,000	July 16, 1901
Randolph, Neb.	No	6,000	Nov. 9, 1916
Rapid City, S.D.	Yes	12,500	Mar. 11, 1914
Raton, N.M.	No	12,000	Jan. 23, 1911
Ravenna, Neb.	No	7,500	Nov. 9, 1916
Raymond, N.H.	Yes	2,000	May 15, 1906
Reading, Mass.	Yes	15,000	Jan. 2, 1902
Reading, Pa.	Yes	111,180	Apr. 16, 1910
Redding, Cal.	Yes	10,000	Mar. 20, 1903
Redfield, S.D.	No	10,000	Mar. 14, 1902
Red Lodge, Mont.	No	15,000	June 11, 1914
Red Oak, Iowa	No	12,500	Nov. 27, 1906
Red Wing, Minn.	Yes	17,000	Dec. 14, 1901
Redwood City, Cal.	Yes	16,000	Feb. 20, 1904
Redwood Falls, Minn.	No	10,000	Nov. 25, 1903
Reedsburg, Wis.	Yes	10,000	Jan. 23, 1911
Reinbeck, Iowa	No	6,000	Mar. 31, 1916
Remington, Ind.	Yes	10,000	Mar. 16, 1915
Reno, Nev.	No	15,000	Mar. 14, 1902
Rensselaer, Ind.	Yes	12,000	Jan. 13, 1903
Renton, Wash.	No	10,000	May 21, 1913
Revere, Mass.	Yes	20,000	Oct. 3, 1901
Rhinelander, Wis.	Yes	15,000	Jan. 2, 1903
Rice Lake, Wis.	Yes	10,000	Dec. 22, 1903
Richfield, Utah	No	10,000	Jan. 6, 1911
Richland Center, Wis.	Yes	10,000	Dec. 22, 1903
Richmond, Cal.	No	17,500	Jan. 14, 1909
Richmond, Utah	No	8,000	Sept. 27, 1912
Ridge Farm, Ill.	Yes	9,000	Apr. 28, 1909
Ridley Park, Pa.	Yes	10,000	June 24, 1911
Ripley, Ohio	No	10,000	Jan. 2, 1913
Ripon, Wis.	Yes	12,000	Apr. 11, 1902
Rising Sun, Ind.	No	10,000	Dec. 3, 1915
Ritzville, Wash.	No	10,500	Dec. 24, 1906
Riverbank, Cal.	No	3,000	June 6, 1917
Riverside, Cal.	Yes	52,500	Aug. 16, 1901
Roachdale, Ind.	Yes	10,000	Jan. 31, 1913
Roann, Ind.	No	10,000	June 11, 1914
Robinson, Ill.	No	11,000	Aug. 6, 1904
Rochelle, Ill.	Yes	10,000	Apr. 25, 1911
Rochester, Ind.	Yes	15,000	Dec. 20, 1904

LOCATION	WAS A PUBLIC LIBRARY ESTABLISHED BEFORE THE CARNEGIE GRANT?	AMOUNT OF CARNEGIE GRANT	DATE
Rochester, N.H.	Yes	$ 20,000	Dec. 22, 1903
Rockford, Ill.	Yes	70,000	Mar. 6, 1901
Rockford, Ohio	Yes	10,000	Jan. 18, 1910
Rockingham, Vt.	Yes	15,000	June 1, 1903
Rockland, Me.	Yes	20,000	Apr. 11, 1902
Rockland, Mass.	Yes	12,500	Jan. 13, 1903
Rockport, Ind.	No	17,000	Jan. 5, 1916
Rockport, Mass.	Yes	10,000	June 18, 1903
Rock Springs, Wyo.	No	12,500	Dec. 13, 1907
Rockville, Ind.	No	12,500	Apr. 13, 1914
Rockville Centre, N.Y.	Yes	10,000	Dec. 14, 1903
Rockwell City, Iowa	No	8,000	Feb. 10, 1908
Rocky Ford, Colo.	Yes	10,000	Dec. 24, 1907
Rome, Ga.	No	15,000	Dec. 24, 1909
Roseville, Cal.	No	10,000	Apr. 25, 1911
Roswell, N.M.	No	10,000	June 1, 1903
Royal Center, Ind.	No	10,000	Sept. 25, 1914
Rumford, Me.	No	10,000	Jan. 22, 1903
Rushville, Ill.	No	7,500	Feb. 13, 1906
Russell, Kan.	Yes	5,800	June 8, 1905
Rutherford College, N.C.	No	2,500	Feb. 21, 1907
Sac City, Iowa	Yes	8,000	Jan. 6, 1911
Sacramento, Cal.	Yes	100,000	Feb. 26, 1914
St. Charles, Ill.	Yes	12,500	Dec. 13, 1906
St. Cloud, Minn.	Yes	25,000	Feb. 16, 1901
St. George, Utah	Yes	8,000	Jan. 31, 1913
St. Helena, Cal.	Yes	8,362	Dec. 13, 1906
St. Joseph, Mich.	Yes	13,500	Dec. 27, 1902
St. Joseph, Mo. (2)	Yes	50,000	Feb. 13, 1901
St. Louis, Mo. (7)	Yes	1,000,000	Mar. 12, 1901
St. Paul, Minn. (3)	Yes	75,000	May 8, 1914
St. Peter, Minn.	Yes	10,000	Jan. 6, 1903
St. Petersburg, Fla.	Yes	17,500	July 9, 1913
Salamanca, N.Y.	No	17,500	Feb. 3, 1917
Salem, Ind.	Yes	16,000	Feb. 20, 1904
Salem, Ohio	Yes	20,000	Jan. 22, 1903
Salem, Ore.	Yes	27,500	Dec. 24, 1907
Salida, Colo.	No	9,000	Dec. 23, 1905
Salina, Kan.	Yes	15,000	Feb. 15, 1902
Salinas, Cal.	Yes	10,000	Mar. 9, 1907
Salt Lake City, Utah	Yes	25,000	Mar. 31, 1916

LOCATION	WAS A PUBLIC LIBRARY ESTABLISHED BEFORE THE CARNEGIE GRANT?	AMOUNT OF CARNEGIE GRANT	DATE
San Anselmo, Cal.	No	$ 10,000	Jan. 14, 1914
San Antonio, Tex.	No	70,000	Jan. 6, 1900
San Bernardino, Cal.	Yes	27,600	Mar. 14, 1902
Sanborn, Iowa	Yes	4,000	Mar. 29, 1911
San Diego, Cal.	Yes	60,000	July 7, 1899
Sandusky, Ohio	Yes	50,000	Oct. 7, 1899
San Francisco, Cal. (8)	Yes	750,000	June 20, 1901
Sanger, Cal.	Yes	10,000	Nov. 17, 1914
San Jose, Cal. (2)	Yes	57,000	Mar. 8, 1901
San Leandro, Cal.	Yes	12,000	Dec. 13, 1907
San Luis Obispo, Cal.	Yes	10,000	Feb. 12, 1903
San Mateo, Cal.	Yes	12,500	Apr. 20, 1905
San Pedro, Cal.	Yes	10,375	Mar. 25, 1905
San Rafael, Cal.	Yes	25,000	Dec. 20, 1904
Santa Ana, Cal.	Yes	15,000	Jan. 22, 1902
Santa Barbara, Cal.	Yes	50,000	May 8, 1914
Santa Cruz, Cal. (4)	Yes	29,000	Feb. 15, 1902
Santa Maria, Cal.	No	10,000	Jan. 8, 1908
Santa Monica, Cal. (2)	Yes	25,000	Apr. 13, 1903
Santa Rosa, Cal.	Yes	26,900	Mar. 14, 1902
Sapulpa, Okla.	No	25,000	Jan. 28, 1916
Saugerties, N.Y.	Yes	12,500	Sept. 25, 1914
Saugus, Mass.	Yes	17,000	Nov. 9, 1916
Sauk Center, Minn.	Yes	11,000	Feb. 12, 1903
Sault Ste. Marie, Mich.	No	30,000	Feb. 6, 1901
Savanna, Ill.	Yes	11,350	Apr. 23, 1903
Savannah, Ga. (2)	No	87,000	Aug. 17, 1910
Schenectady, N.Y.	Yes	50,000	Feb. 13, 1901
Schuyler, Neb.	Yes	9,000	Mar. 29, 1911
Scottsbluff, Neb.	No	15,000	June 6, 1917
Scottsburg, Ind.	No	12,500	Nov. 22, 1917
Seattle, Wash. (7)	Yes	430,000	Jan. 6, 1901
Sebastopol, Cal.	No	7,500	Nov. 21, 1911
Sedalia, Mo.	Yes	50,000	Oct. 28, 1899
Sedro-Woolley, Wash.	Yes	10,000	July 9, 1913
Selma, Ala.	No	11,800	Apr. 13, 1903
Selma, Cal.	No	6,000	Mar. 14, 1905
Seward, Neb.	Yes	8,000	Apr. 3, 1912
Seymour, Ind.	Yes	10,000	Feb. 2, 1903
Sharon, Mass.	Yes	10,000	Mar. 14, 1913
Shawano, Wis.	Yes	10,000	June 11, 1914
Shawnee, Okla.	Yes	15,500	June 2, 1904

236   APPENDIX B

LOCATION	WAS A PUBLIC LIBRARY ESTABLISHED BEFORE THE CARNEGIE GRANT?	AMOUNT OF CARNEGIE GRANT	DATE
Sheboygan, Wis.	Yes	$ 35,000	Mar. 6, 1901
Sheffield, Ill.	Yes	4,000	May 2, 1911
Shelbina, Mo.	No	10,000	Nov. 9, 1916
Shelbyville, Ill.	Yes	10,000	Jan. 22, 1903
Shelbyville, Ind.	Yes	20,000	Dec. 30, 1901
Shelbyville, Ky.	Yes	10,000	Dec. 30, 1901
Sheldon, Ill.	Yes	9,000	June 1, 1915
Sheldon, Iowa	Yes	10,000	Feb. 28, 1906
Shelton, Neb.	Yes	9,000	Apr. 2, 1913
Shenandoah, Iowa	No	10,000	Jan. 22, 1903
Sheridan, Ind.	Yes	12,500	Dec. 7, 1911
Sheridan, Wyo.	Yes	12,500	Mar. 18, 1904
Sherman, Tex.	Yes	20,000	Apr. 3, 1912
Shoals, Ind.	Yes	10,000	Mar. 14, 1913
Sibley, Iowa	Yes	10,000	Sept. 29, 1915
Sidney, Neb.	Yes	6,500	July 9, 1913
Sigourney, Iowa	No	10,000	Jan. 2, 1913
Silverton, Colo.	Yes	12,000	Jan. 19, 1905
Sioux City, Iowa (2)	Yes	85,000	Apr. 8, 1911
Sioux Falls, S.D.	Yes	30,000	Jan. 24, 1901
Sisseton, S.D.	Yes	7,500	June 11, 1914
Smithfield, Utah	Yes	12,000	Jan. 7, 1918
Snohomish, Wash.	Yes	10,000	Mar. 13, 1909
Solvay, N.Y.	Yes	10,000	Jan. 13, 1903
Somerset, Ky.	No	10,000	Dec. 8, 1905
Somerville, Mass. (3)	Yes	123,000	Apr. 8, 1907
Sonoma, Cal.	Yes	6,000	Apr. 25, 1911
South Bend, Wash.	Yes	10,000	Jan. 20, 1908
South Brooklyn, Ohio	No	11,800	Mar. 27, 1903
South Hadley, Mass.	Yes	10,000	Dec. 8, 1905
South Haven, Mich.	Yes	12,500	Dec. 20, 1904
South Milwaukee, Wis.	Yes	15,000	Sept. 29, 1915
South Norwalk, Conn.	Yes	20,000	Apr. 23, 1908
South Omaha, Neb.	Yes	50,000	June 21, 1901
South Pasadena, Cal.	Yes	18,600	Dec. 13, 1906
South San Francisco, Cal.	No	10,000	May 8, 1914
Sparta, Mich.	No	10,000	Mar. 31, 1916
Sparta, Wis.	Yes	12,000	Feb. 4, 1902
Spartanburg, S.C.	No	15,000	June 23, 1903
Spencer, Ind.	Yes	10,000	Jan. 6, 1911
Spencer, Iowa	Yes	10,000	Jan. 13, 1903
Spencer, Neb.	Yes	8,000	Dec. 3, 1915

List of Communities Receiving Carnegie Grants   237

LOCATION	WAS A PUBLIC LIBRARY ESTABLISHED BEFORE THE CARNEGIE GRANT?	AMOUNT OF CARNEGIE GRANT	DATE
Spirit Lake, Iowa	No	$ 8,000	Feb. 1, 1905
Spokane, Wash. (4)	Yes	155,000	Mar. 27, 1903
Springfield, Ill.	Yes	75,000	Mar. 8, 1901
Springfield, Mass. (4)	Yes	260,000	Mar. 30, 1905
Springfield, Mo.	Yes	50,000	Oct. 4, 1901
Spring Valley, Ill.	Yes	15,000	Jan. 27, 1912
Spring Valley, Minn.	Yes	8,000	Mar. 27, 1903
Springville, Utah	Yes	10,000	Nov. 9, 1916
Stambaugh, Mich.	Yes	12,500	Apr. 13, 1914
Stamford, Tex.	No	15,000	June 29, 1908
Stanton, Neb.	Yes	8,000	Apr. 13, 1914
Sterling, Colo.	No	12,500	Dec. 3, 1915
Sterling, Ill.	Yes	17,500	Jan. 2, 1903
Sterling, Kan.	No	10,000	Nov. 9, 1916
Steubenville, Ohio	No	62,000	June 30, 1899
Stevens Point, Wis.	Yes	21,859	Apr. 26, 1902
Stillwater, Minn.	Yes	27,500	July 3, 1901
Stockton, Kan.	No	5,000	Dec. 24, 1909
Stoneham, Mass.	Yes	15,000	Jan. 13, 1903
Storm Lake, Iowa	No	10,000	Dec. 4, 1903
Stoughton, Wis.	Yes	13,000	Dec. 23, 1905
Streator, Ill.	Yes	35,000	Feb. 19, 1901
Stromsburg, Neb.	No	7,500	Mar. 16, 1915
Stuart, Iowa	Yes	6,500	Nov. 14, 1906
Sturgeon Bay, Wis.	Yes	12,500	Apr. 25, 1911
Sturgis, Mich.	Yes	10,000	Dec. 13, 1907
Sullivan, Ind.	Yes	11,000	Jan. 13, 1903
Sulphur Springs, Tex.	No	12,000	Apr. 10, 1909
Summit, N.J.	Yes	21,000	Feb. 1, 1909
Sumter, S.C.	Yes	10,000	Sept. 29, 1915
Sunnyside, Wash.	No	5,000	Apr. 16, 1910
Superior, Neb.	No	7,000	Dec. 24, 1907
Superior, Wis. (2)	Yes	70,000	Mar. 7, 1901
Sutton, Neb.	Yes	5,700	Feb. 1, 1909
Swissvale Boro, Pa.	No	25,000	Nov. 17, 1914
Sycamore, Ill.	Yes	12,000	Jan. 13, 1903
Syracuse, Ind.	Yes	10,000	Feb. 3, 1917
Syracuse, N.Y.	Yes	200,000	Jan. 15, 1901
Tacoma, Wash.	Yes	75,000	Mar. 8, 1901
Tahlequah, Okla.	No	10,000	Mar. 25, 1905
Talladega, Ala.	No	12,500	Feb. 13, 1906

238   APPENDIX B

LOCATION	WAS A PUBLIC LIBRARY ESTABLISHED BEFORE THE CARNEGIE GRANT?	AMOUNT OF CARNEGIE GRANT	DATE
Tama, Iowa	No	$ 8,500	Aug. 30, 1904
Tampa, Fla.	No	50,000	Dec. 30, 1901
Taunton, Mass.	Yes	70,000	Apr. 26, 1902
Taylorville, Ill.	Yes	14,000	Mar. 27, 1903
Tecumseh, Mich.	Yes	10,000	Feb. 2, 1903
Tecumseh, Neb.	Yes	6,000	Nov. 14, 1906
Tekamah, Neb.	No	8,000	Nov. 17, 1914
Tell City, Ind.	Yes	10,000	Mar. 31, 1916
Temple, Tex.	No	15,000	Jan. 22, 1902
Terrell, Tex.	No	10,000	Feb. 20, 1903
The Dalles, Ore.	No	10,000	Mar. 9, 1907
Theresa, N.Y.	Yes	7,500	Jan. 18, 1910
Thermopolis, Wyo.	No	12,500	Apr. 3, 1917
Thief River Falls, Minn.	Yes	12,500	Jan. 31, 1914
Thorntown, Ind.	No	10,000	Sept. 27, 1912
Three Rivers, Mich.	Yes	12,500	Sept. 5, 1902
Ticonderoga, N.Y.	Yes	7,000	Mar. 8, 1904
Tiffin, Ohio	Yes	25,000	Feb. 15, 1912
Tipton, Ind.	Yes	13,000	Mar. 14, 1902
Tipton, Iowa	Yes	10,000	July 9, 1902
Toledo, Ohio (5)	Yes	125,000	Dec. 16, 1905
Tomah, Wis.	Yes	10,000	Mar. 16, 1915
Tooele City, Utah	No	5,000	Jan. 5, 1909
Toulon, Ill.	Yes	6,000	July 23, 1914
Traer, Iowa	No	10,000	June 11, 1914
Traverse City, Mich.	Yes	20,000	Apr. 11, 1902
Trinidad, Colo.	Yes	15,000	Mar. 20, 1903
Troy, Ala.	No	10,000	Apr. 6, 1908
Tucson, Ariz.	Yes	25,000	Oct. 27, 1899
Tulare, Cal.	Yes	10,000	Dec. 30, 1904
Tulsa, Okla.	No	55,000	Nov. 30, 1910
Turlock, Cal.	Yes	10,000	June 1, 1915
Turners Falls, Mass.	Yes	13,500	Mar. 27, 1903
Tuscola, Ill.	Yes	10,000	Apr. 13, 1903
Two Harbors, Minn.	Yes	15,000	Feb. 10, 1908
Two Rivers, Wis.	Yes	12,500	Jan. 9, 1913
Tyler, Tex.	No	15,000	Mar. 20, 1903
Tyndall, S.D.	Yes	7,500	Dec. 3, 1915
Ukiah City, Cal.	Yes	8,000	May 2, 1911
Union, N.J.	Yes	25,000	Feb. 5, 1904
Union, Ore.	Yes	5,500	Apr. 25, 1911

LOCATION	WAS A PUBLIC LIBRARY ESTABLISHED BEFORE THE CARNEGIE GRANT?	AMOUNT OF CARNEGIE GRANT	DATE
Union, S.C.	No	$ 10,000	Jan. 13, 1903
Union City, Ind.	Yes	11,000	Nov. 25, 1903
Union City, Tenn.	No	10,000	Apr. 8, 1910
Union Springs, Ala.	No	7,000	Jan. 6, 1911
Unionville, Conn.	Yes	8,500	Sept. 25, 1914
University Place, Neb.	No	12,500	Mar. 16, 1915
Upland, Cal.	Yes	10,000	May 2, 1911
Upper Sandusky, Ohio	Yes	10,000	Jan. 23, 1911
Vacaville, Cal.	No	12,500	Mar. 14, 1905
Valdosta, Ga.	No	15,000	Apr. 30, 1912
Vallejo, Cal.	Yes	20,000	Dec. 27, 1902
— Valley City, N.D.	Yes	15,000	July 5, 1901
Valparaiso, Ind.	No	20,000	Apr. 22, 1906
Van Buren, Ind.	No	10,000	May 3, 1917
Vancouver, Wash.	No	10,000	Jan. 20, 1908
Vermillion, S.D.	Yes	10,000	Feb. 20, 1903
Vernon, Tex.	No	12,500	Apr. 19, 1915
Verona, N J	Yes	11,000	Mar. 31, 1916
Vevay, Ind.	Yes	12,500	Nov. 7, 1917
Vicksburg, Miss.	No	25,000	July 23, 1914
Vienna, Ill.	Yes	6,000	Jan. 20, 1908
Villisca, Iowa	No	10,000	May 2, 1907
Vinalhaven, Me.	Yes	5,200	Apr. 22, 1906
Vincennes, Ind.	Yes	35,000	Mar. 21, 1910
Vineland, N.J.	Yes	12,000	Feb. 2, 1903
Vinton, Iowa	No	12,500	Jan. 22, 1903
Virginia, Minn.	No	10,000	Dec. 20, 1904
Viroqua, Wis.	Yes	10,000	Feb. 5, 1904
Visalia, Cal.	Yes	10,000	Feb. 2, 1903
Wabash, Ind.	Yes	20,000	Mar. 7, 1901
Waco, Tex.	Yes	30,000	Apr. 28, 1902
Wagner, S.D.	No	5,000	June 1, 1915
Wagoner, Okla.	Yes	10,000	Dec. 7, 1911
Walker, Minn.	Yes	6,500	Apr. 8, 1910
Wallace, Ida.	Yes	12,000	Jan. 18, 1910
Walla Walla, Wash.	Yes	25,000	Nov. 18, 1903
Walnut Creek, Cal.	Yes	2,500	June 1, 1915
Walpole, Mass.	Yes	15,000	July 16, 1901
Walton, Ind.	No	10,000	Nov. 17, 1914
Warren, Ill.	Yes	7,000	Aug. 17, 1910

LOCATION	WAS A PUBLIC LIBRARY ESTABLISHED BEFORE THE CARNEGIE GRANT?	AMOUNT OF CARNEGIE GRANT	DATE
Warren, Ind.	No	$ 10,000	Apr. 3, 1917
Warren, Ohio	Yes	28,384	Apr. 23, 1903
Warsaw, Ind.	Yes	15,000	Sept. 29, 1915
Warsaw, N.Y.	Yes	12,500	Feb. 5, 1904
Washburn, Wis.	Yes	18,000	Feb. 12, 1903
Washington, D.C. (4)	Yes	682,000	Mar. 16, 1899
Washington, Ind.	No	20,000	Mar. 8, 1901
Washington, Kan.	Yes	5,000	Apr. 23, 1908
Washington Court House, Ohio	Yes	15,500	Dec. 30, 1901
Waterloo, Ind.	Yes	9,000	Mar. 14, 1913
Waterloo, Iowa (2)	Yes	45,000	Apr. 11, 1902
Waterman, Ill.	Yes	3,500	Jan. 31, 1913
Watertown, S.D.	Yes	10,000	Apr. 13, 1903
Watertown, Wis.	Yes	20,000	Apr. 20, 1905
Waterville, Me.	Yes	20,000	Apr. 28, 1902
Watsonville, Cal.	Yes	12,000	Apr. 23, 1903
Watts, Cal.	No	10,000	Jan. 9, 1913
Waukegan, Ill.	Yes	27,500	Mar. 20, 1903
Waukesha, Wis.	Yes	15,000	Mar. 14, 1902
Waupaca, Wis.	Yes	10,000	Apr. 28, 1913
Waupun, Wis.	Yes	11,653	Mar. 8, 1904
Wausau, Wis.	Yes	29,000	Jan. 6, 1903
Wauseon, Ohio	No	8,000	Nov. 25, 1903
Wauwatosa, Wis.	Yes	6,000	Feb. 7, 1905
Waveland, Ind.	No	10,000	Feb. 26, 1914
Waverly, Ill.	No	4,500	May 16, 1911
Waverly, Iowa	Yes	10,000	Feb. 20, 1903
Wayne, Neb.	Yes	9,000	Jan. 6, 1911
Waynesboro, Va.	Yes	8,000	Feb. 26, 1914
Webb City, Mo.	No	25,000	Apr. 28, 1913
Wellington, Kan.	No	17,500	Apr. 19, 1915
Wellsville, Ohio	Yes	10,000	Feb. 15, 1912
Wenatchee, Wash.	No	10,000	Mar. 27, 1909
Wessington Springs, S.D.	Yes	7,000	May 3, 1917
West Allis, Wis.	Yes	15,000	Mar. 14, 1913
West End, Ala.	No	10,000	Feb. 1, 1909
Westfield, Ind.	Yes	9,000	Apr. 8, 1910
Westfield, N.J.	No	15,000	Dec. 30, 1904
West Haven, Conn.	No	10,000	Aug. 6, 1906
West Hoboken, N.J.	Yes	25,000	Feb. 4, 1902
West Lebanon, Ind.	No	7,500	Apr. 19, 1915

LOCATION	WAS A PUBLIC LIBRARY ESTABLISHED BEFORE THE CARNEGIE GRANT?	AMOUNT OF CARNEGIE GRANT	DATE
West Liberty, Iowa	Yes	$ 7,500	Feb. 5, 1904
West Point, Miss.	No	10,000	Jan. 31, 1913
West Springfield, Mass.	Yes	25,000	Sept. 29, 1915
West Tampa, Fla.	No	17,500	Jan. 2, 1913
Westville, Ind.	No	8,000	Dec. 8, 1913
Wheatland, Wyo.	Yes	12,500	May 15, 1916
White Bear, Minn.	Yes	5,000	July 13, 1912
Whitefield, N.H.	Yes	7,500	Apr. 23, 1903
White Plains, N.Y.	Yes	40,000	Dec. 20, 1904
Whiting, Ind.	Yes	15,000	Dec. 30, 1904
Whittier, Cal.	Yes	12,500	Dec. 30, 1904
Wichita, Kan.	Yes	75,000	July 13, 1912
Williamsport, Ind.	No	8,000	Mar. 31, 1916
Willits, Cal.	Yes	8,000	Dec. 8, 1913
Willmar, Minn.	No	11,000	Jan. 13, 1903
Willoughby, Ohio	Yes	14,500	Dec. 13, 1906
Willows, Cal.	Yes	10,000	Feb. 12, 1910
Wilmette, Ill.	Yes	11,000	Mar. 20, 1903
Wilmington, Ohio	Yes	12,500	Feb. 4, 1902
Winamac, Ind.	Yes	10,000	Jan. 6, 1911
Winchester, Ill.	Yes	7,500	Feb. 10, 1908
Winchester, Ind.	Yes	12,000	Apr. 23, 1906
Winfield, Kan.	No	15,000	Feb. 15, 1902
Winnsboro, Tex.	No	10,000	Apr. 6, 1908
Winston-Salem, N.C.	No	15,000	Feb. 12, 1903
Winterset, Iowa	Yes	10,000	Feb. 5, 1904
Woodbine, Iowa	Yes	7,500	Apr. 28, 1909
Woodburn, Ore.	Yes	10,000	Jan. 14, 1914
Woodland, Cal.	No	22,000	Feb. 20, 1903
Woodward, Okla.	Yes	10,000	Dec. 3, 1915
Wooster, Ohio	Yes	15,000	Feb. 2, 1903
Worcester, Mass. (3)	Yes	75,000	July 1, 1910
Worthington, Ind.	Yes	10,000	Apr. 3, 1917
Worthington, Minn.	Yes	10,000	June 1, 1903
Wyandotte, Mich.	Yes	17,500	Jan. 23, 1911
Wymore, Neb.	No	10,000	Sept. 25, 1914
Wyoming, Ill.	No	5,600	Nov. 3, 1913
Xenia, Ohio	Yes	23,500	Jan. 10, 1902
Yankton, S.D.	No	12,000	Mar. 14, 1902
Yates Center, Kan.	Yes	7,500	Jan. 31, 1910

LOCATION	WAS A PUBLIC LIBRARY ESTABLISHED BEFORE THE CARNEGIE GRANT?	AMOUNT OF CARNEGIE GRANT	DATE
Yolo, Cal.	Yes	$ 3,000	Sept. 14, 1917
Yonkers, N.Y.	Yes	50,000	Mar. 8, 1901
Youngstown, Ohio	Yes	50,000	Feb. 19, 1908
Yreka, Cal.	Yes	8,000	Mar. 14, 1913
Yuma, Ariz.	No	10,000	Sept. 14, 1917
Zanesville, Ohio	Yes	54,000	Dec. 16, 1905
Zumbrota, Minn.	Yes	6,500	Nov. 27, 1906

LIBRARY GRANTS IN U.S. POSSESSIONS

Honolulu, Hawaii	No	100,000	Nov. 29, 1909
San Juan, Puerto Rico	No	100,000	Oct. 4, 1901

Selected Bibliography

Books

Adams, James Truslow. *The Epic of America*. Boston: Little, 1931.

Alderson, Bernard. *Andrew Carnegie; The Man and His Work*. New York: Doubleday, 1909.

American Library Association. *Public Library Service; A Guide to Evaluation, with Minimum Standards*. Chicago: A.L.A., 1956.

American Library Directory. New York: Bowker, 1923–

Beach, Fred F.; Dunbar, Ralph M.; and Will, Robert F. *The State and Publicly Supported Libraries; Structure and Control at the State Level*. Washington, D.C.: U.S. Office of Education, 1956.

Bowker Annual of Library and Book Trade Information, 1968. New York: Bowker, 1968.

Brett, William Howard. *Abstract of Laws Relating to Libraries in Force in 1915 in the States and Territories of the United States*. Cleveland, Ohio: Privately printed by Lezius Printing Co., 1916.

Brooklyn Public Library. *Agreement Entered into between the City of New York and the Representatives of Andrew Carnegie for the Erection of Branch Libraries in the Borough of Brooklyn*. Brooklyn, N.Y.: Public Library, 1901.

Cannons, Harry G. *Bibliography of Library Economy; A Classified Index to the Professional Periodical Literature in the English Language Relating to Library Economy, Printing, Methods of Publishing, Copyright, Bibliography, etc., from 1876 to 1920*. Chicago: American Library Assn., 1927.

243

244 SELECTED BIBLIOGRAPHY

Carnegie, Andrew. *Autobiography of Andrew Carnegie.* Boston: Houghton, 1920.

————. *A Carnegie Anthology.* Arranged by Margaret Barclay Wilson. New York: Privately printed, 1915.

————. *The Empire of Business.* New York: Doubleday, 1902.

————. *The Gospel of Wealth and Other Timely Essays.* Ed. by Edward C. Kirkland. Cambridge, Mass.: Harvard Univ. Pr., 1962.

Carnegie Corporation of New York. *Andrew Carnegie Centenary, 1835–1935; The Memorial Address by Sir James Colquhoun Irvine, and other Tributes to the Memory of Andrew Carnegie.* New York: Carnegie Corp., 1935.

————. *Annual Reports, 1921–*

————. *Carnegie Corporation Library Program, 1911–1961.* Prep. by Florence Anderson, Secretary. (No. 37 in the "Carnegie Corporation Review Series") New York: Carnegie Corp., 1963.

————. *Carnegie Grants for Library Buildings, 1890–1917.* Comp. by Robert M. Lester. New York: Carnegie Corp., 1943.

————. *Library Interests.* Prep. by Robert M. Lester. (No. 19 in the "Carnegie Corporation Review Series") New York: Carnegie Corp., 1935.

Carnegie Endowment for International Peace. *A Manual of the Public Benefactions of Andrew Carnegie.* Washington, D.C.: Carnegie Endowment for International Peace, 1919.

Clemens, Samuel L. *Mark Twain in Eruption; Hitherto Unpublished Pages about Men and Events.* Ed. by Bernard De Voto. New York: Harper, 1940.

Connor, Martha. *Outline of the History of the Development of the American Public Library.* Chicago: American Library Assn., 1931.

Detroit Public Library. *Annual Reports, 1895–1930.*

Ditzion, Sidney. *Arsenals of a Democratic Culture; A Social History of the American Public Library Movement in New England and the Middle States, 1850–1900.* Chicago: American Library Assn., 1947.

Dumond, Dwight L. *America in Our Time, 1896–1946.* New York: Holt, 1947.

Eastman, Linda A. *Portrait of a Librarian; William Howard Brett.* Chicago: American Library Assn., 1940.

Faulkner, Harold Underwood. *The Quest for Social Justice, 1898–1914.* New York: Macmillan, 1931.

Green, Samuel S. *The Public Library Movement in the United States, 1853–1893.* Boston: Boston Book Co., 1913.

Harlow, Alvin F. *Andrew Carnegie.* New York: Messner, 1953.

Selected Bibliography   245

Hendrick, Burton J. *The Benefactions of Andrew Carnegie.* New York: Carnegie Corp., 1935.
———. *The Life of Andrew Carnegie.* 2 vols. Garden City, N.Y.: Doubleday, 1932.
——— and Henderson, Daniel. *Louise Whitfield Carnegie: The Life of Mrs. Andrew Carnegie.* New York: Hastings, 1950.
Hill, Frank P. *James Bertram; An Appreciation.* New York: Carnegie Corp., 1936.
Joeckel, Carleton B. *The Government of the American Public Library.* Chicago: Univ. of Chicago Pr., 1935.
Johnson, Alvin S. *Pioneer's Progress: An Autobiography.* New York: Viking, 1952.
———. *The Public Library: A People's University.* New York: American Assn. for Adult Education, 1938.
———. *A Report to Carnegie Corporation of New York on the Policy of Donations to Free Public Libraries.* New York: Carnegie Corp., 1919.
Koch, Theodore W. *A Book of Carnegie Libraries.* New York: Wilson, 1917.
Learned, William S. *The American Public Library and the Diffusion of Knowledge.* New York: Harcourt, 1924.
Leigh, Robert D. *The Public Library in the United States; The General Report of the Public Library Inquiry.* New York: Columbia Univ. Pr., 1950.
Lester, Robert M. *Forty Years of Carnegie Giving, A Summary of the Benefactions of Andrew Carnegie and of the Work of the Philanthropic Trusts Which He Created.* New York: Scribner, 1941.
Lynch, Frederick. *Personal Recollections of Andrew Carnegie.* New York: Revell, 1920.
McCloskey, Robert Green. *American Conservatism in the Age of Enterprise; A Study of William Graham Sumner, Stephen J. Field and Andrew Carnegie.* Cambridge, Mass.: Harvard Univ. Pr., 1951.
Morison, Samuel Eliot and Commager, Henry Steele. *The Growth of the American Republic.* Vol.II. 4th ed. New York: Oxford Univ. Pr., 1950.
Munthe, William. *American Librarianship from a European Angle; An Attempt at an Evaluation of Policies and Activities.* Chicago: American Library Assn., 1939.
Schlesinger, Arthur Meier. *Political and Social Growth of the United States: 1852–1933.* New York: Macmillan, 1934.
———. *The Rise of the City.* New York: Macmillan, 1933.

246   SELECTED BIBLIOGRAPHY

Shera, Jesse H. *Foundations of the Public Library; The Origins of the Public Library Movement in New England, 1629-1855.* Chicago: Univ. of Chicago Pr., 1949.

Shippen, Katherine B. *Andrew Carnegie.* New York: Random, 1958.

Stevenson, William M. *Carnegie and His Libraries.* Pittsburgh, Pa.: Privately printed, 1899.

Sullivan, Mark. *Our Times; The United States, 1900-1925.* 6 vols. New York: Scribner, 1926-35.

Tipple, John. *Andrew Carnegie / Henry George: The Problems of Progress.* Cleveland, Ohio: H. Allen, 1960.

U.S. Bureau of Education. *Public Libraries in the United States of America; Their History, Condition, and Management.* Washington, D.C.: Govt. Print. Off., 1876.

———. *Public, Society, and School Libraries.* Washington, D.C.: Govt. Print. Off., 1915.

———. *Public, Society, and School Libraries in the United States with Library Statistics and Legislation of the Various States.* Washington, D.C.: Govt. Print. Off., 1903.

———. *Statistics of Libraries and Library Legislation in the United States, 1895-1896.* Washington, D.C.: Govt. Print. Off., 1897.

———. *Statistics of Public, Society, and School Libraries Having 5,000 Volumes and Over in 1908.* Washington, D.C.: Govt. Print. Off., 1909.

U.S. Bureau of the Census. *Historical Statistics of the United States, Colonial Times to 1957.* Washington, D.C.: Govt. Print. Off., 1960.

Utley, Henry Munson. *The Public Library: Mr. Carnegie's Offer To Provide the Means for Erecting a New Building.* Detroit: Detroit Public Library, 1903.

Vann, Sarah K. *Training for Librarianship before 1923.* Chicago: American Library Assn., 1961.

Wheeler, Joseph L. and Githens, Alfred M. *The American Public Library Building: Its Planning and Design with Special Reference to Its Administration and Services.* New York: Scribner, 1941.

Williamson, Charles C. *Andrew Carnegie; His Contribution to the Public Library Movement. A Commemorative Address.* Cleveland, Ohio: Privately printed, 1920.

———. *Training for Library Service.* New York: Carnegie Corp., 1923.

Wilson, Louis R. *The Geography of Reading: A Study of the Distribution and Status of Libraries in the United States.* Chicago: American Library Assn., 1938.

Winkler, John K. *Incredible Carnegie: The Life of Andrew Carnegie, 1835-1919.* New York: Vanguard, 1931.

Articles and Periodicals

"Andrew Carnegie on Dead Books," *Library Journal,* 37:74 (Feb. 1912).

"Andrew Carnegie, the Patron Saint of Libraries," *Kentucky Library Association Bulletin,* 27:8-19 (April 1963).

Basso, Hamilton. "Andrew Carnegie, or From Rags to Riches— The American as Success Story," in his *Mainstream* (New York: Reynal and Hitchcock, 1943), p.84-112.

Bates, David Homer. "The Turning-Point of Mr. Carnegie's Career," *Century Magazine,* 54:333-40 (July 1908).

Bolton, Sarah Knowles. "Andrew Carnegie and His Libraries," in her *Famous Givers and Their Gifts* (New York: Crowell, 1896), p.58-88.

Borden, Arnold K. "The Sociological Beginnings of the Library Movement," *Library Quarterly,* 1:278-82 (July 1931).

Butler, Nicholas M. "Andrew Carnegie, Benefactor," in his *Family of Nations, Its Need and Its Problems: Essays and Addresses* (New York: Scribner, 1938), p.223-33.

Carnegie, Andrew. "The Best Fields for Philanthropy," *North American Review,* 149:682-90 (Dec. 1889).

———. "Ezra Cornell: An Address Delivered to the Students of Cornell University, April 27, 1907, To Celebrate the One Hundredth Anniversary of the Birth of Ezra Cornell," in *Miscellaneous Writings of Andrew Carnegie,* ed. by Burton J. Hendrick. 2 vols. (Garden City, N.Y.: Doubleday, 1933), I:240-67.

———. "Library Gift Business," *Collier's,* 43:14-15 (June 5, 1909).

———. "Wealth," *North American Review,* 148:653-64 (June 1889).

"Carnegie Libraries Go under Fire," *Wilson Library Bulletin,* 3:261 (May 1928).

"Carnegie Library Grants, February and March, 1918," *Library Journal,* 43:355 (May 1918).

"Carnegie Local Derelictions re Contracts," *Library Journal,* 42:585 (Aug. 1917).

"Dedication of the Washington (D.C.) Carnegie Library Building," *Library Journal,* 28:18-19 (Jan. 1903).

Detroit Free Press, July 2, 1901.

Detroit Journal, Feb. 8, 1901; July 1, 2, and 3, 1901; Aug. 15, 1901; Dec. 10, 1902.

Detroit News, April 2, 1907.

Dewey, Melvil. "The Future of the Library Movement in the United States in the Light of Andrew Carnegie's Recent Gift," *Journal of Social Science,* 39:139–47 (Nov. 1901).

————. "Purpose of Carnegie Gifts," *Library Journal,* 30:80 (Sept. 1905).

Dies, Edward J. "Andrew Carnegie: Steel and Books," in his *Behind the Wall Street Curtain* (Washington, D.C.: Public Affairs Pr., 1952), p.60–67.

Drennan, Henry T. "The Public Library Service Gap," in *National Inventory of Library Needs* (Chicago: American Library Assn., 1965), p.39–44.

————. Kittel, Dorothy; and Winnick, Pauline. "Resources of Public Libraries in the National Education Structure in the 1960's," in *Bowker Annual of Library and Book Trade Information, 1965* (New York: Bowker, 1965), p.8–15.

Dunn, J. P. "Tainted Money," *Public Libraries,* 18:186–87 (May 1913).

Dunne, Finley Peter. "The Carnegie Libraries," in *Mr. Dooley on Ivrything and Ivrybody,* ed. by Robert Hutchinson (New York: Dover, 1963), p.225–29.

"Editorial," *Library Journal,* 40: 226 (April 1915).

Hill, Frank Pierce. "One Phase of Library Development," *Library Journal,* 21:1–9 (Aug. 1906).

Howells, William D. "Examination of Library Gift Horse," *Library Journal,* 26:741–43 (Oct. 1901).

Hutchens, Frank A. "Question Box — Carnegie Libraries," *Wisconsin Library Bulletin,* 1:65–66 (July 1905).

Jewett, Charles C. "Notices of Public Libraries in the United States of America," in Appendix to the *Fourth Annual Report of the Smithsonian Institute* (Washington, D.C.: Printed for the House of Representatives, 1851).

Johnson, Alvin. "Andrew Carnegie, Educator," *Journal of Adult Education,* 8:5–9 (Jan. 1936).

Johnson, Robert. "Public Libraries and Mr. Carnegie," *Library Journal,* 32:440–41 (Oct. 1907).

Josephson, Aksel G. S. "What the Carnegie Institutions Could Do for Librarianship and Bibliography," *Dial,* 39:79 (Feb. 1, 1902).

Keppell, Frederick P. "Andrew Carnegie," in his *Philanthropy and Learning, With Other Papers* (New York: Columbia Univ. Pr., 1936), p.155–75.

Koch, Theodore W. "Purpose of the Carnegie Gifts," *Library Journal,* 30:c78–c81 (Sept. 1905).

Krettek, Germaine and Cooke, Eileen D. "Federal Legislation," in *Bowker Annual of Library and Book Trade Information, 1965* (New York: Bowker, 1965), p.154–60.

Lamb, G. H. "Mr. Carnegie and the Free Library Movement," *Pennsylvania Library Notes,* 10:3 (Jan. 1920).

Lester, Robert M. "Libraries and Librarians from the Side of the Road," *ALA Bulletin,* 29:462–69 (July 1935).

Library Journal. Vols. I–XI (1876–1925). (Particularly regular sections on gifts to libraries and Carnegie grants to libraries)

"Library Suggestion," *Dial,* 46:69–71 (Feb. 1, 1909).

Marcosson, Isaac F. "Giving Carnegie Libraries," *World's Work,* 9:6092–97 (April 1905).

"Mr. Carnegie's Investments," *Library Journal,* 27:329 (June 1902).

"Mr. Carnegie's Library Benefactions," *Current Literature,* 38:99–100 (Feb. 1905).

Munn, Ralph, "Hindsight on the Gifts of Carnegie," *Library Journal,* 76:1966–70 (Dec. 1, 1951).

New York Times. Oct. 23, 1934; Oct. 24, 1934; Nov. 2, 1934; Nov. 23, 1934.

"Outline of Library Movement in America with the Most Important Foreign Events," *Library Journal,* 26:73 (Feb. 1901).

"Pittsburg (Pa.) Carnegie Library," *Library Journal,* 31:144 (March 1906).

"Pittsburg (Pa.), The Carnegie Library," *Library Journal,* 12:300 (Aug. 1887).

Pound, Ezra. "Where Is American Culture?" *Nation,* 126: 443–44 (April 18, 1928).

"Psychological Value of Carnegie Gifts," *Gunton's Magazine,* 20: 557–59 (June 1901).

"Public Libraries and Labor Unions," *Iowa Library Commission Quarterly,* 3: 32 (April 1903).

Putnam, Herbert. "The Relation of Free Public Libraries to the Community," in *Contributions to American Library History,* ed. by Thelma Eaton (Champaign: Illini Bookstore, 1961), p.140–46.

Sherman, Stuart P. "Andrew Carnegie," in his *Americans* (New York: Scribner, 1922), p.246–55.

Today (Detroit). July 2, 1901.

Toepel, M. G. "Legal Responsibility for Public Library Development," *Library Trends,* 9:6–17 (July 1960).

Tyler, Moses Coit. "The Historic Evolution of the Free Public Library in America and Its True Function in the Community," in *Contributions to American Library History*, ed. by Thelma Eaton (Champaign: Illini Bookstore, 1961), p.15-29.

West, Elizabeth Howard. "Texas Libraries," *Library Journal*, 48: 268-70 (Jan. 15, 1923).

Wheeler, Joseph L. "The Library Situation in Ohio," *Library Journal*, 45:877-82 (Nov. 1, 1920).

"Why Mr. Carnegie Founds Free Libraries," *Library Journal*, 25:177 (April 1900).

"Wisdom of the Carnegie Gifts," *Library Journal*, 31:105-6 (March 1906).

Woods, Henry F. "A Suggestion to Mr. Carnegie," *Library Journal* 28:276 (June 1903).

Unpublished Material

Anderson, Florence. Letter to the author, Oct. 12, 1965.

Andrew Carnegie Centennial Scrapbook. 4 vols. A scrapbook of clippings from newspapers in the United States and Great Britain printed between Oct. 17, 1935 and Jan. 4, 1936, mounted and bound by the New York Public Library and located in that library.

Bertram, James. A corrected first draft of a letter to Andrew Carnegie, undated, in the Carnegie Corporation files.

Carnegie Corporation of New York. List of [Carnegie] Bildings in the United States, Canada, United Kingdom and Other English-speaking Countries. March 31, 1913. New York: Privately printed, 1913. (Copy at the General Library of the University of Michigan has letter dated March 2, 1916, from F. M. Coffin to William Bishop, University of Michigan librarian, enclosed in this work. It states that the list formed an accurate record of buildings which had been erected, except for the United Kingdom, as of Dec. 31, 1915. Buildings promised but not erected were struck out. New names were penciled in.)

Carnegie Library Correspondence. Microfilm Reels 1-35: Correspondence and other documents pertaining primarily to Carnegie grants for free public library buildings in the United States, arranged alphabetically by communities. Microfilm Reels 66E, 67, and 68: Correspondence and documents pertaining to buildings promised but lapsed. Microfilm Reels 86 and 87: Cards giving name of community, date of grant, amount of gift, and any additions to the original grant.

Carnegie Scrap-Books 1 and 2; Newspaper clippings relating to Andrew Carnegie, 1901–10. (Carnegie Scrap-Book 1 contains information about $5,200,000 donated for building circulating libraries in New York City) Located in New York Public Library.

Culver, Essae M. Letter to the author, Feb. 1, 1966.

Fyan, Loleta Dawson. Letter to the author, Feb. 4, 1966.

Johnson, Alvin S. Letter to the author, Sept. 3, 1965.

League of Library Commissioners. Correspondence with the Carnegie Corporation of New York, on file in the Corporation offices.

Lester, Robert M. Letter to the author, Nov. 2, 1965.

Miller, Durand R. "My Recollections of J.B." A typewritten manuscript prepared by Durand Miller for Frank Hill on July 31, 1935, when the latter was writing his biography of James Bertram.

Richardson, B. E. Letter to the author, n.d.

Rothrock, Mary. Letter to the author, Feb. 4, 1966.

Schenk, Gretchen Knief. Letter to the author, Feb. 3, 1966.

Vitz, Carl. Letter to the author, Feb. 5, 1966.

Wheeler, Joseph. Letter to the author, Feb. 8, 1966.

Wilson, Louis R. Letter to the author, Feb. 1, 1966.

Index

Index   257